Tarascon Pocket Pharmacopoeia™

2003 Classic Shirt-Pocket Edition

"Desire to take medicines ... distinguishes man from animals." *Sir William Osler*

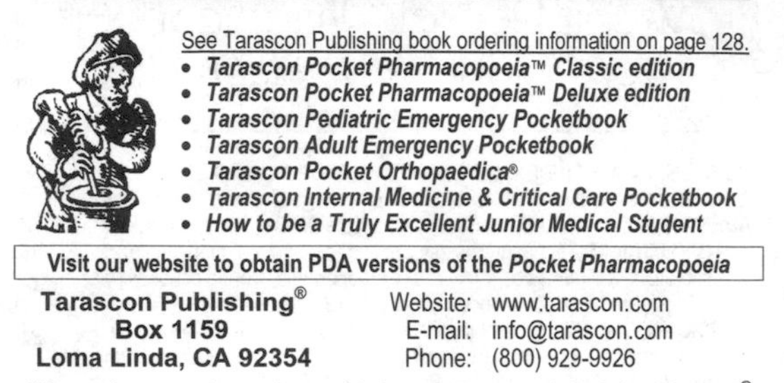

See Tarascon Publishing book ordering information on page 128.

- *Tarascon Pocket Pharmacopoeia™ Classic edition*
- *Tarascon Pocket Pharmacopoeia™ Deluxe edition*
- *Tarascon Pediatric Emergency Pocketbook*
- *Tarascon Adult Emergency Pocketbook*
- *Tarascon Pocket Orthopaedica®*
- *Tarascon Internal Medicine & Critical Care Pocketbook*
- *How to be a Truly Excellent Junior Medical Student*

Visit our website to obtain PDA versions of the *Pocket Pharmacopoeia*

Tarascon Publishing®
Box 1159
Loma Linda, CA 92354

Website: www.tarascon.com
E-mail: info@tarascon.com
Phone: (800) 929-9926

"It's not how much you know, it's how fast you can find the answer."®

Important Caution – Please Read This! The information in the *Pocket Pharmacopoeia* is compiled from sources believed to be reliable, and exhaustive efforts have been put forth to make the book as accurate as possible. *However the accuracy and completeness of this work cannot be guaranteed.* Despite our best efforts this book may contain typographical errors and omissions. The *Pocket Pharmacopoeia* is intended as a quick and convenient reminder of information you have already learned elsewhere. The contents are to be used as a guide only, and health care professionals should use sound clinical judgment and individualize therapy to each specific patient care situation. This book is not meant to be a replacement for training, experience, continuing medical education, studying the latest drug prescribing literature, raw intelligence, good looks, or common sense. This book is sold without warranties of any kind, express or implied, and the publisher and editors disclaim any liability, loss, or damage caused by the contents. ***If you do not wish to be bound by the foregoing cautions and conditions, you may return your undamaged and unexpired book to our office at the above address for a full refund.***

The *Pocket Pharmacopoeia* is edited by a panel of drug information experts with extensive peer review and input from more than 30 practicing clinicians of multiple specialties. Our goal is to provide health professionals focused, core prescribing information in a convenient, organized, & concise fashion. We include FDA-approved dosing indications & those off-label uses that have a reasonable basis to support their use. Tarascon Publishing is independent from & has no affiliation with pharmaceutical companies. Although drug companies purchase and distribute our books as promotional items, the Tarascon editorial staff determines all book content.

Tarascon Pocket Pharmacopoeia™ 2003 Classic Edition

ISBN 1-882742-25-7.

HOW TO USE THE TARASCON POCKET PHARMACOPOEIA™

The *Tarascon Pocket Pharmacopoeia* arranges drugs by clinical class with a comprehensive index in the back. Trade names are italicized and capitalized. Drug doses shown in mg/kg are generally intended for children, while fixed doses represent typical adult recommendations. Brackets indicate currently available formulations, although not all pharmacies stock all formulations. The availability of generic, over-the-counter, and scored formulations are mentioned. Codes are as follows:

METABOLISM & EXCRETION: **L** = primarily liver, **K** = primarily kidney, **LK** = both, but liver > kidney, **KL** = both, but kidney > liver, **LO** = liver & onions

SAFETY IN PREGNANCY: **A** = Safety established using human studies, **B** = Presumed safety based on animal studies, **C** = Uncertain safety; no human studies and animal studies show an adverse effect, **D** = Unsafe - evidence of risk that may in certain clinical circumstances be justifiable, **X** = Highly unsafe - risk of use outweighs any possible benefit. For drugs which have not been assigned a category: **+** Generally accepted as safe, **?** Safety unknown or controversial, **-** Generally regarded as unsafe.

SAFETY IN LACTATION: **+** Generally accepted as safe, **?** Safety unknown or controversial, **-** Generally regarded as unsafe. Many of our "**+**" listings are from the AAP website (www.aap.org/policy/0063.html), and may differ from those recommended by the manufacturer.

DEA CONTROLLED SUBSTANCES: **I** = High abuse potential, no accepted use (eg, heroin, marijuana), **II** = High abuse potential and severe dependence liability (eg, morphine, codeine, hydromorphone, cocaine, amphetamines, methylphenidate, secobarbital). Some states require triplicates. **III** = Moderate dependence liability (eg, *Tylenol #3*, *Vicodin*), **IV** = Limited dependence liability (benzodiazepines, propoxyphene, phentermine), **V** = Limited abuse potential (eg, *Lomotil*).

RELATIVE COST: Cost codes used are "per month" of maintenance therapy (eg, antihypertensives) or "per course" of short-term therapy (eg, antibiotics). Codes are calculated using average wholesale prices (at press time in US dollars) for the most common indication & route of each drug at a typical adult dosage. For maintenance therapy, costs are calculated based upon a 30 day supply or the quantity that might typically be used in a given month. For short-term therapy (ie, 10 days or less), costs are calculated on a single treatment course. When multiple forms are available (eg, generics), these codes reflect the least expensive generally available product. When drugs don't neatly fit into the classification scheme above, we have assigned codes based upon the relative cost of other similar drugs. *These codes should be used as a rough guide only*, as (1) they reflect cost, not charges, (2) pricing often varies substantially from location to location and time to time, and (3) HMOs, Medicaid, and buying groups often negotiate quite different pricing. Your mileage may vary. Check with your local pharmacy if you have any question.

Code	Cost
$	< $25
$$	$25 to $49
$$$	$50 to $99
$$$$	$100 to $199
$$$$$	≥ $200

CANADIAN TRADE NAMES: Unique common Canadian trade names not used in the US are listed after a maple leaf symbol. Trade names used in both nations or only in the US are displayed without such notation.

PAGE INDEX FOR TABLES*

*Please see the *Tarascon Pocket Pharmacopoeia, Deluxe* for extra large format tables as follows. General: P450 Enzymes. CV: CAD 10-year risk, HTN risk stratification & treatment. Heme: Warfarin interactions, Oral anticoagulation goals. Ophth: Visual acuity screen. Pulmonary: Asthma action plan.

ABBREVIATIONS IN TEXT

AAP - American Acad of Pediatrics
ac – before meals
ADHD – attention deficit & hyperactivity disorder
AHA – American Heart Association
ANC – absolute neutrophil count
ASA – aspirin
bid - twice per day
BP – blood pressure
BPH - benign prostatic hypertrophy
CAD – coronary artery disease
cap – capsule
CMV – cytomegalovirus
CNS – central nervous system
COPD – chronic obstructive pulmonary disease
CrCl – creatinine clearance
d - day
D5W - 5% dextrose
DPI – dry powder inhaler
elem – elemental
ET - endotracheal
EPS – extrapyramidal symptoms
g - gram
gtts - drops
GERD - gastroesophageal reflux dz
GU – genitourinary
h - hour
HAART – highly active antiretroviral therapy
HCTZ - hydrochlorothiazide
HRT - hormone replacement therapy
HSV – herpes simplex virus
HTN – hypertension
IM - intramuscular
INR – international normalized ratio
IU - international units
IV - intravenous
JRA - juvenile rheumatoid arthritis
kg – kilogram
LFTs – liver fxn tests
LV – left ventricular
mcg - microgram
MDI – metered dose inhaler
mEq - milliequivalent
mg - milligram
MI - myocardial infarction
min - minute
mL - milliliter
mo – months old
ng - nanogram
NS - normal saline
NYHA – New York Heart Association
N/V -nausea/vomiting
OA – osteoarthritis
pc – after meals
PO - by mouth
PR - by rectum
prn - as needed
q - every
qd - once daily
qhs - at bedtime
qid - four times/day
qod – every other day
q pm – every evening
RA - rheumatoid arthritis
SC - subcutaneous
soln – solution
supp - suppository
susp - suspension
tab – tablet
TB – tuberculosis
TCAs – tricyclic antidepressants
TIA - transient ischemic attack
tid - 3 times/day
TNF – tumor necrosis factor
tiw – 3 times/week
UC – ulcerative colitis
UTI – urinary tract infection
wk - week
yo - years old

CONVERSIONS	*Liquid:*	*Weight:*
Temperature:	1 fluid ounce = 30ml	1 kilogram = 2.2 lbs
F = (1.8) C + 32	1 teaspoon = 5ml	1 ounce = 30 g
C = (F - 32)/(1.8)	1 tablespoon = 15ml	1 grain = 65 mg

If you obtained your *Pocket Pharmacopoeia* from a bookstore, please send us your address (info@tarascon.com). This allows you to be the first to hear of updates! (We don't sell our mailing lists, by the way.) The cover woodcut is *The Apothecary* by Jost Amman, Frankfurt, 1574. If you're not there by 4:30 pm you might miss *The Last Train to Clarksville* (The Monkees, 1966). We will send a free copy of next year's edition to the first 25 who know who put out a major fire with his urine.

Tarascon Pocket Pharmacopoeia Editorial Staff*

**Affiliations are given for information purposes only, and no affiliation sponsorship is claimed*

PEDIATRIC DRUGS		Age	2m	4m	6m	9m	12m	15m	2y	3y	5y
		Kg	5	6½	8	9	10	11	13	15	19
		Lbs	11	15	17	20	22	24	28	33	42
med	**strength**	**freq**	**teaspoons of liquid per dose** (1 tsp= 5 ml)								
Tylenol (mg)		q4h	80	80	120	120	160	160	200	240	280
Tylenol (tsp)	160/t	q4h	½	½	¾	¾	1	1	1¼	1½	1¾
ibuprofen (mg)		q6h	-	-	75†	75†	100	100	125	150	175
ibuprofen (tsp)	100/t	q6h	-	-	¾†	¾†	1	1	1¼	1½	1¾
amoxicillin or	125/t	bid	1	1¼	1½	1¾	1¾	2	2¼	2¾	3½
Augmentin	200/t	bid	½	¾	1	1	1¼	1¼	1½	1¾	2¼
regular dose	250/t	bid	½	½	¾	¾	1	1	1¼	1¼	1¾
	400/t	bid	¼	½	½	½	¾	¾	¾	1	1
amoxicillin or	200/t	bid	--	1¼	1½	1¾	2	2¼	2½	3	4
Augmentin	250/t	bid	--	1¼	1½	1½	1¾	1¾	2¼	2½	3
high OM dose‡	400/t	bid	--	¾	¾	1	1	1¼	1½	1½	2
Augmentin ES‡	600/t	bid	--	½	½	¾	¾	¾	1	1¼	1½
azithromycin*§	100/t	qd	--	½†	½	½	½	½	¾	¾	1
"	200/t	qd	--	¼†	¼	¼	¼	¼	½	½	½
Bactrim/Septra	---	bid	½	¾	1	1	1	1¼	1½	1½	2
cefaclor*	125/t	bid	--	1†	1¼†	1½	1½	1¾	2	2½	3
"	250/t	bid	--	½†	¾†	¾	¾	1	1	1¼	1½
cefadroxil	125/t	bid	½	¾	1	1	1¼	1¼	1½	1¾	2
"	250/t	bid	¼	½	½	½	¾	¾	¾	1	1
cefdinir	125/t	qd	--	¾†	1	1	1	1¼	1½	1¾	2
cefixime	100/t	qd	--	½	¾	¾	¾	1	1	1¼	1½
cefprozil*	125/t	bid	--	¾†	1	1	1¼	1½	1½	2	2¼
"	250/t	bid	--	½†	½	½	¾	¾	¾	1	1¼
cefuroxime	125/t	bid	½	¾	¾	1	1	1	1¼	1½	2
cephalexin	125/t	qid	--	½†	¾†	¾†	1	1	1¼	1½	1¾
"	250/t	qid	--	¼†	¼†	½†	½	½	¾	¾	1
clarithromycin	125/t	bid	--	½†	½†	½	¾	¾	¾	1	1¼
"	250/t	bid	--	¼†	¼†	¼	½	½	½	½	¾
dicloxacillin	62½/t	qid	½	¾	1	1	1¼	1¼	1½	1¾	2
loracarbef*	100/t	bid	--	1†	1¼	1½	1½	1¾	2	2¼	3
nitrofurantoin	25/t	qid	¼	½	½	½	½	¾	¾	¾	1
Pediazole	---	tid	½	½	¾	¾	1	1	1	1¼	1½
penicillin	125/t	qid	½	½	¾	¾	1	1	1¼	1¼	1½
"	250/t	qid	--	¼	¼	½	½	½	¾	¾	1
Benadryl	12.5/t	q6h	½	½	¾	¾	1	1	1¼	1½	2
Dimetapp	---	q4h	-	-	¼†	¼†	½	¾	¾	1	1
prednisolone	15/t	qd	¼	½	½	¾	¾	¾	1	1	1¼
prednisone	5/t	qd	1	1¼	1½	1¾	2	2¼	2½	3	3¾
Robitussin	---	q4h	-	-	¼†	¼†	½	½	¾	¾	1
Rondec	---	q4h	-	-	-	-	¼†	¼†	½	½	1
Triaminic	---	q4h	-	¼	¼	¼	½	½	1	1	1
Tylenol w/ Codeine		q4h	-	-	-	-	-	-	-	1	1
Ventolin	2/t	tid	-	-	-	-	½	½	¾	¾	1
Zyrtec	5/t	qd	-	-	-	-	-	-	½	½	½

* Dose shown is for otitis media only; see dosing in text for alternative indications.
† Dosing at this age/weight not recommended by manufacturer.
‡ High dose (80-90 mg/kg/d) is for otitis media in children at high risk for penicillin-resistant S pneumoniae (age <2 yo, antibiotics within ≤3 months, day care).
§Give a double dose of azithromycin the first day.

PEDIATRIC VITAL SIGNS AND INTRAVENOUS DRUGS

Age		Pre-matr	New-born	2m	4m	6m	9m	12m	15m	2y	3y	5y
Weight	(Kg)	2	3½	5	6½	8	9	10	11	13	15	19
	(Lbs)	4½	7½	11	15	17	20	22	24	28	33	42
Maint fluids	(ml/h)	8	14	20	26	32	36	40	42	46	50	58
ET tube	(mm)	2½	3/3½	3½	3½	3½	4	4	4½	4½	4½	5
Defib	(Joules)	4	7	10	13	16	18	20	22	26	30	38
Systolic BP	(high)	70	80	90	100	110	110	120	120	120	120	120
	(low)	50	60	70	70	70	70	70	70	75	75	80
Pulse rate	(high)	145	145	180	180	180	160	160	160	150	150	135
	(low)	100	100	110	110	110	100	100	100	90	90	65
Resp rate	(high)	45	45	45	40	35	35	30	30	30	24	24
	(low)	35	35	35	30	25	25	20	20	20	16	14
adenosine	(mg)	0.2	0.3	0.5	0.6	0.8	0.9	1	1.1	1.3	1.5	1.9
atropine	(mg)	0.1	0.1	0.1	0.13	0.16	0.18	0.2	0.22	0.26	0.30	0.38
Benadryl	(mg)	-	-	5	6½	8	9	10	11	13	15	19
bicarbonate	(meq)	2	3½	5	6½	8	9	10	11	13	15	19
dextrose	(g)	2	3½	5	6½	8	9	10	11	13	15	19
epinephrine	(mg)	.02	.04	.05	.07	.08	.09	0.1	0.11	0.13	0.15	0.19
lidocaine	(mg)	2	3½	5	6½	8	9	10	11	13	15	19
morphine	(mg)	0.2	0.3	0.5	0.6	0.8	0.9	1	1.1	1.3	1.5	1.9
mannitol	(g)	2	3½	5	6½	8	9	10	11	13	15	19
diazepam	(mg)	0.6	1	1.5	2	2.5	2.7	3	3.3	3.9	4.5	5
lorazepam	(mg)	0.1	0.2	0.3	0.35	0.4	0.5	0.5	0.6	0.7	0.8	1.0
phenobarb	(mg)	30	60	75	100	125	125	150	175	200	225	275
ampicillin	(mg)	100	175	250	325	400	450	500	550	650	750	1000
ceftriaxone	(mg)	-	-	250	325	400	450	500	550	650	750	1000
cefotaxime	(mg)	100	175	250	325	400	450	500	550	650	750	1000
gentamicin	(mg)	6	7	10	13	16	18	20	22	26	30	38

THERAPEUTIC DRUG LEVELS

Drug	Level	Optimal Timing
amikacin peak	20-35 mcg/ml	1 hour after start of 30-60 min infusion
amikacin trough	<5 mcg/ml	Just prior to next dose
carbamazepine trough	4-12 mcg/ml	Just prior to next dose
cyclosporine trough	50-300 ng/ml	Just prior to next dose
digoxin	0.8-2.0 ng/ml	Just prior to next dose
ethosuximide trough	40-100 mcg/ml	Just prior to next dose
gentamicin peak	5-10 mcg/ml	1 hour after start of 30-60 min infusion
gentamicin trough	<2 mcg/ml	Just prior to next dose
lidocaine	1-5 mcg/ml	4-8 hours after start of infusion
lithium trough	0.6-1.2 meq/l	Just prior to first morning dose
NAPA	10-30 mcg/ml	Just prior to next procainamide dose
phenobarbital trough	15-40 mcg/ml	Just prior to next dose
phenytoin trough	10-20 mcg/ml	Just prior to next dose
primidone trough	5-12 mcg/ml	Just prior to next dose
procainamide	4-10 mcg/ml	Just prior to next dose
quinidine	1-4 mcg/ml	Just prior to next dose
theophylline	5-15 mcg/ml	8-12 hrs after once daily dose
tobramycin peak	5-10 mcg/ml	1 hour after start of 30-60 min infusion
tobramycin trough	<2 mcg/ml	Just prior to next dose
valproic acid trough	50-100 mcg/ml	Just prior to next dose
vancomycin trough	5-10 mcg/ml	Just prior to next dose

Alveolar-arterial oxygen gradient = A-a = 148 - 1.2(PaCO2) - PaO2
[normal = 10-20 mmHg, breathing room air at sea level]

Calculated osmolality = 2Na + glucose/18 + BUN/2.8
[norm 280-295 meq/L. Na in meq/L; all others in mg/dL]

Pediatric IV maintenance fluids (see table on page 7)
4 ml/kg/hr **or** 100 ml/kg/day for first 10 kg, plus
2 ml/kg/hr **or** 50 ml/kg/day for second 10 kg, plus
1 ml/kg/hr **or** 20 ml/kg/day for all further kg

mcg/kg/min = $\frac{16.7 \times \text{Drug Conc [mg/ml]} \times \text{Infusion Rate [ml/h]}}{\text{Weight [kg]}}$

Infusion rate [ml/h] = $\frac{\text{Desired mcg/kg/min} \times \text{Weight [kg]} \times 60}{\text{Drug concentration [mcg/ml]}}$

Fractional excretion of sodium = $\left[\frac{\text{urine Na / plasma Na}}{\text{urine creat / plasma creat}}\right] \times 100\%$
[Pre-renal, etc <1%; ATN, etc >1%]

Anion gap = Na – (Cl + HCO3) [normal = 10-14 meq/L]

Creatinine clearance = $\frac{\text{(lean kg)(140 - age)(0.85 if female)}}{\text{(72)(stable creatinine)}}$
[normal >80]

Body surface area (BSA) = square root of: $\left[\frac{\text{height (cm)} \times \text{weight (kg)}}{3600}\right]$
[in m^2]

DRUGS THAT MAY PROLONG THE QT INTERVAL

amiodarone*‡	droperidol*	isradipine	**phenothiazines**§#	sparfloxacin
arsenic trioxide*	erythromycin*‡	levofloxacin*	pimozide*‡	sumatriptan
bepridil*‡	flecainide*†	levomethadyl	polyethylene glycol	tacrolimus†
beta agonists¶	fluconazole*	mefloquine	procainamide*	tamoxifen
chloroquine	fluoxetine*†	metoclopramide*	quetiapine§	tizanidine
cisapride*	fluvoxamine*	moexipril/HCTZ	quinidine*‡	tricyclic anti-
clarithromycin*	foscarnet	moxifloxacin	quinine	depressants
cocaine*	fosphenytoin	naratriptan	rabeprazole†	venlafaxine
disopyramide*‡	gatifloxacin*	nicardipine	risperidone§	*Visicol*
dofetilide*	haloperidol*§	octreotide	sertraline*†	ziprasidone§
dolasetron	ibutilide*‡	paroxetine*	sibutramine†	zolmitriptan†
doxapram†	indapamide*	pentamidine*‡	sotalol*‡	

Risk of drug-induced QT prolongation may be increased in women, elderly, ↓K, ↓Mg, bradycardia, starvation, & CNS injuries. Hepatorenal dysfunction & drug interactions can ↑ the concentration of QT interval-prolonging drugs. Coadministration of QT interval-prolonging drugs can have additive effects. (www.torsades.org) *Torsades reported in product labeling/case reports. †Association unclear. ‡↑Risk in women. § QT prolongation: thioridazine>ziprasidone>risperidone, quetiapine, haloperidol. ¶QT interval prolongation documented for salmeterol. #QT prolongation documented for chlorpromazine*, fluphenazine†, mesoridazine, thioridazine.

DRUG THERAPY REFERENCE WEBSITES (selected)

Professional societies or governmental agencies with drug therapy guidelines		
AHRQ	Agency for Healthcare Research and Quality	www.ahcpr.gov
AAP	American Academy of Pediatrics	www.aap.org
AHA	American Heart Association	www.americanheart.org
AMA	American Medical Association	www.ama-assn.org
ATS	American Thoracic Society	www.thoracic.org
CDC	Centers for Disease Control & Prevention	www.cdc.gov
IDSA	Infectious Diseases Society of America	www.idsociety.org
MHA	Malignant Hyperthermia Association	www.mhaus.org
NHLBI	National Heart, Lung, & Blood Institute	www.nhlbi.nih.gov
Other therapy reference sites		
Emergency Contraception Website		www.not-2-late.com
Int'l Registry for Drug-Induced Arrhythmias		www.qtdrugs.org
Managing Contraception		www.managingcontraception.com

ANALGESICS

Antirheumatic Agents

azathioprine (***Imuran***): RA: Initial dose 1 mg/kg (50-100 mg) PO qd or divided bid. Increase after 6-8 weeks. [Generic/Trade: Tabs 50 mg, scored.] ▶LK ♀D ▶- $$$$

etanercept (***Enbrel***): RA, Psoriatic arthritis: 25 mg SC 2x/week. JRA 4-17 yo: 0.4 mg/kg SC 2x/week, to max single dose of 25 mg. [Supplied in a carton containing four dose trays. Each dose tray contains one 25 mg single-use vial of etanercept, one syringe (1 mL Sterile Bacteriostatic Water for Injection, USP, containing 0.9% benzyl alcohol), one plunger, and two alcohol swabs.] ▶Serum ♀B ▶- $$$$$

hydroxychloroquine sulfate (***Plaquenil***). RA: start 400-600 mg PO qd, then taper to 200-400 mg qd. SLE: 400 PO qd-bid to start, then taper to 200-400 mg qd. [Generic/Trade: Tabs 200 mg, scored.] ▶K ♀C ▶+ $$$

infliximab (***Remicade***); RA: 3 mg/kg IV in combination with methotrexate. ▶Serum ♀B ▶? $$$$$

leflunomide (***Arava***): RA: 100 mg PO qd x 3 days. Maintenance: 10-20 mg PO qd. [Trade: Tabs 10, 20, & 100 mg.] ▶LK ♀X ▶- $$$$$

methotrexate (***Rheumatrex, Trexall***): RA: Start with 7.5 mg/week PO single dose or 2.5 mg PO q12h x 3 doses given as a course once weekly. Max dose 20 mg/week. Supplement with 1 mg/day of folic acid. [Trade: Tabs 5, 7.5, 10 & 15 mg. Generic/Trade: Tabs 2.5 mg, scored.] ▶LK ♀X ▶- $$

sulfasalazine (***Azulfidine, Azulfidine EN-tabs, ✤Salazopyrin EN-Tabs, S.A.S.***): RA: 500 mg PO qd-bid after meals up to 1g PO bid. May turn body fluids, contact lenses or skin orange-yellow. [Generic/Trade: Tabs 500 mg, scored. Enteric coated, Delayed release (EN-Tabs) 500 mg.] ▶L ♀B ▶- $$

Muscle Relaxants

baclofen (***Lioresal***): Spasticity related to MS or spinal cord disease/injury: Start 5 mg PO tid, then increase by 5 mg/dose q3 days until 20 mg PO tid. Max dose 20 mg qid. [Generic/Trade: Tabs 10 & 20 mg, trade scored.] ▶K ♀C ▶+ $$

carisoprodol (***Soma***): Musculoskeletal pain: 350 mg PO tid-qid. Abuse potential. [Generic/Trade:Tabs 350 mg.] ▶LK ♀? ▶- $

chlorzoxazone (***Paraflex, Parafon Forte DSC, Remular-S***): Musculoskeletal pain: 500-750 mg PO tid-qid to start. Decrease to 250 mg tid-qid. [Generic/Trade:Tabs & caplets 250 & 500 mg (Parafon Forte DSC 500 mg scored).] ▶LK ♀C ▶? $$

cyclobenzaprine (***Flexeril***): Musculoskeletal pain: Start 10 mg PO tid, max 60 mg/day. Not recommended in elderly. [Generic/Trade: Tabs 10 mg.] ▶LK ♀B ◗? $

dantrolene (***Dantrium***): Chronic spasticity related to spinal cord injury, stroke, cerebral palsy, MS: 25 mg PO qd to start, up to max of 100 mg bid-qid if necessary. Malignant hyperthermia: 1 mg/kg rapid IV push q6h continuing until symptoms subside or to a maximum cumulative dose of 10 mg/kg. [Trade: Caps 25, 50 & 100 mg.] ▶LK ♀C ◗- $$$$

diazepam (***Valium, Diastat***): Skeletal muscle spasm, spasticity related to cerebral palsy, paraplegia, athetosis, stiff man syndrome: 2-10 mg PO/PR tid-qid. [Generic/Trade: Tabs 2, 5 & 10 mg, trade scored. Generic: Oral soln 5 mg/5 ml & Concentrated soln 5 mg/ml. Trade only: Rectal gel: 2.5 mg & 5 mg (pediatric), 10 mg (pediatric & adult), 15 mg & 20 mg (adult).] ▶LK ♀D ◗- ©IV $$

metaxalone (***Skelaxin***): Musculoskeletal pain: 800 mg PO tid-qid. [Trade: Tabs 400 mg, scored.] ▶LK ♀? ◗? $$$

methocarbamol (***Robaxin, Robaxin-750***): Acute musculoskeletal pain: 1500 mg PO qid or 1000 mg IM/IV tid x 48-72h. Maintenance: 1000 mg PO qid, 750 mg PO q4h, or 1500 mg PO tid. Tetanus: specialized dosing. [Generic/Trade: Tabs 500 & 750 mg. OTC in Canada.] ▶LK ♀C ◗+ $$

orphenadrine (***Norflex***): Musculoskeletal pain: 100 mg PO bid. 60 mg IV/IM bid. [Generic/Trade: 100 mg sustained release. OTC in Canada.] ▶LK ♀C ◗? $$

quinine sulfate: Commonly prescribed for nocturnal leg cramps, but not FDA approved for this indication: 260-325 mg PO qhs. Cinchonism with overdose. Hemolysis with G6PD deficiency, hypersensitivity. [Rx: Generic: Caps 200, 260 & 325 mg. Tabs 260 mg.] ▶L ♀X ◗+ $

tizanidine (***Zanaflex***): Muscle spasticity due to MS/spinal cord injury: 4-8 mg PO q6-8h prn, max 36 mg/d. [Generic/Trade: Tabs 2 & 4 mg, scored.] ▶LK ♀C ◗? $$$$

Non-Opioid Analgesic Combinations

Ascriptin (ASA with Mg/Al hydroxide & Ca carbonate buffers): Multiple strengths. [OTC: Trade: Tabs 325 mg ASA/50 mg Mg hydroxide/50 mg Al hydroxide/calcium carbonate (Asciptin). 325 mg ASA/75 mg Mg hydroxide/75 mg Al hydroxide/calcium carbonate (Ascriptin A/D). 500 mg ASA/80 mg Mg hydroxide/80 mg Al hydroxide/calcium carbonate (Ascriptin Maximum Strength).] ▶K ♀D ◗? $

Esgic (acetaminophen+butalbital+caffeine): 1-2 tabs/caps PO q4h. [Generic/Trade: Tabs/caps acetaminophen 325 mg/butalbital 50 mg/caffeine 40 mg] ▶LK ♀C ◗? $

Fioricet (acetaminophen + butalbital + caffeine): 1-2 tabs PO q4h. [Generic/Trade: Tabs 325 mg acetaminophen//50 mg butalbital/40 mg caffeine.] ▶LK ♀C ◗? $

Fiorinal (ASA + butalbital + caffeine): 1-2 tabs PO q4h. [Generic/Trade: Tabs 325 mg aspirin/50 mg butalbital/40 mg caffeine.] ▶KL ♀D ◗- ©III $$

Norgesic (orphenadrine + ASA + caffeine): Multiple strengths; write specific product on Rx. Norgesic, 1-2 tabs PO tid-qid. Norgesic Forte, 1 tab PO tid-qid. [Trade: Tabs Norgesic 25 mg orphenadrine/385 mg aspirin/30 mg caffeine. Norgesic Forte 50 mg orphenadrine/770 mg aspirin/60 mg caffeine.] ▶KL ♀D ◗? $$$

Robaxisal (methocarbamol + ASA): 2 tabs PO qid. [Generic/Trade: Tabs 400 mg methocarbamol/325 mg ASA.] ▶LK ♀D ◗? $$

Soma Compound (carisoprodol + ASA): 1-2 tabs PO qid. Abuse potential. [Generic/Trade: Tabs 200 mg carisoprodol/325 mg ASA.] ▶LK ♀D ◗- $$$

Ultracet (tramadol + acetaminophen): Acute pain: 2 tabs PO q4-6h prn, max 8 tabs/day for ≤5 days. Adjust dose in elderly & renal dysfunction. Avoid in opioid dependent patients. Seizures may occur if concurrent antidepressants or seizure disorder. [Trade: Tabs 37.5 mg tramadol/325 mg acetaminophen.] ▶KL ♀C ◗- $$

Nonsteroidal Anti-Inflammatories - COX-2 Inhibitors

NOTE: Fewer GI side effects than 1st generation NSAIDs & no effect on platelets, but other NSAID-related side effects (renal dysfunction, fluid retention, CNS) are possible.

celecoxib (***Celebrex***): OA: 200 mg PO qd or 100 mg PO bid. RA: 100-200 mg PO bid. Familial adenomatous polyposis. 400 mg PO bid with food. Acute pain: 400 mg PO x 1, then 200-400 mg PO qd. Dysmenorrhea: 400 mg PO qd. Contraindicated in sulfonamide allergy. [Trade: Caps 100 & 200 mg.] ▶L ♀C (D in 3rd trimester) ▶? $$$

rofecoxib (***Vioxx***): OA: 12.5-25 mg PO qd. Acute pain/dysmenorrhea: 50 mg PO qd. RA: 25 mg PO qd. OK in sulfa allergy. [Trade: Tabs 12.5, 25 & 50 mg. Suspension 12.5 mg/5 ml and 25 mg/5 ml.] ▶Plasma ♀C (D in 3rd trimester) ▶? $$$

valdecoxib (***Bextra***): OA, RA: 10 mg PO qd. Primary dysmenorrhea: 20 mg PO bid. Related to sulfonamides. [Trade: Tabs 10 & 20 mg.] ▶Plasma ♀C (D in 3rd trimester) ▶? $$$

Nonsteroidal Anti-Inflammatories - Salicylic Acid Derivatives

aspirin (***Ecotrin, Bayer, ASA, ♣Asaphen, Entrophen***): 325-650 mg PO/PR q4-6h. [OTC: Tabs 81, 165, 325, 500, 650, controlled release tabs 650 (scored). Rx only: 800 mg controlled release tabs & 975 mg enteric coated. OTC: suppositories 120, 200, 300, & 600 mg.] ▶K ♀D ▶? $

choline magnesium trisalicylate (***Trilisate***): 1500 mg PO bid. [Generic/Trade: Tabs 500,750,&1000 mg, scored. Liquid 500 mg/5 ml] ▶K ♀C (D in 3rd trimest) ▶? $$$

diflunisal (***Dolobid***): 500-1000 mg initially, then 250-500 mg PO q8-12h. [Generic/Trade: Tabs 250 & 500 mg.] ▶K ♀C (D in 3rd trimester) ▶- $$$

salsalate (***Salflex, Disalcid***): 3000 mg/day PO divided q8-12h. [Generic/Trade: Tabs 500 & 750 mg, various scored. Trade only: Caps 500 mg.] ▶K ♀C (D in 3rd trimester) ▶? $$$

Nonsteroidal Anti-Inflammatories - Other

Arthrotec (diclofenac + misoprostol): OA: one 50/200 tab PO tid. RA: one 50/200 tab PO tid-qid. If intolerant, may use 50/200 or 75/200 PO bid. Misoprostol is an abortifacient. [Trade: Tabs 50 mg/200 mcg & 75 mg/200 mcg diclofenac/misoprostol.] ▶LK ♀X ▶- $$$$

diclofenac (***Voltaren, Voltaren XR, Cataflam***): Multiple strengths; write specific product on Rx. Immediate or delayed release 50 mg PO bid-tid or 75 mg PO bid. Extended release (Voltaren XR): 100-200 mg PO qd. [Generic/Trade: Tabs, immediate release (Cataflam) 50 mg. Tabs, delayed release (Voltaren) 25, 50, & 75 mg. Tabs, ext'd release (Voltaren XR) 100 mg.] ▶L ♀B (D in 3rd trimester) ▶- $$$

etodolac (***Lodine, Lodine XL***): Multiple strengths; write specific product on Rx. Immediate release 200-400 mg PO bid-tid. Extended release (Lodine XL): 400-1200 mg PO qd. [Generic/Trade: Tabs, immediate release (Lodine) 400 mg. Trade only: Caps, immediate release (Lodine) 200 & 300 mg. Generic/Trade: Tabs, extended release (Lodine XL) 400,500 & 600 mg.] ▶L ♀C (D in 3rd trimester) ▶- $$$

flurbiprofen (***Ansaid, ♣Froben***): 200-300 mg/day PO divided bid-qid. [Generic/Trade: Tabs immediate release 50 & 100 mg.] ▶L ♀B (D in 3rd trimester) ▶+ $$$

NSAIDSs – If one class fails, consider another. *Salicylic acid derivatives:* aspirin, diflunisal, salsalate, Trilisate. *Propionic acids:* flurbiprofen, ibuprofen, ketoprofen, naproxen, oxaprozin. *Acetic acids:* diclofenac, etodolac, indomethacin, ketorolac, nabumetone, sulindac, tolmetin. *Fenamates:* meclofenamate. *Oxicams:* meloxicam, piroxicam. *COX-2 inhibitors:* celecoxib, rofecoxib, valdecoxib.

ibuprofen (***Motrin, Advil, Nuprin, Rufen***): 200-800 mg PO tid-qid. Peds >6 mo: 5-10 mg/kg PO q6-8h. [OTC: Caps, 200 mg. Tabs 100, 200 mg. Chewable tabs 50 & 100 mg. Caplets 200 mg. Liquid & suspension, 100 mg/5 ml, suspension 100 mg/2.5 ml. Infant drops, 50 mg/1.25 ml (calibrated dropper). Rx only: Tabs 400, 600 & 800 mg.] ▶L ♀B (D in 3rd trimester) ▶+ $$

indomethacin (***Indocin, Indocin SR***): Multiple strengths; write specific product on Rx. Immediate release preparations 25-50 mg cap or supp PO/PR tid. Sustained release: 75 mg cap PO qd-bid. [Generic/Trade: Caps, immediate release 25 & 50 mg. Oral suspension 25 mg/5 ml. Suppositories 50 mg. Caps, sustained release 75 mg.] ▶L ♀B (D in 3rd trimester) ▶+ $

ketoprofen (***Orudis, Orudis KT, Actron, Oruvail***): Immediate release: 25-75 mg PO tid-qid. Extended release: 100-200 mg cap PO qd. [OTC: Tabs immediate release, 12.5 mg. Rx: Generic/Trade: Caps, immediate release 25, 50 & 75 mg. Caps, extended release 100, 150 & 200 mg.] ▶L ♀B (D in 3rd trimester) ▶- $$$

ketorolac (***Toradol***): Moderately severe acute pain: 15-30 mg IV/IM q6h or 10 mg PO q4-6h prn. Combined duration IV/IM and PO is not to exceed 5 days. [Generic/Trade: Tabs 10 mg.] ▶L ♀C (D in 3rd trimester) ▶+ $

meclofenamate: 50-100 mg PO tid-qid. [Generic caps 50,100 mg] ▶L ♀D ▶- $$$$$

meloxicam (***Mobic***): OA: 7.5 mg tab PO qd. [Trade: Tabs 7.5 mg] ▶L ♀C (D in 3rd trimester) ▶? $$$

nabumetone (***Relafen***): RA/OA: Initial: two 500 mg tabs (1000mg) PO qd. May increase to 1500-2000 mg PO qd or divided bid. [Generic/Trade: Tabs 500 & 750 mg.] ▶L ♀C (D in 3rd trimester) ▶- $$$

naproxen (***Naprosyn, Aleve, Anaprox, EC-Naprosyn, Naprelan***, ✤***Naxen***): Immediate release: 250-500 mg PO bid. Delayed release: 375-500 mg PO bid (do not crush or chew). Controlled release: 750-1000 mg PO qd. JRA ≤13 kg: 2.5 ml PO bid. 14-25 kg: 5 ml PO bid. 26-38 kg: 7.5 ml PO bid. 500 mg naproxen = 550 mg naproxen sodium. [OTC: Generic/Trade: Tabs immed release 200 mg. Rx: Generic/Trade: Tabs immed release 250, 375 & 500 mg. Rx: Trade: Tabs (Naprelan), delay release enteric coated, 375 & 500 mg. Tabs, control release 375 & 500 mg. Generic/Trade: Susp 125 mg/5 ml.] ▶L ♀B (D in 3rd trimester) ▶+ $$$

oxaprozin (***Daypro***): 1200 mg PO qd. [Generic/Trade: Caplets 600 mg, trade scored.] ▶L ♀C (D in 3rd trimester) ▶- $$$

piroxicam (***Feldene, Fexicam***): 20 mg PO qd. [Generic/Trade: Caps 10 & 20 mg.] ▶L ♀B (D in 3rd trimester) ▶+ $

sulindac (***Clinoril***): 150-200 mg PO bid. [Generic/Trade: Tabs 150 & 200 mg.] ▶L ♀B (D in 3rd trimester) ▶- $

tolmetin (***Tolectin***): 200-600 mg PO tid. [Generic/Trade: Tabs 200 (trade scored) & 600 mg. Caps 400 mg.] ▶L ♀C (D in 3rd trimester) ▶+ $$$

Opioid Agonist-Antagonists

buprenorphine (***Buprenex***): 0.3-0.6 mg IV/IM q6-8h prn. ▶L ♀C ▶? ©V $

butorphanol (***Stadol, Stadol NS***): 0.5-2 mg IV or 1-4 mg IM q3-4h prn. Nasal spray (Stadol NS): 1 spray (1 mg) in 1 nostril q3-4h. Abuse potential. [Generic/Trade: Nasal spray 1 mg/spray, 2.5 ml bottle (14-15 doses/bottle).] ▶LK ♀C ▶+ ©IV $$$

FENTANYL TRANSDERMAL DOSE (based on ongoing morphine requirement)

morphine (IV/IM)	*morphine (PO)*	*Transdermal fentanyl*
8-22 mg/day	45-134 mg/day	25 mcg/hr
23-37 mg/day	135-224 mg/day	50 mcg/hr
38-52 mg/day	225-314 mg/day	75 mcg/hr
53-67 mg/day	315-404 mg/day	100 mcg/hr

nalbuphine (***Nubain***): 10-20 mg IV/IM/SC q3-6h. ▶LK ♀? ▶? $

pentazocine (***Talwin, Talwin NX***): 30 mg IV/IM q3-4h prn (Talwin). 1 tab PO q3-4h. (Talwin NX = 50 mg pentazocine/0.5 mg naloxone). [Generic/Trade: Tabs 50 mg with 0.5 mg naloxone, trade scored.] ▶LK ♀C ▶? ©IV $$$

Opioid Agonists

NOTE: Patients with chronic pain may require more frequent & higher dosing. All opioids are pregnancy class D if used for prolonged periods or in high doses at term.

codeine: 0.5-1 mg/kg up to 15-60 mg PO/IM/IV/SC q4-6h. Do not use IV in children. [Generic: Tabs 15, 30, & 60 mg. Oral soln: 15 mg/5 ml.] ▶LK ♀C ▶+ ©II $

fentanyl (***Duragesic Patches, Actiq***): Transdermal (Duragesic): 1 patch q72 hrs (some chronic pain pts may req q48 h dosing). May wear more than one patch to achieve the correct analgesic effect. Transmucosal lozenge for breakthrough cancer pain (Actiq): 200-1600 mcg, max dose 4 lozenges on a stick/day. [Trade: Transdermal patches 25, 50, 75, & 100 mcg/h (Duragesic). Transmucosal forms: lozenges on a stick, raspberry flavored 200, 400, 600, 800, 1,200, & 1,600 mcg (Actiq lozenges on a stick).] ▶L ♀C ▶+ ©II $$$$$

hydromorphone (***Dilaudid, Dilaudid-5***): Adults: 2-4 mg PO q4-6h. Titrate dose as high as necessary to relieve cancer pain or other types of non-malignant pain where chronic opioids are necessary. 0.5-2 mg IM/SC or slow IV q4-6h. 3 mg PR q6-8h. Peds ≤12 yo: 0.03-0.08 mg/kg PO q4-6h prn. 0.015 mg/kg/dose IV q4-6h prn. [Generic/Trade: Tabs 2, 4, & 8 mg (8 mg trade scored). Liquid 5 mg/5 ml (Dilaudid). Suppositories 3 mg. Trade only: Tabs 1 & 3 mg.] ▶L ♀C ▶? ©II $$$$$

levorphanol (***Levo-Dromoran***): 2 mg PO/SC q6-8h. [Trade: Tabs 2 mg, scored.] ▶L ♀C ▶? ©II $$$$

meperidine (***Demerol***): 1-1.8 mg/kg up to 150 mg IM/SC/PO or slow IV q3-4h. 75 mg meperidine IV,IM,SC = 300 mg PO. [Generic/Trade:Tabs 50 (trade scored) & 100 mg. Syrup 50 mg/5 ml (trade banana flavored).] ▶LK ♀C but + ▶+ ©II $

methadone (***Dolophine, Methadose***): Severe pain: 2.5-10 mg IM/SC/PO q3-4h prn. Titrate dose as high as necessary to relieve cancer pain or other types of non-malignant pain where chronic opioids are necessary. Detoxification: 15-40 mg PO qd to start, then decrease by 20% q1-2 days. [Generic/Trade: Tabs 5, 10, various scored. Dispersable tabs 40 mg. Oral concentrate: 10 mg/ml. Generic only: Oral soln 5 & 10 mg/5 ml.] ▶L ♀C ▶? ©II $$$

morphine sulfate (***MS Contin, Kadian, Avinza, Roxanol, Oramorph SR, MSIR, ♣Statex, M-Eslon***): Controlled-release tabs (MS Contin, Oramorph SR): Start at 30 mg PO q8-12h. Controlled release caps (Kadian): 20 mg PO q12-24h. Extended release caps (Avinza): Start at 30 mg PO qd. Do not break, chew, or crush MS Contin or Oramorph SR. Kadian & Avinza caps may be opened & sprinkled in applesauce for easier administration, however the pellets should not be crushed or chewed. 0.1-0.2 mg/kg up to 15 mg IM/SC or slow IV q4h. Titrate dose as high as necessary to relieve cancer pain or other types of non-malignant pain where chronic opioids are necessary. [Generic/Trade: Tabs, immed release 15,30 mg. Trade: Caps 15,30 mg. Generic/Trade: Oral soln (Roxanol) 10 mg/5 ml, 10 mg/2.5 ml, 20 mg/5 ml, 20 mg/ml (concentrate) & 100 mg/5 ml (concentrate). Rectal suppositories 5,10,20,30 mg. Control release tabs (MS Contin, Oramorph SR) 15,30, 60,100; 200 mg MS Contin only. Control release caps (Kadian) 20,30,50,60,100 mg. Extended release caps (Avinza) 30, 60, 90 & 120 mg.] ▶LK ♀C ▶+ ©II $$$$

oxycodone (***Roxicodone, OxyContin, Percolone, OxyIR, OxyFAST, ♣Endocodone, Supeudol***): Immediate release preparations: 5 mg PO q6h prn. Controlled release (OxyContin): 10-40 mg PO q12h (No supporting data for shorter dosing intervals for controlled release tabs.) Titrate dose as high as necessary to relieve

OPIOIDS*

Opioid Agonists	Approximate equianalgesic		Recommended starting dose			
			Adults >50kg		Children/Adults 8 to 50 kg	
	IV / SC / IM	PO	IV / SC / IM	PO	IV / SC / IM	PO
morphine	10 mg q3-4h	†30 mg q3-4h †60 mg q3-4h	10 mg q3-4h	30 mg q3-4h	0.1 mg/kg q3-4h	0.3 mg/kg q3-4h
codeine	75 mg q3-4h	130 mg q3-4h	60 mg q2h	60 mg q3-4h	n/r	1 mg/kg q3-4h
fentanyl	0.1 mg q1h	n/a	0.1 mg q1h	n/a	n/r	n/a
hydromorphone	1.5 mg q3-4h	7.5 mg q3-4h	1.5 mg q3-4h	6 mg q3-4h	0.015 mg/kg q3-4h	0.06 mg/kg q3-4h
hydrocodone	n/a	30 mg q3-4h	n/a	10 mg q3-4h	n/a	0.2 mg/kg q3-4h
levorphanol	2 mg q6-8h	4 mg q6-8h	2 mg q6-8h	4 mg q6-8h	0.02 mg/kg q6-8h	0.04 mg/kg q6-8h
meperidine§	100 mg q3h	300 mg q2-3h	100 mg q3h	n/r	0.75 mg/kg q2-3h	n/r
oxycodone	n/a	30 mg q3-4h	n/a	10 mg q3-4h	n/a	0.2 mg/kg q3-4h
oxymorphone	1 mg q3-4h	n/a	1 mg q3-4h	n/a	n/r	n/r
Opioid Agonist-Antagonist and Partial Agonist						
buprenorphine	0.3-0.4 mg q6-8h	n/a	0.4 mg q6-8h	n/a	0.004 mg/kg q6-8h	n/a
butorphanol	2 mg q3-4h	n/a	2 mg q3-4h	n/a	n/r	n/a
nalbuphine	10 mg q3-4h	n/a	10 mg q3-4h	n/a	0.1 mg/kg q3-4h	n/a
pentazocine	60 mg q3-4h	150 mg q3-4h	n/r	50 mg q4-6h	n/r	n/r

*Approximate dosing, adapted from 1992 AHCPR guidelines, www.ahcpr.gov. All PO dosing is with immediate-release preparations. Individualize all dosing, especially in the elderly, children, and patients with chronic pain, opioid tolerance, or hepatic/renal insufficiency. Many recommend initially using lower than equivalent doses when switching between different opioids. Not available = "n/a". Not recommended = "n/r". Methadone is excluded due to poor consensus on equivalence.

†30 mg with around the clock dosing, and 60 mg with a single dose or short-term dosing (ie, the opioid-naïve).

cancer pain or other types of non-malignant pain where chronic opioids are necessary. Do not break, chew, or crush controlled release preparations. [Generic/Trade: Immediate release: Tabs (scored) & caps 5 mg. Oral soln 5 mg/5 ml. Oral concentrate 20 mg/ml. Trade: Controlled release tabs (OxyContin): 10,20,40,80,160 mg.] ▶L ♀C ▶- ©II $$$$

oxymorphone (***Numorphan***): 1-1.5 mg IM/SC q4-6h prn. 0.5 mg IV q4-6h prn, increase dose until pain adequately controlled. 5 mg PR q4-6h prn. [Trade only: Suppositories 5 mg.] ▶L ♀C ▶? ©II $

propoxyphene (***Darvon-N, Darvon Pulvules***): 65-100 mg PO q4h prn. [Generic/Trade: Caps 65 mg. Trade only: 100 mg (Darvon-N).] ▶L ♀C ▶+ ©IV $

Opioid Analgesic Combinations

NOTE: Refer to individual components for further information. May cause drowsiness and/or sedation, which may be enhanced by alcohol & other CNS depressants. Opioids, carisoprodol, and butalbital may be habit-forming. Avoid exceeding 4 g/day of acetaminophen in combination products. Caution people who drink >3 alcoholic drinks/day to limit acetaminophen use due to additive liver toxicity. Opioids commonly cause constipation.

Anexsia (hydrocodone + acetaminophen): Multiple strengths; write specific product on Rx. 1 tab PO q4-6h prn. [Generic/Trade: Tabs 5/500, 7.5/650, 10/660 mg hydrocodone/mg acetaminophen, scored.] ▶LK ♀C ▶- ©III $

Capital with Codeine suspension (acetaminophen + codeine): 15 ml PO q4h prn. >12yo use adult dose. 7-12 yo 10 ml/dose q4-6h prn. 3-6 yo 5 ml/dose q4-6h prn. [Generic = oral soln. Trade = suspension. Both codeine 12 mg/acetaminophen 120 mg/5 ml (trade, fruit punch flavor).] ▶LK ♀C ▶? ©V $

Darvocet (propoxyphene + acetaminophen): Multiple strengths; write specific product on Rx. 50/325, 2 tabs PO q4h prn. 100/650, 1 tab PO q4h prn. [Generic/Trade: Tabs 50/325 (Darvocet N-50) & 100/650 (Darvocet N-100), mg propoxyphene/mg acetaminophen.] ▶L ♀C ▶+ ©IV $$

Darvon Compound-65 Pulvules (propoxyphene + ASA + caffeine): 1 cap PO q4h prn. [Generic/Trade: Caps, 65 mg propoxyphene/389 mg ASA/32.4 mg caffeine.] ▶LK ♀D ▶- ©IV $

Empirin with Codeine (ASA + codeine, ***♣Frosst 292***): Multiple strengths; write specific product on Rx.1-2 tabs PO q4h prn. [Generic/Trade: Tabs 325/30& 325/60 mg ASA/mg codeine. Empirin brand no longer made.] ▶LK ♀D ▶- ©III $

Fioricet with Codeine (acetaminophen + butalbital + caffeine + codeine): 1-2 caps PO q4h prn. [Generic/Trade: Caps, 325 mg acetaminophen/50 mg butalbital/40 mg caffeine/30 mg codeine.] ▶LK ♀C ▶- ©III $$$

Fiorinal with Codeine (ASA + butalbital + caffeine + codeine): 1-2 caps PO q4h prn. [Trade: Caps, 325 mg ASA/50 mg butalbital /40 mg caffeine/30 mg codeine.] ▶LK ♀D ▶- ©III $$$

Lorcet (hydrocodone + acetaminophen): Multiple strengths; write specific product on Rx. 5/500: 1-2 tabs PO q4-6h prn; 7.5/650 & 10/650 : 1 tab PO q4-6h prn. [Generic/Trade: Caps, 5/500. (Lorcet HD) Tabs, 7.5/650 (Lorcet Plus). Trade: Lorcet 10/650, mg hydrocodone/mg acetaminophen, scored.] ▶LK ♀C ▶- ©III $$

Lortab (hydrocodone + acetaminophen): Multiple strengths; write specific product on Rx. 1-2 tabs PO q4-6h prn (2.5/500 & 5/500). 1 tab PO q4-6h prn (7.5/500 & 10/500). Elixir: 15 ml PO q4-6h prn. [Trade: Tabs Lortab 2.5/500. Generic/Trade: Lortab 5/500 (scored), Lortab 7.5/500 (trade scored) & Lortab 10/500 mg hydrocodone/mg acetaminophen. Elixir: 7.5/500 mg hydrocodone/mg acetaminophen/15 ml.] ▶LK ♀C ▶- ©III $$

Maxidone (hydrocodone + acetaminophen): 1 tab PO q4-6h prn, max dose 5 tabs/day. [Trade: Tabs 10/750 mg hydrocodone/mg acetamin.] ▶LK ♀C ▶- ©III $$

Norco (hydrocodone + acetaminophen): 1 tab PO q4-6h prn, max 6/day. [Trade: Tabs: 5/325, 7.5/325 & 10/325 mg hydroc./mg acet. scored.] ▶L ♀C ▶? ©III $$

Percocet (oxycodone + acetaminophen): Multiple strengths; write specific product on Rx. 1-2 tabs PO q6h prn (2.5/325 & 5/325). 1 tab PO q6 prn (7.5/500 & 10/650). [Trade: Tabs Percocet 2.5/325, Percocet 7.5/325, Percocet 7.5/500, Percocet 10/325, Percocet 10/650. Generic/Trade: Tabs Percocet 5/325 mg oxycodone/mg acetaminophen.] ▶L ♀C ▶- ©II $

Percodan (oxycodone + ASA): 1 tab PO q6h prn (5/325 mg). 1-2 tabs PO q6h prn (2.5/325). [Generic/Trade: Tabs Perodan 5/325 (trade scored). Trade only: 2.5/325(Percodan Demi) scored, mg oxycodone/mg ASA.] ▶LK ♀D ▶- ©II $

Roxicet (oxycodone + acetaminophen): Multiple strengths; write specific product on Rx. 1 tab PO q6h prn. Soln: 5 ml PO q6h prn. [Generic/Trade: Tablet Roxicet 5/325, scored. Caplet Roxicet 5/500, scored. Generic: Caps 5/500. Trade only: Roxicet oral soln 5/325 per 5 ml, mg oxycodone/mg acetam.] ▶L ♀C ▶- ©II $$

Soma Compound with Codeine (carisoprodol + ASA + codeine): Moderate to severe musculoskeletal pain:1-2 tabs PO qid prn. [Trade: Tabs 200 mg carisoprodol/325 mg ASA/16 mg codeine.] ▶L ♀C ▶- ©III $$$

Talacen (pentazocine + acetaminophen): 1 tab PO q4h prn. [Trade: Tabs 25 mg pentazocine/650 mg acetaminophen, scored.] ▶L ♀C ▶? ©IV $$$

Tylenol with Codeine (codeine + acetaminophen): Multiple strengths; write specific product on Rx. 1-2 tabs PO q4h prn. Elixir 3-6 yo 5 ml/dose. 7-12 yo 10 ml/dose q4-6h prn. [Generic/Trade: Tabs Tylenol #2 (15/300), Tylenol #3 (30/300), Tylenol #4 (60/300). Tylenol with Codeine Elixir 12/120 per 5 ml, mg codeine/mg acetaminophen.] ▶LK ♀C ▶? ©III (Tabs), V(elixir) $

Tylox (oxycodone + acetaminophen): 1 cap PO q6h prn. [Generic/Trade: Caps, 5 mg oxycodone/500 mg acetaminophen.] ▶L ♀C ▶- ©II $

Vicodin (hydrocodone + acetaminophen): Multiple strengths; write specific product on Rx. 5/500 & 7.5/750: 1-2 tabs PO q4-6h prn. 10/660: 1 tab PO q4-6h prn. [Generic/Trade: Tabs Vicodin (5/500), Vicodin ES (7.5/750), Vicodin HP (10/660), scored, mg hydrocodone/mg acetaminophen.] ▶LK ♀C ▶? ©III $

Vicoprofen (hydrocodone + ibuprofen): 1 tab PO q4h prn. [Trade: Tabs 7.5 mg hydrocodone/200 mg ibuprofen.] ▶LK ♀- ▶? ©III $$$

Wygesic (propoxyphene + acetaminophen): 1 tab PO q4h prn. [Generic/Trade: Tabs 65 mg propoxyphene/650 mg acetaminophen.] ▶L ♀C ▶? ©IV $$

Zydone (hydrocodone + acetaminophen): Multiple strengths; write specific product on Rx: 1-2 tabs PO q4-6h prn [5/400]. 1 tab q4-6h prn [7.5/400,10/400]. [Trade: Tabs (5/400), (7.5/400) & (10/400) mg hydrocodone/mg acetaminophen.] ▶LK ♀C ▶? ©III $$

Opioid Antagonists

nalmefene (***Revex***): Opioid overdose: 0.5 mg/70 kg IV. If needed, this may be followed by a second dose of 1 mg/70kg, 2-5 minutes later. Max cumulative dose 1.5 mg/70 kg. If suspicion of opioid dependency, initially administer a challenge dose of 0.1 mg/70 kg. Post-operative opioid reversal: 0.25 mcg/kg IV followed by 0.25 mcg/kg incremental doses at 2-5 minute intervals, stopping as soon as the desired degree of opioid reversal is obtained. Max cumulative dose 1mcg/kg. [Trade: Injection 100 mcg/ml nalmefene for postoperative reversal (blue label). 1 mg/ml nalmefene for opioid overdose (green label).] ▶L ♀B ▶? $$$

naloxone (***Narcan***): Opioid overdose: 0.4-2.0 mg q2-3 min prn. Adult post-op reversal 0.1-0.2 mg. Ped post-op reversal: 0.005-0.01 mg. IV/IM/SC/ET. ▶LK ♀B ▶? $

Other Analgesics

acetaminophen (***Tylenol, Panadol, Tempra***): 325-650 mg PO/PR q4-6h prn. Max dose 4g/day. OA: 2 extended release caplets (ie, 1300 mg) PO q8h around the clock. Peds: 10-15 mg/kg/dose PO/PR q4-6h prn. [OTC: Tabs 160, 325, 500, 650 mg. Chewable Tabs 80 mg. Gelcaps 500 mg. Caps 325 & 500 mg. Sprinkle Caps 80 & 160 mg. Extended release caplets 650 mg. Liquid 80 mg/2.5 ml, 80, 120, 160 mg/5 ml, 500 mg/15 ml. Drops 80 mg/0.8 ml & 80 mg/1.66 ml, & 100 mg/ml. Suppositories 80, 120, 125, 300, 325, & 650 mg.] ▶LK ♀B ▶+ $

lidocaine (***Lidoderm, Xylocaine***): Postherpetic neuralgia: apply up to 3 patches to affected area at once for up to 12h within a 24h period. [Trade: Patch 5%, box of 30.] ▶LK ♀B ▶+ $$$$

tramadol (***Ultram***): Moderate to moderately severe pain: 50-100 mg PO q4-6h prn, max 400 mg/day. Adjust dose in elderly, renal & hepatic dysfunction. Avoid in the opioid dependent. Seizures may occur with concurrent antidepressants or seizure disorder. [Generic/Trade: Tabs immediate release 50 mg.] ▶KL ♀C ▶- $$$

Women's Tylenol Menstrual Relief (acetaminophen + pamabrom): 2 caplets PO q4-6h. [OTC: Caplets 500 mg acet. /25 mg pamabrom (diuretic).] ▶LK ♀B ▶+ $

ANESTHESIA

Anesthetics & Sedatives

dexmedetomidine (***Precedex***): ICU sedation <24h: Load 1 mcg/kg over 10 min followed by infusion 0.2-0.7 mcg/kg/h titrated to desired sedation endpoint. Beware of bradycardia and hypotension. ▶LK ♀C ▶? $$$$

etomidate (***Amidate***): Induction 0.3 mg/kg IV. ▶L ♀C ▶? $

fentanyl (***Sublimaze***): Procedural sedation: 50 mcg (1 mcg/kg in children) IV, may repeat q3 min, adjust to desired effect. IV adjunct to anesthesia: specialized dosing. ▶L ♀C ▶? ©II $

ketamine (***Ketalar***): 1-2 mg/kg IV over 1-2 min or 4 mg/kg IM induces 10-20 min dissociative state. Concurrent atropine minimizes hypersalivation. ▶L ♀? ▶? ©III $

methohexital (***Brevital***): Induction 1-1.5 mg/kg IV, duration 5 min. ▶L ♀B ▶? ©IV $

midazolam (***Versed***): Adult sedation/anxiolysis: 5 mg or 0.07 mg/kg IM; or 1 mg IV slowly q2-3 min up to 5 mg. Peds: 0.25-1.0 mg/kg to max of 20 mg PO, or 0.1-0.15 mg/kg IM. IV route (6 mo to 5 yo): Initial dose 0.05-0.1 mg/kg IV, then titrated to max 0.6 mg/kg. IV route (6-12 yo): Initial dose 0.025-0.05 mg/kg IV, then titrated to max 0.4 mg/kg. Monitor for resp depression. [Oral liquid 2 mg/ml] ▶LK ♀D ▶- ©IV $

propofol (***Diprivan***): 40 mg IV q10 sec until induction (2-2.5 mg/kg) ICU ventilator sedation: infusion 5-50 mcg/kg/min. ▶L ♀B ▶- $$$

thiopental (***Pentothal***): Induction 3-5 mg/kg IV, duration 5 min. ▶L ♀C ▶? ©III $

Local Anesthetics

articaine (***Septocaine***): 4% injection (includes epinephrine). [4% (includes epinephrine 1:100,000)] ▶LK ♀C ▶? ?

bupivacaine (***Marcaine, Sensorcaine***): 0.25% injection. [0.25%. With epinephrine: 0.25%] ▶LK ♀C ▶? $

levobupivacaine (***Chirocaine***): Local & epidural anesthesia, nerve block. [2.5, 5, 7.5 mg/ml injection.] ▶LK ♀B ▶? ?

lidocaine (***Xylocaine***): 0.5-1% injection with and without epinephrine. [0.5,1,1.5,2%. With epi: 0.5,1,1.5,2%.] ▶LK ♀B ▶? $

mepivacaine (***Carbocaine***): 1-2% injection. [1,1.5,2,3%.] ▶LK ♀C ▶? $

Neuromuscular Blockers

Should be administered only by those skilled in airway management & respiratory support.

atracurium (***Tracrium***): 0.4-0.5 mg/kg IV. Duration 15-30 min. ▶Plasma ♀C ▶? $
cisatracurium (***Nimbex***): 0.1-0.2 mg/kg IV. Duration 30-60 min. ▶Plasma ♀B ▶? $$
doxacurium (***Nuromax***): 0.05 mg/kg IV. Duration ~100 minutes. ▶K ♀C ▶? $
mivacurium (***Mivacron***): 0.15 mg/kg IV. Duration 20 minutes. ▶Plasma ♀C ▶? $
pancuronium (***Pavulon***): 0.04 to 0.1 mg/kg IV. Duration 45 min. ▶LK ♀C ▶? $
rocuronium (***Zemuron***): 0.6 mg/kg IV. Duration 30 min. ▶L ♀B ▶? $$
succinylcholine (***Anectine, Quelicin***): 0.6-1.1 mg/kg IV. Peds: 2 mg/kg IV, preceded by atropine 0.02 mg/kg if <5 yo. ▶Plasma ♀C ▶? $
vecuronium (***Norcuron***): 0.08-0.1 mg/kg IV. Duration 15-30 min. ▶LK ♀C ▶? $

ANTIMICROBIALS

Aminoglycosides

NOTE: See also dermatology and ophthalmology

amikacin (***Amikin***): 15 mg/kg up to 1500 mg/day IM/IV divided q8-12h. Peak 20-35 mcg/ml, trough <5 mcg/ml. Alternative 15 mg/kg IV q24h. ▶K ♀D ▶? $$$$
gentamicin (***Garamycin***): Adults: 3-5 mg/kg/day IM/IV divided q8h. Peak 5-10 mcg/ml, trough <2 mcg/ml. Alternative 5-7 mg/kg IV q24h. Peds: 2-2.5 mg/kg q8h. ▶K ♀D ▶+ $$
streptomycin: Combo therapy for tuberculosis: 15 mg/kg up to 1 g IM qd. Peds: 20-40 mg/kg up to 1 g IM qd. Adults/peds: 25-30 mg/kg up to 1.5 g IM 2-3 times weekly. Nephrotoxicity, ototoxicity. [Generic: 1 g vials for parenteral use.] ▶K ♀D ▶+ $$$$$
tobramycin (***Nebcin, TOBI***): Adults: 3-5 mg/kg/day IM/IV divided q8h. Peak 5-10 mcg/ml, trough <2 mcg/ml. Alternative 5-7 mg/kg IV q24h. Peds: 2-2.5 mg/kg q8h. Cystic fibrosis (TOBI): 300 mg neb bid 28 days on, then 28 days off. [TOBI 300 mg ampules for nebulizer.] ▶K ♀D ▶? $$$$

Antifungal Agents

amphotericin B deoxycholate (***Fungizone***): Test dose 0.1 mg/kg up to 1 mg slow IV. Wait 2-4 h, and if tolerated then begin 0.25 mg/kg IV qd & advance to 0.5-1.5 mg/kg/day depending on fungal type. Maximum dose 1.5 mg/kg/day. Oral candidiasis: 1 ml oral suspension swish & swallow qid given between meals x at least 2 weeks. [Trade: Oral susp 100 mg/ml.] ▶Tissues ♀B for IV, C for PO ▶? $$$$
amphotericin B lipid formulations (***Amphotec, Abelcet, AmBisome***): Abelcet: 5 mg/kg/day IV at 2.5 mg/kg/hr. AmBisome: 3-5 mg/kg/day IV over 2 h. Amphotec: Test dose of 10 ml over 15-30 minutes, observe for 30 minutes, then 3-4 mg/kg/day IV at 1 mg/kg/h. ▶? ♀B ▶? $$$$$
caspofungin (***Cancidas***): 70 mg loading dose on day 1, then 50 mg qd. Infuse IV over 1 h. ▶KL ♀C ▶? $$$$$
clotrimazole (***Mycelex***, ♣***Canesten***): Oral troches 5 times/day x 14 days. [Trade: Oral troches 10 mg.] ▶L ♀C ▶? $$$
fluconazole (***Diflucan***): Vaginal candidiasis: 150 mg PO single dose. All other regimens IV/PO. Oropharyngeal/ esophageal candidiasis: 200 mg first day, then 100 mg qd. Systemic candidiasis, cryptococcal meningitis: 400 mg qd. Peds: Oropha-

yngeal/esophageal candidiasis: 6 mg/kg first day, then 3 mg/kg qd. Systemic candidiasis: 6-12 mg/kg qd. Cryptococcal meningitis: 12 mg/kg on first day, then 6 mg/kg qd. [Trade: Tabs 50,100,150,200 mg; susp 10&40 mg/ml.] ▶K ♀C ▶+ $$$$

flucytosine (***Ancobon***): 50-150 mg/kg/day PO divided qid. Myelosuppression. [Trade: Caps 250, 500 mg.] ▶K ♀C ▶ $$$$$

griseofulvin microsize (***Fulvicin-U/F, Grifulvin-V, Grisactin 500***): Tinea: 11 mg/kg up to 500 mg PO qd x 4-6 weeks. [Generic/Trade: Tabs 500 mg. Trade: Tabs 250, susp 125 mg/5 ml.] ▶Skin ♀C ▶? $$

itraconazole (***Sporanox***): Oral caps for onychomycosis "pulse dosing": 200 mg PO bid for 1st wk of month x 2 months (fingernails) or 3-4 months (toenails). Oral sol'n for oropharyngeal or esophageal candidiasis: 100-200 mg PO qd or 100 mg bid swish & swallow in 10 ml increments on empty stomach. For life-threatening infections, load with 200 mg IV bid x 4 doses or 200 mg PO tid x 3 days. Empiric therapy of suspected fungal infection in febrile neutropenia: 200 mg IV bid x 4 doses, then 200 mg IV qd for ≤14 days. Continue with oral sol'n 200 mg (20 ml) PO bid until significant neutropenia resolved. Contraindicated with cisapride, dofetilide, lovastatin, PO midazolam, pimozide, quinidine, simvastatin, triazolam. Negative inotrope, do not use for onychomycosis if ventricular dysfunction. [Trade: Cap 100 mg, oral soln 10 mg/ml.] ▶L ♀C ▶- $$$$$

ketoconazole (***Nizoral***): 200-400 mg PO qd. Hepatotoxicity. Contraindicated with cisapride, midazolam, pimozide, triazolam. H2 blockers, proton pump inhibitors, antacids impair absorption. [Generic/Trade: Tabs 200 mg.] ▶L ♀C ▶?+ $$$$

nystatin (***Mycostatin***, ***✤Nilstat, Nyaderm***): Thrush: 4-6 ml PO swish & swallow qid. Infants: 2 ml/dose with 1 ml in each cheek qid. [Generic/Trade: Susp 100,000 units/ml. Trade: Troches 200,000 units.] ▶Not absorbed ♀B ▶? $

terbinafine (***Lamisil***): Onychomycosis: 250 mg PO qd x 6 weeks for fingernails, x 12 weeks for toenails. "Pulse dosing": 500 mg PO qd for first week of month x 2 months (fingernails) or 4 months (toenails). [Trade: Tabs 250 mg.] ▶LK ♀B ▶- $$$$$

voriconazole (***Vfend***): IV: 6 mg/kg q12h x 2, then 4 mg/kg IV q12h. Infuse over 2 h. PO: 200 mg q12h if >40 kg, 100 mg PO q12 h if <40 kg. Many drug interactions. [Trade: Tabs 50,200 mg (contains lactose).] ▶L ♀D ▶? $$$$$

Antimalarials

> **NOTE:** For help treating malaria or getting antimalarials, call the CDC "malaria hotline" (770) 488-7788 Monday-Friday 8 am to 4:30 pm EST. After hours / weekend (404) 639-2888. Information is also available at: http://www.cdc.gov

chloroquine phosphate (***Aralen***): Malaria prophylaxis, chloroquine-sensitive areas: 8 mg/kg up to 500 mg PO q wk from 1-2 weeks before exposure to 4 weeks after. Chloroquine resistance widespread. [Generic: Tabs 250 mg. Generic/Trade: Tabs 500 mg (500 mg phosphate equivalent to 300 mg base).] ▶KL ♀C but + ▶+ $

doxycycline (***Vibramycin, Vibra-Tabs, Doryx, Monodox***): Malaria prophylaxis: 2 mg/kg/day up to 100 mg PO qd starting 1-2 days before exposure until 4 weeks after. 100 mg IV/PO bid for severe infections. [Generic/Trade: Tabs 100 mg, caps 50,100 mg. Trade: Susp 25 mg/5 ml, syrup 50 mg/5 ml.] ▶LK ♀D ▶? $

Fansidar (sulfadoxine + pyrimethamine): Chloroquine-resistant P falciparum malaria: 2-3 tabs PO single dose. Peds: 5-10 kg: ½ tab. 11-20 kg: 1 tab. 21-30 kg: 1½ tab. 31-45 kg: 2 tabs. >45 kg: 3 tabs. Stevens Johnson syndrome, toxic epidermal necrolysis. Fansider resistance common in many malarious areas. [Trade: Tabs sulfadoxine 500 mg + pyrimethamine 25 mg.] ▶KL ♀C ▶- $

Malarone (atovaquone + proguanil): Malaria prevention: 1 adult tab PO qd from 1-2 days before exposure until 7 days after. Treatment: 4 adult tabs PO qd x 3 days. Take with food or milky drink. [Trade: Adult tabs atovaquone 250 mg + proguanil 100 mg; pediatric tabs 62.5 mg + 25 mg.] ▶Fecal excretion; LK ♀C ◗? $$$$

mefloquine (***Lariam***): Malaria prophylaxis for chloroquine-resistant areas: 250 mg PO q week from 1 week before exposure to 4 weeks after. Treatment: 1250 mg PO single dose. [Generic/trade: Tabs 250 mg.] ▶L ♀C ◗? $$

primaquine phosphate: 26.3 mg PO qd x 14 days. [Generic: Tabs 26.3 mg (equiv to 15 mg base).] ▶L ♀- ◗- $

quinidine gluconate: Life-threatening malaria: Load with 10 mg/kg (max 600 mg) IV over 1-2 h, then 0.02 mg/kg/min. Treat x 72 h, until parasitemia <1%, or PO meds tolerated. ▶LK ♀C ◗+ $$$$

quinine sulfate: Malaria: 600-650 mg PO tid. Peds: 25-30 mg/kg/day up to 2 g/day PO divided q8h. Treat for 3-7 days. Also give doxycycline or Fansidar. [Generic: Tabs 260 mg, caps 200,325 mg.] ▶L ♀X ◗+? $

Antimycobacterial Agents

NOTE: Two or more drugs are needed for the treatment of active mycobacterial infections. See guidelines at http://www.thoracic.org/statements/.

clofazimine (***Lamprene***): Mycobacterium avium complex disease treatment: 100 mg PO qd. [Trade: Caps 50 mg.] ▶Fecal excretion ♀C ◗?- $

dapsone, (♣***Avlosulfon***): Pneumocystis prophylaxis, leprosy: 100 mg PO qd. Pneumocystis treatment: 100 mg PO qd with trimethoprim 5 mg/kg PO tid x 21 days. [Generic: Tabs 25,100 mg.] ▶LK ♀C ◗+? $

ethambutol (***Myambutol***, ♣***Etibi***): 15-25 mg/kg up to 2500 mg PO qd. [Generic/Trade: Tabs 100,400 mg.] ▶LK ♀B ◗+ $$$$$

isoniazid (***INH***): Adults: 5 mg/kg up to 300 mg PO qd. Peds: 10-20 mg/kg up to 300 mg PO qd. Hepatotoxicity. Consider supplemental pyridoxine 10-50 mg PO qd. [Generic: Tabs 100,300 mg, syrup 50 mg/5 ml.] ▶LK ♀C but + ◗+ $

pyrazinamide, ♣***Tebrazid***: 15-30 mg/kg up to 2000 mg PO qd. [Generic: Tabs 500 mg.] ▶LK ♀C ◗? $$$

rifabutin (***Mycobutin***): 300 mg PO qd or 150 mg PO bid. [Trade: Caps 150 mg.] ▶L ♀B ◗? $$$$$

Rifamate (isoniazid + rifampin): 2 caps PO qd. [Trade: Caps isoniazid 150 mg + rifampin 300 mg.] ▶LK ♀C ◗+ $$$$

rifampin (***Rimactane, Rifadin***): 10-20 mg/kg up to 600 mg PO/IV qd. [Generic/Trade: Caps 150,300 mg. Pharmacists can make oral susp.] ▶L ♀C ◗+ $$$

rifapentine (***Priftin***): 600 mg PO twice weekly x 2 months, then q week x 4 months (twice weekly if HIV). [Trade: Tabs 150 mg.] ▶Esterases, fecal ♀C ◗? $$$

Rifater (isoniazid + rifampin + pyrazinamide): 6 tabs PO qd if ≥55 kg, 5 qd if 45-54 kg, 4 qd if ≤ 44 kg. [Trade: Tab Isoniazid 50 mg + rifampin 120 mg + pyrazinamide 300 mg.] ▶LK ♀C ◗? $$$$$

Antiparasitics

albendazole (***Albenza***): Hydatid disease, neurocysticercosis: 400 mg PO bid. 15 mg/kg/day up to 800 mg/day if <60 kg. [Trade: Tabs 200 mg.] ▶L ♀C ◗? $$$

atovaquone (***Mepron***): Pneumocystis treatment: 750 mg PO bid x 21 days. Pneumocystis prevention: 1500 mg PO qd. Take with meals. [Trade: Susp 750 mg/5 ml, foil pouch 750 mg/5 ml.] ▶Fecal ♀C ◗? $$$$$

iodoquinol (***Yodoxin, diiodohydroxyquin***, ♣***Diodoquin***): Intestinal amebiasis: 40 mg/kg/day up to 650 mg PO tid after meals x 20 days. [Generic/Trade: Tabs 650 mg. Trade: Tabs 210 mg.] ▶Not absorbed ♀? ◗? $$

ivermectin (***Stromectol***): Single PO dose of 200 mcg/kg for strongyloidiasis, scabies (not for children <15 kg), 150 mcg/kg for onchocerciasis. [Trade: Tab 3 mg.] ▶L ♀C ◗+ $

mebendazole (***Vermox***): Pinworm: 100 mg PO x 1; may repeat in 2 wks. Roundworm, whipworm, hookworm: 100 mg PO bid x 3d. [Trade/Generic: Chew tab 100 mg.] ▶L ♀C ◗? $

metronidazole (***Flagyl***): Trichomoniasis: 2g PO single dose for patient & sex partners. Giardia: 250 mg PO tid x 5-7 days. [Generic/Trade: Tabs 250,500 mg. Trade: Caps 375 mg, Flagyl ER tabs 750 mg.] ▶KL ♀B ◗?- $

paromomycin (***Humatin***): 25-35 mg/kg/day PO divided tid with or after meals. [Generic/Trade: Caps 250 mg.] ▶Not absorbed ♀C ◗- $$$$

pentamidine (***Pentam, NebuPent***, ***✤Pentacarina***): Pneumocystis treatment: 4 mg/kg IM/IV qd x 14-21 days. Pneumocystis prevention: 300 mg nebulized q 4 weeks. [Trade: Aerosol 300 mg.] ▶K ♀C ◗- $$$$$

praziquantel (***Biltricide***): Schistosomiasis: 20 mg/kg PO q4-6h x 3 doses. Neurocysticercosis: 50 mg/kg/day PO divided tid x 15 days (up to 100 mg/kg/day for peds). [Trade: Tabs 600 mg.] ▶LK ♀B ◗- $$$

pyrantel (***Pin-X, Pinworm***, ***✤Combantrin***): Pinworm/roundworm: 11 mg/kg up to 1 g PO single dose. [OTC: Caps 62.5 mg, liquid 50 mg/ml.] ▶Not absorbed ♀- ◗? $

pyrimethamine (***Daraprim***): Toxoplasmosis: 50-75 mg PO qd x 1-3 weeks, then reduce dose by 50% for 4-5 more weeks. CNS toxoplasmosis in AIDS: 200 mg PO x 1, then 75-100 mg qd. Secondary prevention after CNS toxoplasmosis in AIDS: 25-75 mg PO qd. Give with leucovorin and sulfadiazine or clindamycin. Reduce initial dose in seizure disorders. Peds: 1 mg/kg/day PO divided bid x 2-4 days, then reduce by 50% x 1 month. [Trade: Tabs 25 mg.] ▶L ♀C ◗+ $$

thiabendazole (***Mintezol***): Helminths: 22 mg/kg/dose up to 1500 mg PO bid after meals. Treat x 2 days for strongyloidiasis, cutaneous larva migrans. [Trade: Chew tab 500 mg, susp 500 mg/5 ml.] ▶LK ♀C ◗? $

trimetrexate (***Neutrexin***): 45 mg/m2 IV infused over 1h qd x 21 days. Give leucovorin 20 mg/m2 IV/PO q6h x 24 days (until 72 h after last trimetrexate dose). ▶LK ♀D ◗- $$$$$

Antiviral Agents - Anti-CMV

cidofovir (***Vistide***): CMV retinitis in AIDS: 5 mg/kg IV q wk x 2, then 5 mg/kg q2 wks. Nephrotoxicity. ▶K ♀C ◗- $$$$$

foscarnet (***Foscavir***): CMV retinitis: 60 mg/kg IV (over 1 h) q8h or 90 mg/kg IV (over 1.5-2 h) q12h x 2-3 weeks, then 90-120 mg/kg/day IV over 2h. HSV infection: 40 mg/kg (over 1 h) q8-12h. Nephrotoxicity, seizures. ▶K ♀C ◗? $$$$$

ganciclovir (***DHPG, Cytovene***): CMV retinitis: Induction 5 mg/kg IV q12h for 14-21 days. Maintenance 6 mg/kg IV qd for 5 days per week. Oral: 1000 mg PO tid or 500 mg 6 times daily. Myelosuppression. Potential carcinogen, teratogen. May impair fertility. [Trade: Caps 250, 500 mg.] ▶K ♀C ◗- $$$$$

valganciclovir (***Valcyte***): CMV retinitis: 900 mg PO bid x 21 days, then 900 mg PO qd. Give with food. Impaired fertility, myelosuppression, potential carcinogen & teratogen. [Trade: Tabs 450 mg.] ▶K ♀C ◗- $$$$$

Antiviral Agents - Anti-Herpetic

acyclovir (***Zovirax***): 5-10 mg/kg IV q8h, each dose over 1 h. Genital herpes: 400 mg PO tid x 7-10 days for first episode, x 5 days for recurrent episodes. Herpes prophylaxis: 400 mg PO bid. Zoster: 800 mg PO 5 times/day x 7-10 days. Varicella: 20 mg/kg up to 800 mg PO qid x 5 days. [Generic/Trade: Caps 200 mg, tabs 400,800 mg. Trade: Susp 200 mg/5 ml.] ▶K ♀B ◗+ $

famciclovir (***Famvir***): First-episode genital herpes: 250 mg PO tid x 7-10 days. Recurrent genital herpes: 125 mg PO bid x 5 days. Herpes prophylaxis: 250 mg PO bid. Recurrent oral/genital herpes in HIV patients: 500 bid x 7 days. Zoster: 500 mg PO tid for 7 days. [Trade: Tabs 125,250,500 mg.] ▶K ♀B ◗? $$$

valacyclovir (***Valtrex***): First-episode genital herpes: 1000 mg PO bid x 10 days. Recurrent genital herpes: 500 mg PO bid x 3 days. Herpes prophylaxis: 500-1000 mg PO qd. Zoster: 1000 mg PO tid x 7 days. [Trade: Tabs 500,1000 mg.] ▶K ♀B ◗? $$$$

Antiviral Agents - Anti-HIV - Non-Nucleoside Reverse Transcript. Inhibitors

NOTE: AIDS treatment guidelines available online at www.hivatis.org. Many serious drug interactions - always check before prescribing! Consider monitoring LFTs in patients receiving highly active anti-retroviral therapy (HAART).

delavirdine (***Rescriptor, DLV***): Adults & children >16yo: 400 mg PO tid. [Trade: Tabs 100,200 mg.] ▶L ♀C ◗- $$$$$

efavirenz (***Sustiva, EFV***): Adults & children >40kg: 600 mg PO qhs. [Trade: Caps 50,100,200 mg, tabs 600 mg.] ▶L ♀C ◗- $$$$$

nevirapine (***Viramune, NVP***): 200 mg PO qd x 14 days initially. If tolerated, increase to 200 mg PO bid. Severe skin reactions & hepatotoxicity. [Trade: Tabs 200 mg, susp 50 mg/5 ml.] ▶LK ♀C ◗- $$$$$

Antiviral Agents - Anti-HIV - Nucleoside Reverse Transcriptase Inhibitors

NOTE: AIDS treatment guidelines available online at www.hivatis.org. Consider monitoring LFTs in patients receiving highly active anti-retroviral therapy (HAART).

abacavir (***Ziagen, ABC***): Adult: 300 mg PO bid. Children >3 mo: 8 mg/kg up to 300 mg PO bid. Potentially fatal hypersensitivity; never rechallenge if this occurs. [Trade: Tabs 300 mg, oral soln 20 mg/ml.] ▶L ♀C ◗- $$$$$

Combivir (lamivudine + zidovudine): 1 tab PO bid. [Trade: Tabs lamivudine 150 mg + zidovudine 300 mg.] ▶LK ♀C ◗- $$$$$

didanosine (***Videx, Videx EC, ddI***): Adult, buffered tabs: 200 mg PO bid if ≥60 kg, 125 mg PO bid if <60 kg. Peds: 120 mg/m2 PO bid. Videx EC, adults: 400 mg PO qd if ≥60 kg, 250 mg PO qd if <60 kg. Take all formulations on empty stomach. [Trade: chew/dispersible buffered tabs 25,50,100,150,200 mg, packets of buffered powder for oral soln 100,167,250 mg, pediatric powder for oral soln 10 mg/ml (buffered with antacid). Delayed-release caps (Videx EC) 125,200,250,400 mg.] ▶LK ♀B ◗- $$$$$

lamivudine (***Epivir, Epivir-HBV, 3TC, ♣Heptovir***): Epivir for HIV infection. Adults: 2 mg/kg up to 150 mg PO bid. Peds: 4 mg/kg up to 150 mg PO bid. Epivir-HBV for hepatitis B: Adults: 100 mg PO qd [Trade: Epivir, 3TC: Tabs 150, 300 mg, oral soln 10 mg/ml. Epivir-HBV, Heptovir: Tabs 100 mg, oral soln 5 mg/ml.] ▶K ♀C ◗- $$$$$

stavudine (***Zerit, d4T***): 40 mg PO q12h, or 30 mg q12h if <60 kg. Peds (<30 kg): 1 mg/ kg PO bid. [Trade: Caps 15,20,30,40 mg; oral soln 1 mg/ml.] ▶LK ♀C ◗- $$$$$

tenofovir (***Viread***): 300 mg PO qd with meal. [Trade: Tab 300 mg.] ▶K ♀B ◗- $$$$$

Trizivir (abacavir + lamivudine + zidovudine): 1 tab PO bid. [Trade: Tabs abacavir 300 mg + lamivudine 150 mg + zidovudine 300 mg.] ▶LK ♀C ◗- $$$$$

zalcitabine (***Hivid, ddC***): 0.75 mg PO q8h. [Trade: Tabs 0.375, 0.75 mg.] ▶K ♀C ◗- $$$$$

zidovudine (***Retrovir, AZT***): 200 mg PO tid or 300 bid. Peds: 180 mg/m2 up to 200 mg q6h. [Trade: Cap 100 mg, tab 300 mg, syrup 50 mg/5 ml.] ▶LK ♀C ◗- $$$$$

Antiviral Agents - Anti-HIV - Protease Inhibitors

NOTE: Many serious drug interactions - always check before prescribing!

amprenavir (***Agenerase, APV***): 1200 mg PO bid. Peds >4yo: caps 20 mg/kg up to 1200 mg PO bid. Oral soln 22.5 mg/kg PO bid up to 2800 mg/day. [Trade: Caps 50,150 mg, oral soln 15 mg/ml.] ▶L ♀C ◗- $$$$$

indinavir (***Crixivan, IDV***): 800 mg PO q8h between meals with water (at least 48 ounces per day to prevent kidney stones). [Trade: Caps 100,200,333,400 mg.] ▶LK ♀C ◗- $$$$$

Kaletra (lopinavir + ritonavir): 3 caps or 5 ml PO bid. May increase to 4 caps or 6.5 ml PO bid with efavirenz/ nevirapine. Peds, 6 mo-12 yo: lopinavir 12 mg/kg PO bid for 7-14.9 kg, 10 mg/kg PO bid for 15-40 kg. With efavirenz/ nevirapine, may increase to 13 mg/kg PO bid for 7-14.9 kg, 11 mg/kg PO bid for 15-45 kg. Take with food. [Trade: Caps 133.3 mg lopinavir + 33.3 mg ritonavir. Oral soln 80 mg lopinavir + 20 mg ritonavir/ml.] ▶L ♀C ◗- $$$$$

nelfinavir (***Viracept, NFV***): 750 mg PO tid or 1250 mg PO bid with meals. [Trade: Tab 250 mg, powder 50 mg/g.] ▶L ♀B ◗- $$$$$

ritonavir (***Norvir, RTV***): Begin 300 mg PO bid with meals, and increase over 1-2 weeks to 600 mg bid. [Trade: Cap 100 mg, oral soln 80 mg/ml.] ▶L ♀B ◗- $$$$$

saquinavir (***Fortovase, Invirase, SQV, FTV***): Fortovase: 1200 mg PO tid. Invirase: 600 mg PO tid. [illegible] with/after meals. [Trade: Fortovase (soft gel), Invirase (hard gel) caps 200 mg.] [illegible] ◗? $$$$$

Antiviral Agents - Anti-Influenza

amantadine (***Symmetrel***): Influenza A: 100 mg PO bid. Elderly: 100 mg qd. Peds: 5 mg/kg up to 150 mg/day. [Generic: Cap 100 mg. Trade: Tab 100 mg. Generic/Trade: Syrup 50 mg/5 ml.] ▶K ♀C ◗? $

oseltamivir (***Tamiflu***): 75 mg PO bid x 5 days starting within 2 days of symptom onset. 75 mg PO qd for prophylaxis. Peds treatment: 2 mg/kg PO bid x 5 days. [Trade: Caps 75 mg, susp 12 mg/ml.] ▶LK ♀C ◗? $$$

rimantadine (***Flumadine***): Influenza A: 100 mg PO bid x 7 days. Peds: 5 mg/kg PO qd up to 150 mg/day. [Trade: Tabs 100 mg, syrup 50 mg/5 ml.] ▶LK ♀C ◗- $$

zanamivir (***Relenza***): Influenza treatment: 2 puffs bid x 5 days. [Trade: Rotadisk inhaler 5 mg/puff (20 puffs).] ▶K ♀C ◗? $$

Antiviral Agents - Other

interferon alfa-2b (***Intron A***): Chronic hepatitis B: 5 million units/day or 10 million units 3 times/week SC/IM x 4 mo. Chronic hepatitis C: 3 million units SC/IM 3 times/week x 4 mo. Continue for 18-24 mo if ALT normalized. [Trade: Powder/sol'n for injection 3,5,10 million units/vial. Sol'n for injection 18,25 million units/multidose vial. Multidose injection pens 3,5,10 million units/dose (6 doses/pen).] ▶K? ♀C ◗?+ $$$$$

interferon alfacon-1 (***Infergen***): Chronic hepatitis C: 9 mcg SC 3 times/week x 24 weeks. If relapse/no response, increase to 15 mcg SC 3 times/week. If intolerable adverse effects, reduce to 7.5 mcg SC 3 times/week. [Trade: Vials injectable soln 9,15 mcg.] ▶Plasma ♀C ◗? $$$$$

palivizumab (***Synagis***): Prevention of respiratory syncytial virus pulmonary disease in high-risk children: 15 mg/kg IM q month during RSV season. ▶L ♀C ◗? $$$$$

peginterferon alfa-2b (***PEG-Intron***): Chronic hepatitis C not previously treated with alpha interferon. Give SC once weekly for 1 year. Monotherapy 1 mcg/kg/week. In combo oral ribavirin: 1.5 mcg/kg/week. May cause or worsen severe autoimmune, neuropsychiatric, ischemic, & infectious diseases. Frequent clinical & lab monitoring. [Trade: 50,80,120,150 mcg/0.5 ml single-use vials with diluent, 2 syringes, and alcohol swabs.] ▶K? ♀C ▶- $$$$$

Rebetron (interferon alfa-2b + ribavirin): Chronic hepatitis C: Interferon alfa-2b 3 million units SC 3 times/week and ribavirin (Rebetol) 600 mg PO bid if >75 kg; 400 mg q am and 600 q pm if ≤75 kg. Ribavirin dose adjusted according to hemoglobin. Contraindicated in pregnant women or their male partners. [Trade: Each kit contains a 2-week supply of interferon alfa-2b, ribavirin caps 200 mg.] ▶K ♀X ▶- $$$$$

ribavirin - inhaled (***Virazole***): Severe respiratory syncytial virus infection in children: Aerosol 12-18 h/day x 3-7 days. Beware of sudden pulmonary deterioration; ventilator dysfunction due to drug precipitation. ▶Lung ♀X ▶- $$$$$

ribavirin - oral (***Rebetol***): Hepatitis C. In combo with interferon alfa 2b: 600 mg PO bid if >75 kg; 400 mg q am and 600 q pm if ≤75 kg. In combo with peginterferon alfa 2b: 400 mg PO bid. Lower dose if hemoglobin decreases. [Trade: Caps 200 mg.] ▶Cellular, K ♀X ▶- $$$$$

Carbapenems

ertapenem (***Invanz***): 1 g IV/IM q24h. ▶K ♀B ▶? $$$$$

imipenem-cilastatin (***Primaxin***): 250-1000 mg IV q6-8h. ▶K ♀C ▶? $$$$$

meropenem (***Merrem IV***): 1 g IV q8h. Peds: 20-40 mg/kg up to 2g IV q8h. ▶K ♀B ▶? $$$$$

CEPHALOSPORINS – GENERAL ANTIMICROBIAL SPECTRUM

1st generation: gram positive (including Staph aureus); basic gram neg. coverage
2nd generation: diminished Staph aureus, improved gram negative coverage compared to 1st generation; some with anaerobic coverage
3rd generation: further diminished Staph aureus, further improved gram negative coverage compared to 1st & 2nd generation; some with Pseudomonal coverage & diminished gram positive coverage
4th generation: same as 3rd generation plus coverage against Pseudomonas

Cephalosporins - 1st Generation

cefadroxil (***Duricef***): 1-2 g/day PO divided qd-bid. Peds: 30 mg/kg/day divided bid. [Generic/Trade: Tabs 1 g, caps 500 mg. Trade: Susp 125,250, & 500 mg/5 ml.] ▶K ♀B ▶+ $$$

cefazolin (***Ancef, Kefzol***): 0.5-1.5 g IM/IV q6-8h. Peds: 25-50 mg/kg/day divided q6-8h, severe infections 100 mg/kg/day. ▶K ♀B ▶+ $$$

cephalexin (***Keflex, Keftab***): 250-500 mg PO qid. Peds 25-50 mg/kg/day. Not for otitis media, sinusitis. [Generic/Trade: Caps 250,500 mg, tabs 500 mg, susp 125 & 250 mg/5 ml. Generic: Tabs 250 mg. Keftab: 500 mg.] ▶K ♀B ▶? $

Cephalosporins - 2nd Generation

cefaclor (***Ceclor***): 250-500 mg PO tid. Peds: 20-40 mg/kg/day PO divided bid for otitis media & group A streptococcal pharyngitis, tid for other infections. Extended release (Ceclor CD): 375-500 mg PO bid. Serum sickness-like reactions with repeated use. [Generic/Trade: Caps 250,500 mg, susp 125,187,250, 375 mg/5 ml. Generic/Trade: Extended release (Ceclor CD): 375,500 mg.] ▶K ♀B ▶? $$

cefotetan (***Cefotan***): 1-2 g IM/IV q12h. ▶K/Bile ♀B ▶? $$$$$

cefoxitin (***Mefoxin***): 1-2 g IM/IV q6-8h. ▶K ♀B ▶+ $$$$$

OVERVIEW OF BACTERIAL PATHOGENS (selected)

Gram Positive Aerobic Cocci: *Staph epidermidis* (coagulase negative), *Staph aureus* (coagulase positive), Streptococci: *S pneumoniae* (pneumococcus), *S pyogenes* (Group A), *S agalactiae* (Group B), enterococcus
Gram Positive Aerobic / Facultatively Anaerobic Bacilli: *Bacillus, Corynebacterium diphtheriae, Erysipelothrix rhusiopathiae, Listeria monocytogenes, Nocardia*
Gram Negative Aerobic Diplococci: *Moraxella catarrhalis, Neisseria gonorrhoeae, Neisseria meningitidis*
Gram Negative Aerobic Coccobacilli: *Haemophilus ducreyi, Haemoph. influenzae*
Gram Negative Aerobic Bacilli: *Acinotobacter, Bartonella* species, *Bordetella pertussis, Brucella, Burkholderia cepacia, Campylobactor, Francisella tu larensis, Helicobacter pylori, Legionella pneumophila, Pseudomonas aeruginosa, Stenotrophomonas maltophilia, Vibrio cholerae, Yersinia*
Gram Neg Facultatively Anaerobic Bacilli: *Aeromonas hydrophila, Eikenella corrodens, Pasteurella multocida,* Enterobacteriaceae: *E coli, Citrobacter, Shigella, Salmonella, Klebsiella, Enterobacter, Hafnia, Serratia, Proteus, Providencia*
Anaerobes: *Actinomyces, Bacteroides fragilis, Clostridium botulinum, Clostridium difficile, Clostridium perfringens, Clostridium tetani, Fusobacterium, Lactobacillus, Peptostreptococcus*
Defective Cell Wall Bacteria: *Chlamydia pneumoniae, Chlamydia psittaci, Chlamydia trachomatis, Coxiella burnetii, Myocoplasma pneumoniae, Rickettsia prowazekll, Rickettsia rickettsii, Rickettsia typhi, Ureaplasma urealyticum*
Spirochetes: *Borrelia burgdorferi, Leptospira, Treponema pallidum*
Mycobacteria: *M avium complex, M kansasii, M leprae, M tuberculosis*

cefprozil (***Cefzil***): 250-500 mg PO bid. Peds otitis media: 15 mg/kg/dose PO bid. Peds group A streptococcal pharyngitis (2nd-line to penicillin): 7.5 mg/kg/dose PO bid x 10d. [Trade: Tabs 250,500 mg, susp 125 & 250 mg/5 ml.] ▶K ♀B ▶+ $$$

cefuroxime (***Zinacef, Ceftin***): 750-1500 mg IM/IV q8h. Peds: 60-100 mg/kg/day IV divided q6-8h, not for meningitis. 250-500 mg PO bid. Peds: 20-30 mg/kg/day susp PO divided bid. [Generic/trade. Tabs 125,250,500 mg. Trade: Susp 125 & 250 mg/5 ml.] ▶K ♀B ▶? $$$

loracarbef (***Lorabid***): 200-400 mg PO bid. Peds: 30 mg/kg/day for otitis media (15 mg/kg/day for other infections) divided bid. [Trade: Caps 200,400 mg, susp 100 & 200 mg/5 ml.] ▶K ♀B ▶? $$$

Cephalosporins - 3rd Generation

cefdinir (***Omnicef***): 14 mg/kg/day up to 600 mg/day PO divided qd or bid. [Trade: Cap 300 mg, susp 125 mg/5 ml.] ▶K ♀B ▶? $$$

cefditoren (***Spectracef***): 200-400 mg PO bid with food. [Trade: Tabs 200 mg.] ▶K ♀B ▶? $$

cefixime (***Suprax***): 400 mg PO qd or 200 mg bid. Gonorrhea: 400 mg PO single-dose. Peds: 8 mg/kg/day divided qd-bid. [Trade: Tabs 200,400 mg, susp 100 mg/5 ml.] ▶K/Bile ♀B ▶? $$$

cefoperazone (***Cefobid***): Usual dose 2-4 g/day IM/IV given q12h. Maximum dose: 6-12 g/day IV given q6-12 h. Possible clotting impairment. ▶Bile/K ♀B ▶? $$$$$

cefotaxime (***Claforan***): Usual dose: 1-2 g IM/IV q6-8h. Peds: 50-180 mg/kg/day IM/IV divided q4-6h. Use high end of dosage range for meningitis. ▶KL ♀B ▶+ $$$$$

cefpodoxime (***Vantin***): 100-400 mg PO bid. Peds: 10 mg/kg/day divided bid. [Trade: Tabs 100,200 mg, susp 50 & 100 mg/5 ml.] ▶K ♀B ▶? $$$

SEXUALLY TRANSMITTED DISEASES & VAGINITIS*

Bacterial vaginosis: 1) metronidazole 5 g of 0.75% gel intravaginally qd for 5 days. 2) metronidazole 500 mg PO bid for 7 days . 3) clindamycin 5 g of 2% cream intravaginally qhs for 7 days. In pregnancy: 1) metronidazole 250 mg PO tid for 7 days. 2) clindamycin 300 mg PO bid for 7 days.

Candidal vaginitis: 1) intravaginal clotrimazole, miconazole, terconazole, nystatin, tioconazole, or butoconazole. 2) fluconazole 150 mg PO single dose.

Chancroid: 1) azithromycin 1 g PO single dose. 2) ceftriaxone 250 mg IM single dose.

Chlamydia: 1) azithromycin 1 g PO single dose. 2) doxycycline 100 mg PO bid for 7 days. 3) ofloxacin 300 mg PO bid for 7 days. 4) levofloxacin 500 mg PO qd for 7 days. 5) erythromycin base 500 mg PO qid for 7 days.

Chlamydia (in pregnancy): 1) erythromycin base 500 mg PO qid for 7 days or 250 mg PO qid for 14 days. 2) amoxicillin 500 mg PO tid for 7 days. 3) azithromycin 1 g PO single dose.

Epididymitis: 1) ceftriaxone 250 mg IM single dose + doxycycline 100 mg PO bid x 10 days. 2) ofloxacin 300 mg PO bid or levofloxacin 500 mg PO qd for 10 days if enteric organisms suspected, cephalosporin/doxycycline allergic, or >35 yo.

Gonorrhea: 1) ceftriaxone 125 mg IM single dose. 2) cefixime 400 mg PO single dose. 3) ciprofloxacin 500 mg PO single dose. 4) ofloxacin 400 mg PO single dose. 5) levofloxacin 250 mg PO single dose. Treat chlamydia empirically. Due to high resistance rates, quinolones not recommended in Hawaii or California, or for infections acquired in Asia or the Pacific.

Herpes simplex (genital, first episode): 1) acyclovir 400 mg PO tid for 7-10 days. 2) famciclovir 250 PO tid for 7-10 days. 3) valacyclovir 1 g PO bid for 7-10 days.

Herpes simplex (genital, recurrent): 1) acyclovir 400 mg PO tid for 5 days. 2) famciclovir 125 mg PO bid for 5 days. 3) valacyclovir 500 mg PO bid for 3-5 days. 4) valacyclovir 1 g PO qd for 5 days.

Herpes simplex (suppressive therapy): 1) acyclovir 400mg PO bid. 2) famciclovir 250 mg PO bid. 3) valacyclovir 500-1000 mg PO qd.

Herpes simplex (genital, recurrent in HIV infection): 1) Acyclovir 400 mg PO tid for 5-10 days. 2) famciclovir 500 mg PO bid for 5-10 days. 3) Valacyclovir 1 g PO bid for 5-10 days.

Herpes simplex (suppressive therapy in HIV infection): 1) Acyclovir 400-800 mg PO bid-tid. 2) Famciclovir 500 mg PO bid. 3) Valacyclovir 500 mg PO bid.

Pelvic inflammatory disease (PID), outpatient treatment: 1) ceftriaxone 250 mg IM single dose + doxycycline 100 mg PO bid +/- metronidazole 500 mg PO bid for 14 days. 2) ofloxacin 400 mg PO bid/ levofloxacin 500 mg PO qd +/- metronidazole 500 mg PO bid for 14 days.

Sexual assault prophylaxis: ceftriaxone 125 mg IM single dose + metronidazole 2 g PO single dose + azithromycin 1 g PO single dose/doxycycline 100 mg PO bid for 7 days. Consider giving antiemetic.

Syphilis (primary and secondary): 1) benzathine penicillin 2.4 million units IM single dose. 2) doxycycline 100 mg PO bid for 2 weeks if penicillin allergic.

Trichomonal vaginitis: metronidazole 2 g PO single dose or 500 mg bid for 7days. Can use 2 g single dose in pregnant women.

Urethritis, Cervicitis: Test for chlamydia and gonorrhea. Treat based on test results or treat for both if testing not available or if patient unlikely to return for follow-up.

* MMWR 2002;51:RR-6 or http://www.cdc.gov/std/.

Treat sexual partners for all except herpes, candida, and bacterial vaginosis.

ceftazidime (***Ceptaz, Fortaz, Tazidime, Tazicef***): 1 g IM/IV or 2 g IV q8-12h. Peds: 30-50 mg/kg IV q8h. ▶K ♀B ▶+ $$$$$

ceftibuten (***Cedax***): 400 mg PO qd. Peds: 9 mg/kg up to 400 mg PO qd. [Trade: Cap 400 mg, susp 90 mg/5 ml.] ▶K ♀B ▶? $$$

ceftizoxime (***Cefizox***): 1-2 g IV q8-12h. Peds: 50 mg/kg/dose IV q6-8h. ▶K ♀B ▶? $$$$$

ceftriaxone (***Rocephin***): 1-2 g IM/IV q24h. Meningitis: 2 g IV q12h. Gonorrhea: single dose 125 mg IM (250 mg if PID). Peds: 50-75 mg/kg/day up to 2 g divided q12-24h. Meningitis: 100 mg/kg/day up to 4 g/day. Otitis media: 50 mg/kg up to 1 g IM single dose. Dilute in 1% lidocaine for IM. ▶K/Bile ♀B ▶+ $$$$$

Cephalosporins - 4th Generation

cefepime (***Maxipime***): 0.5-2 g IM/IV q12h. ▶K ♀B ▶? $$$$$

Macrolides

azithromycin (***Zithromax***): 500 mg IV qd. PO: 10 mg/kg up to 500 mg on day 1, then 5 mg/kg up to 250 mg qd to complete 5 days. Group A streptococcal pharyngitis (second-line to penicillin): 12 mg/kg up to 500 mg qd x 5 d. Short regimens for peds otitis media: 30 mg/kg PO single dose or 10 mg/kg PO qd x 3 days. Chlamydia, chancroid: 1 g single dose. Prevention of disseminated Mycobacterium avium complex disease: 1200 mg q week. [Trade: Tab 250,600 mg, packet 1000 mg, susp 100 & 200 mg/5 ml. Z-Pak: #6, 250 mg tab. Tri-Pak: #3, 500 mg tab.] ▶L ♀B ▶? $$

clarithromycin (***Biaxin, Biaxin XL***): 250-500 mg PO bid. Peds: 7.5 mg/kg PO bid. H pylori: See table in GI section. See table for prophylaxis of bacterial endocarditis. Mycobacterium avium complex disease prevention: 7.5 mg/kg up to 500 mg PO bid. Biaxin XL: 1000 mg PO qd with food. [Trade: Tab 250,500 mg, susp 125, 187.5 & 250 mg/5 ml; Extended release (Biaxin XL) 500 mg, Biaxin XL-Pak: #14, 500 mg tabs.] ▶KL ♀C ▶? $$$

dirithromycin (***Dynabac***): 500 mg PO qd with food or within 1 h of eating. [Trade: Tab 250 mg, Dynabac D5-Pak: 250 mg, #10.] ▶L ♀C ▶? $$$

erythromycin base (***Eryc, E-mycin***). 250-500 mg PO qid, 333 mg PO tid, or 500 mg PO bid. [Generic/Trade: Tab 250,333,500 mg, delayed-release 250.] ▶L ♀B ▶+ $

erythromycin ethyl succinate (***EES, Eryped***): 400 mg PO qid. Peds: 30-50 mg/kg/day divided qid. [Generic/Trade: Tab 400 tab, susp 200 & 400 mg/5 ml. Trade: Chew tab 200 tab.] ▶L ♀B ▶+ $

erythromycin lactobionate: 15-20 mg/kg/day (max 4g) IV divided q6h. Peds: 15-50 mg/kg/day IV divided q6h. ▶L ♀B ▶+ $$$$

Pediazole (erythromycin ethyl succinate + sulfisoxazole): 50 mg/kg/day (based on EES dose) PO divided tid-qid. [Generic/Trade: Susp, erythromycin ethyl succinate 200 mg + sulfisoxazole 600 mg/5 ml.] ▶KL ♀C ▶- $

Penicillins - 1st generation - Natural

benzathine penicillin (***Bicillin L-A***): 1.2 million units IM. Peds <27 kg 0.3-0.6 MU IM, ≥27 kg 0.9 MU IM. Doses last 2-4 wks. [600,000 units/ml; 1, 2, and 4 ml syringes.] ▶K ♀B ▶? $

benzylpenicilloyl polylysine (***Pre-Pen***): Skin test for penicillin allergy: 1 drop in needle scratch, then 0.01-0.02 ml intradermally if no reaction. ▶K ♀? ▶? $

Bicillin CR (procaine + benzathine penicillin): For IM use. [Trade: mixes of 1.2/1.2 million, 300/300, 600/600, 300/900 thousand units procaine/benz.] ▶K ♀B ▶? $

PENICILLINS - GENERAL ANTIMICROBIAL SPECTRUM

1st generation: Most streptococci; oral anaerobic coverage
2nd generation: Most streptococci; Staph aureus
3rd generation: Most streptococci; basic gram negative coverage
4th generation: Pseudomonas

penicillin G: Pneumococcal pneumonia & severe infections: 250,000-400,000 units/kg/day (8-12 million units in adult) IV divided q4-6h. Pneumococcal meningitis: 250,000 units/kg/day (24 million U. in an adult) IV divided q2-4h. ▶K ♀B ▶? $$$

penicillin V (***Pen-Vee K, Veetids***): Adults: 250-500 mg PO qid. Peds: 25-50 mg/kg/day divided bid-qid. AHA doses for pharyngitis: 250 mg (peds) or 500 mg (adults) PO bid-tid x 10 days. [Generic/Trade: Tabs 250,500 mg, oral soln 125 & 250 mg/5 ml.] ▶K ♀B ▶? $

procaine penicillin (***Wycillin***): 0.6-1.0 million units IM qd (peak 4h, lasts 24h). ▶K ♀B ▶? $$$

Penicillins - 2nd generation - Penicillinase-Resistant

dicloxacillin (***Dynapen***): 125-500 mg PO qid. Peds: 12.5-25 mg/kg/day divided qid. [Generic: Caps 250. Generic/Trade: Caps 500 mg. Trade: Susp 62.5 mg/5 ml.] ▶KL ♀B ▶? $

nafcillin (***Nallpen***): 1-2 g IM/IV q4h. Peds: 50-200 mg/kg/day divided q4-6h. ▶L ♀B ▶? $$$$$

oxacillin (***Bactocill***): 1-2 g IM/IV q4-6h. Peds 150-200 mg/kg/day IM/IV divided q4-6h. ▶KL ♀B ▶? $

PROPHYLAXIS FOR BACTERIAL ENDOCARDITIS*

For dental, oral, respiratory tract, or esophageal procedures	
Standard regimen	amoxicillin[1] 2 g PO 1h before procedure
Unable to take oral meds	ampicillin[1] 2 g IM/IV within 30 minutes before procedure
Allergic to penicillin	clindamycin[2] 600 mg PO; or cephalexin[1] or cefadroxil[1] 2 g PO; or azithromycin[3] or clarithromycin[3] 500 mg PO 1h before procedure
Allergic to penicillin and unable to take oral meds	clindamycin[2] 600 mg IV; or cefazolin[4] 1 g IM/IV within 30 minutes before procedure
For genitourinary and gastrointestinal (excluding esophageal) procedures	
High-risk patients	ampicillin[1] 2 g IM/IV plus gentamicin 1.5 mg/kg (max 120 mg) within 30 min of starting procedure; 6h later ampicillin[4] 1 g IM/IV or amoxicillin[4] 1 g PO.
High-risk patients allergic to ampicillin	vancomycin[2] 1 g IV over 1-2h plus gentamicin 1.5 mg/kg IV/IM (max 120 mg) complete within 30 minutes of starting procedure
Moderate-risk patients	amoxicillin[1] 2 g PO or ampicillin[1] 2 g IM/IV within 30 minutes of starting procedure
Moderate-risk patients allergic to ampicillin	vancomycin[2] 1 g IV over 1-2h complete within 30 minutes of starting procedure

**JAMA 1997; 277:1794* or http://www.americanheart.org

Footnotes for pediatric doses: 1 = 50 mg/kg; 2 = 20 mg/kg; 3 = 15 mg/kg; 4 = 25 mg/kg. Total pediatric dose should not exceed adult dose.

Penicillins - 3rd generation - Aminopenicillins

amoxicillin (***Amoxil, Polymox, Trimox***): 250-500 mg PO tid, or 500-875 mg PO bid. Acute sinusitis with antibiotic use in past month &/or drug-resistent S pneumoniae rate >30%: 3-3.5 g/day PO. Peds: 40 mg/kg/day PO divided tid or 45 mg/kg/day divided bid. Otitis media/sinusitis in children at high risk for penicillin-resistant S pneumoniae (age <2 yo, antibiotics within ≤3 months, day care): 90 mg/kg/day PO divided bid-tid x 10 days for <2 yo, x 5-7 days for ≥ 2 yo. Prevention of recurrent otitis media: 20 mg/kg PO qd. [Generic/Trade: Caps 250,500 mg, tabs 500,875 mg, chews 125,250 mg, susp 125, 250 mg/5 ml. Trade: chews 200,400 mg, susp 200 & 400mg/5 ml, infant drops 50 mg/ml.] ▸K ♀B ▸+ $

amoxicillin-clavulanate (***Augmentin, Augmentin ES-600, Augmentin XR, *Clavulin***): *Augmentin XR*: 2 tabs PO q12h with meals. *Augmentin*: 500-875 mg PO bid or 250-500 mg tid. Peds: 45 mg/kg/day PO divided bid or 40 mg/kg/day divided tid for otitis, sinusitis, pneumonia; 25 mg/kg/day divided bid or 20 mg/kg/day divided tid for less severe infections. *Augmentin ES-600* susp for recurrent/persistent otitis media with risk factors (antibiotics for otitis in past 3 mo and either age ≤2 yo or daycare): 90 mg/kg/day PO divided bid with food x 10d. [Trade (amox+clav): Tabs 250+125, 500+125, 875+125 mg, chewables and susp 125+31.25, 200 +28.5, 250+62.5, 400+57 mg per tab or 5 ml. *Augmentin ES-600* susp 600+42.9 mg/5 ml. Extended-release tabs (*Augmentin XR*) 1000+62.5 mg.] ▸K ♀B ▸? $$$

ampicillin (***Principen***): Pneumonia, soft tissue infections: 250-500 mg IM/IV/PO q6h. Gastrointestinal infections, UTIs: 500 mg IM/IV/PO q6h. Sepsis, meningitis: 150-200 mg/kg/day IV divided q3-4h. Peds: 50-400 mg/kg/day IM/IV divided q4-6h. [Generic/Trade: Caps 250,500 mg, susp 125 & 250 mg/5 ml.] ▸K ♀B ▸? $$$

ampicillin-sulbactam (***Unasyn***): 1.5-3 g IM/IV q6h. Peds: 100-400 mg/kg/day of ampicillin divided q6h. ▸K ♀B ▸? $$$$$

Penicillins - 4th generation - Extended Spectrum

piperacillin (***Pipracil***): 3-4 g IM/IV q4-6h. ▸K/Bile ♀B ▸? $$$$$

piperacillin-tazobactam (***Zosyn***): 3.375 g IV q4-6h. ▸K ♀B ▸? $$$$$

ticarcillin (***Ticar***): 3-4 g IM/IV q4-6h. Peds: 200 300 mg/kg/d divided q4-6h. ▸K ♀B ▸+ $$$$$

ticarcillin-clavulanate (***Timentin***): 3.1 g IV q4-6h. Peds. 50 mg/kg up to 3.1 g IV q4-6h. ▸K ♀B ▸? $$$$$

Quinolones - 1st Generation

nalidixic acid (***NegGram***): 1 g PO qid. [Trade: Tabs 0.25,0.5,1 g, susp 250 mg/5 ml.] ▸KL ♀C ▸? $$$$

Quinolones - 2nd Generation

ciprofloxacin (***Cipro***): 200-400 mg IV q8-12h. 250-750 mg PO bid. Simple UTI: 100 mg bid x 3d. Gonorrhea: 250 mg PO single dose (not for use in California, Hawaii, or for infections acquired in Asia or the Pacific). [Trade: Tabs 100,250,500,750 mg, susp 250 & 500 mg/5 ml.] ▸LK ♀C but teratogenicity unlikely ▸?+ $$$

enoxacin (***Penetrex***): Gonorrhea. 400 mg PO single dose (not for use in California or Hawaii or for infections acquired in Asia or the Pacific). Simple UTI: 200 mg PO bid x 7 days. Double dose and duration for complicated UTI. Take on empty stomach. [Trade: Tabs 200,400 mg.] ▸LK ♀C ▸? $$$

lomefloxacin (***Maxaquin***): 400 mg PO qd. Take at night. Photosensitivity. [Trade: Tabs 400 mg.] ▸LK ♀C ▸? $$$

norfloxacin (***Noroxin***): Simple UTI: 400 mg PO bid x 3 days. [Trade: Tabs 400 mg.] ▸LK ♀C ▸? $$

ofloxacin (***Floxin***): 200-400 mg IV/PO q12h. [Trade: Tabs 200,300,400 mg.] ▶LK ♀C ◗?+ $$$$

Quinolones - 3rd Generation

levofloxacin (***Levaquin***): 250-500 mg PO/IV qd. [Trade: Tabs 250,500,750 mg.] ▶KL ♀C ◗? $$$

Quinolones - 4th Generation

gatifloxacin (***Tequin***): 400 mg IV/PO qd. Simple UTI: 400 mg PO single dose or 200 mg PO qd x 3 d. Gonorrhea: 400 mg PO single dose (not for use in California or Hawaii, or for patients who became infected in Asia or the Pacific). [Trade: Tabs 200,400 mg.] ▶K ♀C ◗- $$$

moxifloxacin (***Avelox***): 400 mg PO qd. [Trade: Tabs 400 mg.] ▶LK ♀C ◗- $$$

trovafloxacin (***Trovan, alatrofloxacin***): 200-300 mg IV q24h then 200 mg PO x ≤14 days. Hepatotoxicity. Only for inpatient treatment of serious or life-threatening infections. [Trade: Tabs 100, 200 mg.] ▶LK ♀C ◗- $$$$$

QUINOLONES- GENERAL ANTIMICROBIAL SPECTRUM

<u>1st generation</u>: gram negative (excluding Pseudomonas), urinary tract only
<u>2nd generation</u>: gram negative (including Pseudomonas); Staph aureus but not pneumococcus; some atypicals
<u>3rd generation</u>: gram negative (including Pseudomonas); gram positive (including Staph aureus and pneumococcus); expanded atypical coverage
<u>4th generation</u>: same as 3rd generation plus broad anaerobic coverage

Sulfonamides

Bactrim, Septra, Sulfatrim (trimethoprim + sulfamethoxazole, TMP/SMX, cotrimoxazole): One tab PO bid, double strength (DS, 160 mg/800 mg) or single strength (SS, 80 mg/400 mg). Pneumocystis treatment: 15-20 mg/kg/day (based on TMP) IV divided q6-8h or PO divided q6h x 21 days total. Pneumocystis prophylaxis: 1 DS tab PO qd. Peds: 5 ml susp/10 kg (up to 20 ml)/dose PO bid. [Generic/Trade: Tabs 80 mg TMP/400 mg SMX (single strength), 160 mg TMP/800 mg SMX (double strength; DS), susp 40 mg TMP/200 mg SMX per 5 ml. 20 ml susp = 2 SS tabs = 1 DS tab.] ▶K ♀C ◗+ $

Pediazole (erythromycin ethyl succinate + sulfisoxazole): 50 mg/kg/day (based on EES dose) PO divided tid-qid. [Generic/Trade: Susp, erythromycin ethyl succinate 200 mg, sulfisoxazole 600 mg/5 ml.] ▶KL ♀C ◗- $

Sulfadiazine (✤***Coptin***): Toxoplasmosis: 100-200 mg/kg/day PO up to 1-1.5 g qid with pyrimethamine and leucovorin. [Generic: Tab 500 mg.] ▶K ♀C ◗+ $$$$$

sulfisoxazole (***Gantrisin Pediatric***): Peds prophylaxis for recurrent otitis media: 50 mg/kg PO qhs. [Trade: susp 500 mg/5ml. Generic: Tabs 500 mg.] ▶KL ♀C ◗+ $

Tetracyclines

doxycycline (***Vibramycin, Doryx, Monodox***, ✤***Doxycin***): 100 mg PO bid first day, then 50 mg bid or 100 mg qd. 100 mg PO/IV bid for severe infections. Periostat for periodontitis: 20 mg PO bid. [Generic/Trade: Tabs 100 mg, caps 50,100 mg. Trade: Susp 25 mg/5 ml, syrup 50 mg/5 ml, Periostat: Caps 20 mg.] ▶LK ♀D ◗? $

minocycline (***Minocin, Dynacin***): 200 mg IV/PO initially, then 100 mg q12h. [Generic/Trade: Caps 50,75,100 mg. Trade: Susp 50 mg/5 ml.] ▶LK ♀D ◗? $

tetracycline (***Sumycin***): 250-500 mg PO qid. [Generic/Trade: Caps 250,500 mg. Trade: Tabs 250, 500 mg, susp 125 mg/5 ml.] ▶LK ♀D ◗?+ $

Other Antimicrobials

aztreonam (***Azactam***): 0.5-2 g IM/IV q6-12h. Peds: 30 mg/kg q6-8h. ▶K ♀B ▶+ $$$$$

chloramphenicol (***Chloromycetin***): 50-100 mg/kg/day IV divided q6h. Aplastic anemia. ▶LK ♀C ▶- $$$$$

clindamycin (***Cleocin***): 600-900 mg IV q8h. Each IM injection should be ≤600 mg. 150-450 mg PO qid. Peds: 20-40 mg/kg/day IV divided q6-8h or 8-25 mg/kg/day susp PO divided tid-qid. [Generic/Trade: Cap 150 mg. Trade: Cap 75,300 mg, oral soln 75 mg/5 ml.] ▶L ♀B ▶?+ $$

drotrecogin alfa (***Xigris***): To reduce mortality in sepsis: 24 mcg/kg/h IV x 96 h. ▶Plasma ♀C ▶? $$$$$

fosfomycin (***Monurol***): Simple UTI: One 3 g packet PO single-dose. [Trade: 3 g packet of granules.] ▶K ♀B ▶? $$

linezolid (***Zyvox***): 400-600 mg IV/PO q12 h. Infuse over 30-120 minutes. Myelosuppression. MAO inhibitor. [Trade: Tabs 600 mg, susp 100 mg/5 ml. 400 mg tab FDA-approved, but not marketed.] ▶Esterase, fecal excretion ♀C ▶? $$$$$

metronidazole (***Flagyl, Trikacide***): Bacterial vaginosis: 500 mg PO bid x 7 days or Flagyl ER 750 mg PO qd x 7 days. H pylori: See table in GI section. Anaerobic bacterial infections: Load 1 g or 15 mg/kg IV, then 500 mg or 7.5 mg/kg IV/PO q6h, each IV dose over 1h (not to exceed 4 g/day). [Generic/Trade: Tabs 250,500 mg. Trade: Caps 375 mg. Flagyl ER tabs 750 mg.] ▶KL ♀B ▶?- $

nitrofurantoin (***Furadantin, Macrodantin, Macrobid***): 50-100 mg PO qid. Peds: 5-7 mg/kg/day divided qid. Sustained release: 100 mg PO bid. [Macrodantin: Caps 25,50,100 mg. Generic: Caps 50,100 mg. Furadantin: Susp 25 mg/5 ml. Macrobid: Caps 100 mg.] ▶KL ♀B ▶+? $

rifampin (***Rimactane, Rifadin, Rofact***): Neisseria meningitidis carriers: 600 mg PO bid x 2 days. [Generic/Trade: Caps 150,300 mg. Pharmacists can make oral suspension.] ▶L ♀C ▶+ $$$

Synorcid (quinupristin + dalfopristin): 7.5 mg/kg IV q8-12 h, each dose over 1 h. Not active against E. faecalis. ▶Bile ♀B ▶? $$$$$

trimethoprim (***Primsol***, ***✤Proloprim***): 100 mg PO bid or 200 mg PO qd. [Generic/Trade: Tabs 100,200 mg. Primsol: Oral soln 50 mg/5 ml.] ▶K ♀C ▶- $

vancomycin (***Vancocin***): 1g IV q12h, each dose over 1h. Peds: 10-15 mg/kg IV q6h. Clostridium difficile diarrhea: 40 mg/kg up to 2000 mg/day PO divided tid-qid x 7-10 days. IV administration ineffective for this indication. [Generic/Trade: oral soln 1 g/20 ml bottle. Trade: Caps 125,250 mg; oral soln 500 mg/6 ml.] ▶K ♀C ▶? $$$$

CARDIOVASCULAR

ACE Inhibitors

NOTE: See also antihypertensive combinations. To minimize the risk of hypotension in diuretic treated patients, hold diuretic dose (if possible) for 2-3 days before starting an ACE inhibitor and use a low ACE inhibitor dose. If diuretics can not be held, then reduce the dose (if possible). Use with caution in volume depleted or hyponatremic patients. Hyperkalemia possible, especially if used concomitantly with other drugs that increase K+ and in patients with CHF or renal impairment.

benazepril (***Lotensin***): HTN: Start 10 mg PO qd, usual maintenance dose 20-40 mg PO qd or divided bid, max 80 mg/day. [Trade: Tabs, non-scored 5,10,20,40 mg.] ▶LK ♀C (1st trimester) D (2nd & 3rd) ▶? $$

captopril (***Capoten***): HTN: Start 25 mg PO bid-tid, usual maintenance dose 25-50 mg bid-tid, max 450 mg/day. CHF: Start 6.25-12.5 mg PO tid, usual dose 50-100 mg PO tid. [Generic/Trade: Tabs, scored 12.5,25,50,100 mg.] ▶LK ♀C (1st trimester) D (2nd & 3rd) ◗+ $$$

enalapril (***Vasotec***): HTN: Start 5 mg/day PO qd, usual maintenance dose 10-40 mg PO qd or divided bid, max 40 mg/day. CHF: Start 2.5 mg PO bid, usual dose 10-20 mg PO bid. [Generic/Trade: Tabs, scored 2.5,5, non-scored 10, 20 mg.] ▶LK ♀C (1st trimester) D (2nd & 3rd) ◗+ $$

fosinopril (***Monopril***): HTN: Start 10 mg PO qd, usual maintenance dose 20-40 mg PO qd, max 80 mg/day. CHF: Start 10 mg PO qd, usual dose 20-40 mg PO qd. [Trade: Tabs, scored 10, non-scored 20,40 mg.] ▶LK ♀C (1st trimester) D (2nd & 3rd) ◗? $$

lisinopril (***Prinivil, Zestril***): HTN: Start 10 mg PO qd, usual maintenance dose 20-40 mg PO qd, max 80 mg/day. CHF, acute MI: Start 2.5-5 mg PO qd, usual dose 5-20 mg PO qd, max dose 40 mg. [Generic/Trade: Tabs, non-scored 2.5,10,20,40, scored 5 mg.] ▶K ♀C (1st trimester) D (2nd & 3rd) ◗? $$

moexipril (***Univasc***): HTN: Start 7.5 mg PO qd, usual maintenance dose 7.5-30 mg PO qd or divided bid, max 30 mg/day. [Trade: Tabs, scored 7.5,15 mg.] ▶LK ♀C (1st trimester) D (2nd & 3rd) ◗? $

perindopril (***Aceon***, ***✤Coversyl***): HTN: Start 4 mg PO qd, usual maintenance dose 4-8 mg PO qd, max 16 mg/day. [Trade: Tabs, scored 2,4,8 mg.] ▶K ♀C (1st trimester) D (2nd & 3rd) ◗? $$

quinapril (***Accupril***): HTN: Start 10 mg PO qd, usual maintenance dose 20-80 mg PO qd or divided bid, max 80 mg/day. CHF: Start 5 mg PO bid, usual maintenance dose 20-40 mg bid. [Trade: Tabs, scored 5, non-scored 10,20,40 mg.] ▶LK ♀C (1st trimester) D (2nd & 3rd) ◗? $$

ramipril (***Altace***): HTN: 2.5 mg PO qd, usual maintenance dose 2.5-20 mg PO qd or divided bid, max 20 mg/day. CHF: Start 2.5 mg PO bid, usual maintenance dose 5 mg PO bid. [Trade: Caps, 1.25,2.5,5,10 mg.] ▶LK ♀C (1st trimester) D (2nd & 3rd) ◗? $$

trandolapril (***Mavik***): HTN: Start 1 mg PO qd, usual maintenance dose 2-4 mg PO qd, max 8 mg/day. CHF/post MI: Start 0.5-1 mg PO qd, usual maintenance dose 4 mg PO qd. [Trade: Tabs, scored 1, non-scored 2,4 mg.] ▶LK ♀C (1st trimester) D (2nd & 3rd) ◗? $$

Angiotensin Receptor Blockers (ARBs)

NOTE: See also antihypertensive combinations. To minimize the risk of hypotension in diuretic treated patients, hold diuretic dose (if possible) for 2-3 days before starting an ARB and use a low ARB dose. If diuretics can not be held, reduce the dose (if possible). Use with caution in volume depleted or hyponatremic patients.

candesartan (***Atacand***): HTN: Start 16 mg PO qd, maximum 32 mg/day. [Trade: Tabs, non-scored 4,8,16,32 mg.] ▶K ♀C (1st trimester) D (2nd & 3rd) ◗? $$

eprosartan (***Teveten***): HTN: Start 600 mg PO qd, maximum 800 mg/day given qd or divided bid. [Trade: tab, scored 400, non-scored 600 mg.] ▶Fecal excretion ♀C (1st trimester) D (2nd & 3rd) ◗? $$

irbesartan (***Avapro***): HTN: Start 150 mg PO qd, maximum 300 mg/day. [Trade: Tabs, non-scored 75,150,300 mg.] ▶L ♀C (1st trimester) D (2nd & 3rd) ◗? $$

losartan (***Cozaar***): HTN: Start 50 mg PO qd, max 100 mg/d given qd or divided bid. [Trade: Tabs, non-scored 25,50,100 mg.] ▶L ♀C (1st trim) D (2nd & 3rd) ◗? $$

olmesartan (***Benicar***): HTN: Start 20 mg PO qd, max 40 mg/day. [Trade: Tabs, non-scored 5,20,40 mg.] ▶K ♀C (1st trimester) D (2nd & 3rd) ◗? $$

telmisartan (***Micardis***): HTN: Start 40 mg PO qd, maximum 80 mg/day. [Trade: Tabs, non-scored 40,80 mg.] ▶L ♀C (1st trimester) D (2nd & 3rd) ▶? $$

valsartan (***Diovan***): HTN: Start 80-160 mg PO qd, max 320 mg/day. [Trade: Tabs 80, 160, 320 mg.] ▶L ♀C (1st trimester) D (2nd & 3rd) ▶? $$

ACE INHIBITOR DOSING	Hypertension		Heart Failure		
	Initial	*Max*	*Initial*	*Target*	*Max*
benazepril (*Lotensin*)	10 mg qd*	80/d	-	-	-
captopril (*Capoten*)	25 mg bid/tid	450/d	6.25-12.5 mg tid	50 mg tid	150 mg tid
enalapril (*Vasotec*)	5 mg qd/bid*	40/d	2.5 mg bid	10 mg bid	20 mg bid
fosinopril (*Monopril*)	10 mg qd	80/d	5-10 mg qd	20 mg qd	40 mg qd
lisinopril (*Zestril/Prinivil*)	10 mg qd	80/d	5 mg qd	20 mg qd	40 mg qd
moexipril (*Univasc*)	7.5 mg qd*	30/d	-	-	-
perindopril (Aceon)	4 mg qd	16/d	2 mg qd	4 mg qd	8 mg qd
quinapril (*Accupril*)	10 mg qd*	80/d	2.5-5 mg bid	10 mg bid	20 mg bid
ramipril (*Altace*)	2.5 mg qd*	20/d	1.25-2.5 mg bid	5 mg bid	10 mg bid
trandolapril (*Mavik*)	1-2 mg qd	8/d	0.5-1 mg qd	4 mg qd	4 mg qd

**May require bid dosing for 24-hour BP control.*

Antiadrenergic Agents

clonidine (***Catapres***): HTN: Start 0.1 mg PO bid, usual maintenance dose 0.2 to 1.2 mg/day divided bid-tid, max 2.4 mg/day. Can get rebound HTN with abrupt discontinuation, especially at doses ≥ 0.8 mg/d. Transdermal (Catapres-TTS): Start 0.1 mg/24 hour patch q week, titrate to desired effect, max effective dose 0.6 mg/24 hour (two, 0.3 mg/24 hour patches). [Generic/Trade: Tabs, non-scored 0.1,0.2,0.3 mg. Trade only: Patch, 0.1,0.2,0.3 mg/24 hours.] ▶KL ♀C ▶? $

doxazosin (***Cardura***): HTN: Start 1 mg PO qhs, max 16 mg/day. Take first dose at bedtime to avoid orthostatic hypotension. BPH: see urology section. [Generic/Trade: Tabs, scored 1,2,4,8 mg.] ▶L ♀C ▶? $$

guanfacine (***Tenex***): Start 1 mg PO qhs, increase to 2-3 mg qhs if needed after 3-4 weeks, max 3 mg/day. [Generic/Trade: Tabs, non-scored 1,2 mg.] ▶K ♀B ▶? $

methyldopa (***Aldomet***): HTN: Start 250 mg PO bid-tid, maximum 3000 mg/day. May cause hemolytic anemia. [Generic/Trade: Tabs, non-scored 125,250,500 mg.] ▶LK ♀B ▶+ $

prazosin (***Minipress***): HTN: Start 1 mg PO bid-tid, max 40 mg/day. Take first dose at bedtime to avoid orthostatic hypotension. [Generic/Trade: Caps 1,2,5 mg.] ▶L ♀C ▶? $$

reserpine (***Serpasil***): HTN: Start 0.05-0.1 mg PO qd or 0.1 mg PO qod, max 0.25 mg/day. [Generic: Tabs, scored, 0.1,0.25 mg.] ▶LK ♀C ▶- $

terazosin (***Hytrin***): HTN: Start 1 mg PO qhs, usual effective dose 1-5 mg PO qd or divided bid, max 20 mg/day. Take first dose at bedtime to avoid orthostatic hypotension . [Generic (Tabs)/Trade (Caps). 1,2,5,10 mg.] ▶LK ♀C ▶? $$

Anti-Dysrhythmics / Cardiac Arrest

adenosine (***Adenocard***): PSVT conversion (not A-fib): Adult and peds ≥ 50 kg: 6 mg rapid IV & flush, preferably through a central line. If no response after 1-2 mins then 12 mg. A third dose of 12 mg may be given prn. Peds <50 kg: initial dose 50-100 mcg/kg, subsequent doses 100-200 mcg/kg q1-2 min prn up to a max single dose of 300 mcg/kg or 12 mg. Half-life is <10 seconds. Need higher dose if on theophylline or caffeine, lower dose if on dipyridamole or carbamazepine. ▶Plasma ♀C ▶? $$$

amiodarone (***Cordarone, Pacerone***): Life-threatening ventricular arrhythmia: Load

150 mg IV over 10 min, then 1 mg/min x 6h, then 0.5 mg/min x 18h. Mix in D5W. Oral loading dose 800-1600 mg PO qd for 1-3 weeks, reduce to 400-800 mg PO qd for 1 month when arrhythmia is controlled, reduce to lowest effective dose thereafter, usually 200-400 mg PO qd. Photosensitivity with oral therapy. Pulmonary & hepatic toxicity. Hypo or hyperthyroidism possible. May increase digoxin levels by 70% and INRs with warfarin by 100%. IV therapy may cause hypotension. Contraindicated with marked sinus bradycardia and second or third degree heart block in the absence of a functioning pacemaker. [Generic/Trade: Tabs, scored 200 mg.] ▶L ♀D ◗- $$$$

atropine: Bradyarrhythmia/CPR: 0.5-1.0 mg IV q3-5 min to max 0.04 mg/kg. Peds: 0.02 mg/kg/dose; minimum single dose, 0.1 mg; max cumulative dose, 1 mg. ▶K ♀C ◗- $

bicarbonate sodium: Severe acidosis: 1 mEq/kg IV up to 50-100 mEq/dose. ▶K ♀C ◗? $

bretylium (***Bretylol***): Ventricular arrhythmia: Initial 5 mg/kg IV bolus over 1 minute, then 10 mg/kg if needed at 5-30 minute intervals up to a total 30-35 mg/kg. Infusion 500 mg in 50 ml D5W (10 mg/mL) at 1-3 mg/min (6-18 mL/h). ▶K ♀C ◗? $$

digoxin (***Lanoxin, Lanoxicaps, Digitek***): Atrial fibrillation/CHF: 0.125-0.25 mg PO qd. Rapid A-fib: Load 0.5 mg IV, then 0.25 mg IV q6h x 2 doses, maintenance 0.125-0.375 mg IV/PO qd. [Generic/Trade: Tabs, scored (Lanoxin, Digitek) 0.125, 0.25, 0.5 mg; elixir 0.05 mg/mL. Trade only: Caps (Lanoxicaps), 0.05,0.1,0.2 mg.] ▶KL ♀C ◗+ $

digoxin-immune Fab (***Digibind, Digifab***): Digoxin toxicity: 2-20 vials IV, one formula is: Number vials = (serum dig level in ng/mL) x (kg) / 100. ▶K ♀C ◗? $$$$$

disopyramide (***Norpace, Norpace CR***, ♣***Rythmodan-LA***): Rarely indicated, consult cardiologist. Ventricular arrhythmia: 400-800 mg PO daily in divided doses (immediate-release, q6h or extended-release, q12h). Proarrhythmic. [Generic/Trade: caps, immediate-release, 100,150 mg; extended-release, 100,150 mg.] ▶KL ♀C ◗+ $$$$

dofetilide (***Tikosyn***): A-fib/flutter: Specialized dosing based on creatinine clearance and QTc interval. [Trade: Caps, 0.125,0.25,0.5 mg.] ▶KL ♀C ◗- $$$$

epinephrine (***EpiPen, EpiPen Jr***): Cardiac arrest: 1 mg IV. Anaphylaxis: 0.1-0.5 mg SC/IM, may repeat SC dose every 10-15 minutes. [Adults: EpiPen Auto-injector delivers 0.3 mg (1:1,000 soln) IM dose. Children: EpiPen Jr. Autoinjector delivers 0.15 mg (1:2,000 solution) IM dose.] ▶Plasma ♀C ◗- $

flecainide (***Tambocor***): Rarely indicated, consult cardiologist. Proarrhythmic. [Generic/Trade: Tabs, non-scored 50, scored 100,150 mg.] ▶K ♀C ◗- $$$$

ibutilide (***Corvert***): A-fib/flutter: 0.01 mg/kg up to 1 mg IV over 10 mins, may repeat once if no response after 10 additional minutes. Keep on cardiac monitor ≥4 hours. ▶K ♀C ◗? $$$$$

isoproterenol (***Isuprel***): Refractory bradycardia or third degree AV block: 0.02-0.06 mg IV bolus or infusion 2 mg in 250 ml D5W (8 mcg/mL) at 5 mcg/min. 5 mcg/min = 37 mL/h. Peds: 0.05-2 mcg/kg/min. 10 kg: 0.1 mcg/kg/min = 8 mL/h. ▶LK ♀C ◗? $$

lidocaine (***Xylocaine, Xylocard***): Ventricular arrhythmia: Load 1 mg/kg IV, then 0.5 mg/kg q8-10min as needed to max 3 mg/kg. IV infusion: 4 gm in 500 mL D5W (8 mg/ml) at 1-4 mg/min. Peds: 20-50 mcg/kg/min. ▶LK ♀B ◗? $

mexiletine (***Mexitil***): Rarely indicated, consult cardiologist. Ventricular arrhythmia: Start 200 mg PO q8h with food or antacid, max dose 1,200 mg/day. Proarrhythmic. [Generic/Trade: Caps, 150,200,250 mg.] ▶L ♀C ◗- $$$

procainamide (***Procanbid, Pronestyl***): Ventricular arrhythmia: 500 - 1250 mg PO q6h or 50 mg/kg/day. Extended-release: 500-1000 mg PO q12h. Load 100 mg IV q10min or 20 mg/min (150 mL/h) until: 1) QRS widens >50%, 2) dysrhythmia suppressed, 3) hypotension, or 4) total of 17 mg/kg or 1000 mg. Infusion 2g in 250 ml D5W (8 mg/mL) at 2-6 mg/min (15-45 mL/h). Proarrhythmic. [Generic/Trade: tabs, immediate-release, non-scored and caps (Pronestyl) 250,375,500 mg. Generic only: tabs, sustained-release, non-scored (generic procainamide SR, q6h dosing), 250,500,750 mg. Trade only: tabs, extended-release, non-scored (Procanbid, q12h dosing) 500,1000 mg.] ▶LK ♀C ◗? $$$

propafenone (***Rythmol***): Rarely indicated, consult cardiologist. Proarrhythmic. [Trade: Tabs, scored 150,225,300 mg.] ▶L ♀C ◗? $$$$

quinidine gluconate (***Quinaglute, Quinalan, Quinate***): A-fib/flutter: 324-648 mg PO q8-12h. Proarrhythmic. [Generic/Trade: Tabs, extended-release, non-scored (Quinaglute) 324, scored (Quinalan) 324 mg.] ▶LK ♀C ◗? $$

quinidine sulfate (***Quinidex, Quinora***): A-fib/flutter: Immediate-release: 200-400 mg PO 6-8h. Extended-release: 300-600 mg PO q8-12h. Proarrhythmic. [Generic/Trade: Tabs, non-scored immediate-release 200,300 mg (Quinora). Generic/Trade: Tabs, extended release 300 mg (Quinidex Extentabs).] ▶LK ♀C ◗? $

sotalol (***Betapace, Betapace AF, ♣Rylosol, Sotacar***): Ventricular arrhythmia (Betapace), A-fib/A-flutter (Betapace AF): Start 80 mg PO bid, max 640 mg/d. Proarrhythmic. [Generic/Trade: Tabs, scored 80,120,160,240 mg. Trade only: 80,120,160 mg (Betapace AF).] ▶K ♀B ◗- $$$$

vasopressin (***Pitressin, ADH, ♣Pressyn***): Ventricular fibrillation: 40 units IV once. ▶LK ♀C ◗? $

Anti-Hyperlipidemic Agents - Bile Acid Sequestrants

cholestyramine (***Questran, Questran Light, Prevalite, LoCHOLEST, LoCHOLEST Light***): Elevated LDL cholesterol: Powder: Start 4 g PO qd-bid before meals, increase up to max 24 g/day. [Generic/Trade: Powder for oral suspension, 4 g cholestyramine resin / 9 g powder (Questran, LoCHOLEST), 4 g cholestyramine resin / 5 g powder (Questran Light), 4 g cholestyramine resin / 5.5 g powder (Prevalite, LoCHOLEST Light).] ▶Fecal excretion ♀C ◗+ $$$

colesevelam (***Welchol***): Elevated LDL cholesterol: 3 Tabs bid with meals or 6 Tabs once daily with a meal, max dose 7 Tabs/day. [Trade: Tabs, non-scored, 625 mg.] ▶Not absorbed ♀B ◗+ $$$$

colestipol (***Colestid, Colestid Flavored***): Elevated LDL cholesterol: Tabs: Start 2 g PO qd-bid, max 16 g/day. Granules: Start 5 g PO qd-bid, max 30 g/day. [Trade: Tab 1 g. Granules for oral susp, 5 g / 7.5 g powder.] ▶Fecal excretion ♀B ◗+ $$$

LIPID RESPONSE* *(%change)*	*Cholesterol*	*LDL*	*HDL*	*Triglycerides*	**LFT MONITORING FOR STATINS****
Advicor 1000/20 mg	N/R	-30%	+20%	-32%	B, 6 to 12 wk, 24 wk, semiannually
atorvastatin 10 mg	-29%	-39%	+6%	-19%	B, 12 wk, semiannually
fluvastatin 40 mg	-19%	-25%	+4%	-14%	B, 12 wk
lovastatin 20 mg	-17%	-24%	+7%	-10%	B, 6 & 12 wk, semiannually
pravastatin 40 mg	-25%	-34%	+12%	-24%	B
simvastatin 20 mg	-28%	-38%	+8%	-15%	B, 6 mo, 12 mo ***

*Doses are recommended starting doses. Data taken from prescribing information. *Advicor* = lovastatin + niacin. **Schedule for LFT monitoring when starting therapy and after each dosage increase. Stop statin therapy if LFTs are > 3 times upper limit of normal. ***For first year only or after last dose increase. Get LFTs 3,6,12 months after increasing to 80 mg. B = baseline, LDL = low-density lipoprotein, LFT = liver function tests, HDL = high-density lipoprotein. N/R = not reported.

LDL CHOLESTEROL GOALS[1]

Risk Category	*LDL Goal (mg/dL)*	*Lifestyle Changes at LDL (mg/dL)*[2]	*Also Consider Meds at LDL (mg/dL)*
CHD or equivalent risk[3] (10-year risk >20%)	<100	≥100	≥130 (100-129: Rx optional)
2+ risk factors[4] (10-year risk ≤20%)	<130	≥130	10-yr risk 10-20%: ≥130 10-yr risk <10%: ≥160
0 to 1 risk factor (10-year risk <10%)	<160	≥160	≥190 (160-189: Rx optional)

1. CHD=coronary heart disease. LDL=low density lipoprotein. Adapted from NCEP: *JAMA* 2001; 285:2486. All 10-year risks based upon Framingham stratification. **2**. Dietary modification, weight reduction, exercise. **3**. Equivalent risk defined as diabetes, other atherosclerotic disease (peripheral artery disease, abdominal aortic aneurysm, symptomatic carotid artery disease), or multiple risk factors such that 10 year risk >20%. **4**. Risk factors: Cigarette smoking, HTN (BP≥140/90 mmHg or on antihypertensive meds), low HDL (<40 mg/dL), family hx of CHD (1° relative: ♂ <55 yo, ♀ <65 yo), age (♂ ≥45 yo, ♀ ≥55 yo).

Anti-Hyperlipidemic Agents - HMG-CoA Reductase Inhibitors ("Statins")

NOTE: Hepatotoxicity - monitor LFTs periodically (see table). Myopathy a concern especially when combined with fibric acid agents (gemfibrozil, fenofibrate) and niacin. Weigh potential risk of combination therapy against potential benefit.

Advicor (lovastatin + niacin): Hyperlipidemia: 1 tab PO qhs with a low-fat snack. Establish dose using extended-release niacin first, or if already on lovastatin substitute combo product with lowest niacin dose. Aspirin or ibuprofen 30 min prior may decrease niacin flushing reaction. [Trade: Tabs, non-scored extended release niacin/lovastatin 500/20, 750/20, 1000/20 mg.] ▶LK ♀X ▶- $$$

atorvastatin (***Lipitor***): Hypercholesterolemia: Start 10-40 mg PO qd, max 80 mg/day. [Trade: Tabs, non-scored 10,20,40,80 mg.] ▶L ♀X ▶- $$$

fluvastatin (***Lescol, Lescol XL***): Hypercholesterolemia: Start 20-80 mg PO qhs, max 80 mg qd or divided bid. [Trade: Caps, 20,40 mg; tab, extended-release, non-scored 80 mg.] ▶L ♀X ▶- $$

lovastatin (***Mevacor, Altocor***): Reduced cardiovascular morbidity, hyperlipidemia: Start 20 mg PO q pm, max 80 mg/day qd or divided bid. [Generic/Trade: Tabs, non-scored 10,20,40 mg. Trade only: Tabs, extended-release (Altocor) 10,20,40,60 mg.] ▶L ♀X ▶- $$$

pravastatin (***Pravachol***): Reduced cardiovascular morbidity/mortality, hyperlipidemia: Start 40 mg PO qd, max 80 mg/day. [Trade: Tabs, non-scored 10,20,40,80 mg.] ▶L ♀X ▶- $$$

simvastatin (***Zocor***): Reduced cardiovascular morbidity/mortality, hyperlipidemia: Start 20-40 mg PO q pm, max 80 mg/d. [Trade: Tabs, non-scored 5,10,20,40,80 mg.] ▶L ♀X ▶- $$$$

Anti-Hyperlipidemic Agents - Other

fenofibrate (***Tricor***): Hypertriglyceridemia: 54-160 mg PO qd with a meal. Max 160 mg qd. [Trade: Tabs, non-scored, 54,160 mg.] ▶LK ♀C ▶- $$$

gemfibrozil (***Lopid***, ***✤Lipidil Micro***): Hypertriglyceridemia: 600 mg PO bid. [Generic/Trade: Tabs, scored 600 mg.] ▶LK ♀C ▶? $$

niacin (***nicotinic acid,*** **vitamin B3,** ***Niacor, Nicolar, Niaspan***): Hyperlipidemia: Start 50-100 mg PO bid-tid with meals, increase slowly, usual maintenance range 1.5-3 g/day, max 6 g/d. Extended-release (Niaspan): Start 500 mg qhs, increase monthly as needed up to max 2000 mg. Extended-release formulations not listed here may have greater hepatotoxicity. Titrate slowly and use aspirin or ibuprofen 30 minutes before niacin doses to decrease flushing reaction. [Generic (OTC): Tabs, scored 25,50,100,150,500 mg. Trade: Tabs, immediate-release, scored (Niacor), 500 mg; extended-release, non-scored (Niaspan), 500,750,1000 mg.] ▶K ♀C ▶? $

omega-3 fatty acid (fish oil) (***Promega, Cardio-Omega 3, Sea-Omega, Marine Lipid Concentrate, SuperEPA 1200***): Hypertriglyceridemia: 3-5 gm EPA+DHA content daily. Marine Lipid Concentrate, Super EPA 1200 mg cap contains EPA 360 mg + DHA 240 mg, daily dose = 5-8 Caps. [Trade/Generic: cap, shown as EPA+DHA mg content, 240 (Promega Pearls), 300 (Cardi-Omega 3, Max EPA), 400 (Promega), 500 (Sea-Omega), 600 (Marine Lipid Concentrate, SuperEPA 1200), 875 mg (SuperEPA 2000).] ▶L ♀? ▶? $$

Antihypertensive Combinations

NOTE: Dosage should first be adjusted by using each drug separately. See component drugs for metabolism, pregnancy, and lactation.

By type: ACE Inhibitor/Diuretic: *Accuretic, Capozide, Lotensin HCT, Monopril HCT, Prinizide, Uniretic, Vaseretic, Zestoretic.* ACE Inhibitor/Calcium Channel Blocker: *Lexxel, Lotrel, Tarka.* ARB/Diuretic: *Atacand HCT, Avalide, Diovan HCT, Hyzaar, Micardis HCT.* Beta-blocker/Diuretic: *Corzide, Inderide, Inderide LA, Lopressor HCT, Tenoretic, Timolide, Ziac.* Diuretic combinations: *Aldactazide, Dyazide, Maxzide, Maxzide-25, Moduretic, Moduret.* Diuretic/miscellaneous antihypertensive: *Aldoclor-250, Aldoril-15, Aldoril-25, Aldoril D30, Aldoril D50, Apresazide, Combipres, Diutensin-R, Enduronyl, Enduronyl Forte, Minizide, Rauzide, Renese-R, Salutensin, Salutensin-Demi, Ser-Ap-Es.*

By name: ***Accuretic*** (quinapril + HCTZ): Trade: Tabs, 10/12.5, 20/12.5, 20/25. ***Aldactazide*** (spironolactone + HCTZ). Generic/Trade: Tabs, non-scored 25/25, scored 50/50 mg. ***Aldoclor 250*** (methyldopa + chlorothiazide): Trade: Tabs, non-scored, 250/250 mg. ***Aldoril*** (methyldopa + HCTZ): Generic/Trade: Tabs, non-scored, 250/15 (Aldoril-15), 250/25 mg (Aldoril-25). Trade: Tabs, non-scored, 500/30 (Aldoril D30), 500/50 mg (Aldoril D50). ***Apresazide*** (hydralazine + HCTZ): Generic/Trade: Caps 25/25, 50/50, 100/50. ***Atacand HCT*** (candesartan + HCTZ): Trade: tab, non-scored 16/12.5, 32/12.5 mg. ***Avalide*** (irbesartan + HCTZ): Trade: Tabs, non-scored 150/12.5, 300/12.5 mg. ***Capozide*** (captopril + HCTZ): Generic/Trade: Tabs, scored 25/15, 25/25, 50/15, 50/25 mg. ***Combipres*** (clonidine + chlorthalidone): Generic/Trade: Tabs, non-scored 0.1/15, 0.2/15, 0.3/15 mg. ***Corzide*** (nadolol + bendroflumethiazide): Trade: Tabs, scored 40/5, 80/5 mg. ***Diovan HCT*** (valsartan + HCTZ): Trade: Tabs, non-scored 80/12.5, 160/12.5, 160/25 mg. ***Diutensen-R*** (reserpine + methyclothiazide): Trade: Tabs, non-scored, 0.1/2.5 mg. ***Dyazide*** (triamterene + HCTZ): Generic/Trade: Caps, (Dyazide) 37.5/25, (generic only) 50/25 mg. ***Enduronyl*** (deserpidine, methyclothiazide): Trade: Tabs, non-scored, 0.25/5 (Enduronyl), 0.5/5 mg (Enduronyl Forte). ***Hyzaar*** (losartan + HCTZ): Trade: Tabs, non-scored 50/12.5, 100/25 mg. ***Inderide*** (propranolol + HCTZ): Generic/Trade: Tabs, scored 40/25, 80/25 mg. ***Inderide LA*** (propranolol + HCTZ): Generic/Trade:Caps, extended-release 80/50, 120/50, 160/50 mg. ***Lexxel*** (enalapril + felodipine): Trade: Tabs, non-scored 5/2.5, 5/5 mg. ***Lopressor HCT*** (metoprolol + HCTZ): Trade: Tabs, scored 50/25, 100/25, 100/50 mg. ***Lotensin HCT*** (benazepril + HCTZ): Trade: Tabs, scored 5/6.25, 10/12.5, 20/12.5, 20/25 mg.

Lotrel (amlodipine + benazepril): Trade: cap, 2.5/10, 5/10, 5 /20 10/20 mg. ***Maxzide*** (triamterene + HCTZ): Generic/Trade: Tabs, scored (Maxzide-25) 37.5/25 (Maxzide) 75/50 mg. ***Maxzide-25*** (triamterene + HCTZ): Generic/Trade: Tabs, scored (Maxzide-25) 37.5/25 (Maxzide) 75/50 mg. ***Micardis HCT*** (telmisartan + HCTZ): Trade: Tabs, non-scored 40/12.5, 80/12.5 mg. ***Minizide*** (prazosin + polythiazide): Trade: cap, 1/0.5, 2/0.5, 5/0.5 mg. ***Moduretic*** (amiloride + HCTZ): Generic/Trade: Tabs, scored 5/50 mg. ***Monopril HCT*** (fosinopril + HCTZ): Trade: Tabs, non-scored 10/12.5, scored 20/12.5 mg. ***Prinzide*** (lisinopril + HCTZ): Generic/Trade: Tabs, non-scored 10/12.5, 20/12.5, 20/25 mg. ***Rauzide*** (rauwolfia + bendroflumethiazide): Trade: Tabs, non-scored, 50/4 mg. ***Renese-R*** (reserpine + polythiazide): Trade: Tabs, scored, 0.25/2 mg. ***Salutensin*** (reserpine + hydroflumethiazide): Trade: Tabs, non-scored, 0.125/25 (Salutensin-Demi), 0.125/50 mg (Salutensin) ***Ser-Ap-Es*** (hydralazine + HCTZ + reserpine): Generic: Tabs, non-scored, 25/15/0.1 mg. ***Tarka*** (trandolapril + verapamil): Trade: Tabs, non-scored 2/180, 1/240, 2/240, 4/240 mg. ***Tenoretic*** (atenolol + chlorthalidone): Generic/ Trade: Tabs, scored 50/25, non-scored 100/25 mg. ***Teveten HCT*** (eprosartan + HCTZ): Trade: Tabs, non-scored 600/12.5, 600/25 mg. ***Timolide*** (timolol + HCTZ): Trade: Tabs, non-scored 10/25 mg. ***Uniretic*** (moexipril + HCTZ): Trade: Tabs, scored 7.5/12.5, 15/12.5, 15/25 mg. ***Vaseretic*** (enalapril + HCTZ): Generic/Trade: Tabs, non-scored 5/12.5, 10/25 mg. ***Zestoretic*** (lisinopril + HCTZ): Generic/Trade: Tabs, non-scored 10/12.5, 20/12.5, 20/25 mg. ***Ziac*** (bisoprolol + HCTZ): Generic/Trade: Tabs, non-scored 2.5/6.25, 5/6.25, 10/6.25 mg.

Antihypertensives - Miscellaneous

diazoxide (***Hyperstat***): Severe HTN: 1-3 mg/kg (up to 150 mg) IV q5-15 min until BP is controlled. ▶L ♀C ◗- $$$$

fenoldopam (***Corlopam***): Severe HTN: 10 mg in 250 ml D5W (40 mcg/mL), start at 0.1 mcg/kg/min titrate q15 min, usual effective dose 0.1-1.6 mcg/kg/min. ▶LK ♀B ◗? $$$$$

hydralazine (***Apresoline***): Hypertensive emergency: 10-50 mg IM or 10-20 mg IV, repeat as needed. HTN: Start 10 mg PO bid-qid, max 400 mg/day. Headaches, peripheral edema, lupus syndrome. [Generic/Trade: Tabs, non-scored 10,25,50, 100 mg.] ▶LK ♀C ◗+ $

minoxidil (***Loniten***): Refractory HTN: Start 2.5-5 mg PO qd, max 100 mg/day. [Generic/Trade: Tabs, scored, 2.5,10 mg.] ▶K ♀C ◗+ $$

nitroprusside sodium (***Nipride, Nitropress***): Hypertensive emergency: 50 mg in 250 mL D5W (200 mcg/mL), start at 0.3 mcg/kg/min (for 70 kg adult = 6 mL/h). Max 10 mcg/kg/min. Protect from light. Cyanide toxicity with high doses, hepatic/renal impairment, and prolonged infusions, check thiocyanate levels. ▶RBC's ♀C ◗- $

phenoxybenzamine (***Dibenzyline***): Pheochromocytoma: Start 10 mg PO bid, then ↑ slowly qod as needed, 120 mg/day. [Trade: Caps, 10 mg.] ▶KL ♀C ◗? $$$$$

phentolamine (***Regitine, Rogitine***): Diagnosis of pheochromocytoma: 5 mg increments IV/IM. Peds 0.05-0.1 mg/kg IV/IM up to 5 mg per dose. Extravasation: 5-10 mg in 10 mL NS local injection. ▶Plasma ♀C ◗? $$

tolazoline (***Priscoline***): Persistent pulmonary HTN in newborns: Test dose 1-2 mg/kg IV over 10 minutes via a scalp vein, then IV infusion 0.5-2 mg/kg/h. ▶L ♀C ◗? $$

Antiplatelet Drugs

abciximab (***ReoPro***): Platelet aggregation inhibition, percutaneous coronary intervention: 0.25 mg/kg IV bolus via separate infusion line before procedure, then 0.125 mcg/kg/min (max 10 mcg/min) IV infusion for 12h. ▶Plasma ♀C ▶? $$$$$

Aggrenox (dipyridamole + aspirin): Platelet aggregation inhibition: 1 cap bid. [Trade: Caps, 200/25 mg.] ▶LK ♀D ▶? $$$

aspirin (***Ecotrin, Empirin, Halfprin, Bayer, ASA***, ♣***Entrophen***): Platelet aggregation inhibition: 81-325 mg PO qd. [Generic/Trade (OTC): tabs, 325,500 mg; chewable 81 mg; enteric-coated 81,165 mg (Halfprin), 81,325,500 mg (Ecotrin), 650,975 mg. Trade only: tabs, controlled-release 650,800 mg (ZORprin, Rx). Generic only (OTC): suppository 120,200,300,600 mg.] ▶K ♀D ▶? $

clopidogrel (***Plavix***): Platelet aggregation inhibition: 75 mg PO qd. Acute coronary syndrome (unstable angina or non Q-wave MI). 300 mg loading dose, then 75 mg PO qd in combination with aspirin 81-325 mg PO qd. Rare TTP. [Trade: Tab, non-scored 75 mg.] ▶LK ♀B ▶? $$$$

dipyridamole (***Persantine***): Antithrombotic: 75-100 mg PO qid. [Generic/Trade: Tabs, non-scored 25,50,75 mg.] ▶L ♀B ▶? $

eptifibatide (***Integrilin***): Acute coronary syndromes: Load 180 mcg/kg IV bolus, then infusion 2 mcg/kg/min for up to 72 hr. Discontinue infusion prior to CABG. Percutaneous cardiovascular intervention: Load 180 mcg/kg IV bolus just before procedure, followed by infusion 2 mcg/kg/min and a second 180 mcg/kg IV bolus 10 min after the first bolus. Continue infusion for 18-24 hr after procedure. ▶K ♀B ▶? $$$$$

ticlopidine (***Ticlid***): Due to high incidence of neutropenia and TTP, other drugs preferred. Platelet aggregation inhibition/reduction of thrombotic stroke: 250 mg PO bid with food. Neutropenia, TTP. [Generic/Trade: Tab, non-scored 250 mg.] ▶L ♀B ▶? $$$$

tirofiban (***Aggrastat***): Acute coronary syndromes: Start 0.4 mcg/kg/min IV infusion for 30 mins, then decrease to 0.1 mcg/kg/min for 48-108 hr or until 12-24 hr after coronary intervention. Half dose with CrCl < 30 ml/min. Use concurrent heparin to keep PTT twice normal. ▶K ♀B ▶? $$$$$

β-BLOCKER DOSING	Hypertension		Heart Failure		
	Initial	*Max*	*Initial*	*Target*	*Max*
bisoprolol (*Zebeta*)	2.5-5 mg qd	20/d	1.25 mg qd	10 mg qd	10 qd
carvedilol (*Coreg*)	6.25 mg bid	50/d	3.125 mg bid	25-50 mg bid*	50 bid
metoprolol (*Lopressor*)	50 mg bid	450/d	6.25 mg bid†	75 mg bid	75 bid
metoprolol (*Toprol XL*)	50-100 mg qd	400/d	12.5-25 mg qd	200 mg qd	200 qd

*Target dose for patients >85 kg is 50 mg bid. †Lowest strength tablet available is 50 mg. Adapted from ACC/AHA practice guidelines for chronic heart failure in adults: www.acc.org

Beta Blockers

NOTE: See also antihypertensive combinations. Abrupt discontinuation may precipitate ischemia if underlying CAD. Discontinue by tapering over 2 weeks. Avoid using nonselective beta-blockers and use agents with beta1 selectivity cautiously in asthma / COPD. Beta 1 selectivity diminishes at high doses.

acebutolol (***Sectral***): HTN: Start 400 mg PO qd or 200 mg PO bid, maximum 1200 mg/day. Beta1 receptor selective. [Generic/Trade: Caps, 200,400 mg.] ▶LK ♀B ▶- $$

atenolol (***Tenormin***): Acute MI: 5 mg IV over 5 min, repeat in 10 min. HTN: Start 25-50 mg PO qd or divided bid, maximum 100 mg/day. Beta1 receptor selective. [Generic/Trade: Tabs, non-scored 25,100; scored, 50 mg.] ▶K ♀D ▶- $

betaxolol (***Kerlone***): HTN: Start 5-10 mg PO qd, max 20 mg/day. Beta1 receptor selective. [Trade: Tabs, scored 10, non-scored 20 mg.] ▶LK ♀C ◗? $$

bisoprolol (***Zebeta***): HTN: Start 2.5-5 mg PO qd, max 20 mg/day. Beta1 receptor selective. [Generic/Trade: Tabs, scored 5, non-scored 10 mg.] ▶LK ♀C ◗? $$

carteolol (***Cartrol***): HTN: Start 2.5 mg PO qd, max 10 mg qd. [Trade: Tabs, non-scored, 2.5,5 mg.] ▶K ♀C ◗? $$

carvedilol (***Coreg***): CHF: Start 3.125 mg PO bid with food, double dose q2 weeks as tolerated up to max of 25 mg bid (if <85 kg) or 50 mg bid (if >85 kg). HTN: Start 6.25 mg PO bid, max 50 mg/day. Not first line agent for HTN. Alpha1, beta1, and beta2 receptor blocker. [Trade: Tabs, non-scored 3.125, scored, 6.25,12.5,25 mg.] ▶L ♀C ◗? $$$$

esmolol (***Brevibloc***): SVT/HTN emergency: Mix infusion 5 g in 500 mL (10 mg/mL), load with 500 mcg/kg over 1 minute (70 kg: 35 mg or 3.5 mL) then infusion 50-200 mcg/kg/min (70 kg: 100 mcg/kg/min = 40 mL/h). Half-life = 9 minutes. Beta1 receptor selective. ▶K ♀C ◗? $$

labetalol (***Trandate, Normodyne***): HTN: Start 100 mg PO bid, max 2400 mg/day. HTN emergency: Start 20 mg IV slow injection, then 40-80 mg IV q10 min prn up to 300 mg or IV infusion 0.5-2 mg/min. Peds: Start 0.3-1 mg/kg/dose (max 20 mg). Alpha1, beta1, and beta2 receptor blocker. [Generic/Trade: Tabs, scored 100,200 (Trandate, Normodyne), 300 (Trandate), non-scored 300 mg (Normodyne).] ▶LK ♀C ◗+ $$

metoprolol (***Lopressor, Toprol XL***, ✤***Betaloc***): Acute MI: 5 mg increments IV q5-15 min up to 15 mg followed by oral therapy if tolerated. HTN (immediate release): Start 100 mg PO qd or 50 mg bid, increase as needed up to 450 mg/day. HTN (extended release): Start 50-100 mg PO qd, increase as needed up up to 400 mg/day. CHF: Start 12.5-25 mg (extended-release) PO qd, double dose every 2 weeks as tolerated up to max 200 mg/day. Beta1 receptor selective.[Generic/Trade: tabs, scored 50,100 mg. Trade only: tabs, extended-release, scored (Toprol XL) 25,50,100,200 mg.] ▶L ♀C ◗? $$

nadolol (***Corgard***): HTN: Start 20-40 mg PO qd, max 320 mg/day. Beta1 and beta2 blocker. [Generic/Trade: Tabs, scored 20,40,80,120,160 mg.] ▶K ♀C ◗- $$

penbutolol (***Levatol***): HTN: Start 20 mg PO qd, max 80 mg/day. [Trade: Tabs, scored 20 mg.] ▶LK ♀C ◗? $$$

pindolol (***Visken***): HTN: Start 5 mg PO bid, max 60 mg/day. Beta1 and beta2 receptor blocker. [Generic/Trade: Tabs, scored 5,10 mg.] ▶K ♀B ◗? $$$

propranolol (***Inderal, Inderal LA***): HTN: Start 20-40 mg PO bid or 60-80 mg PO qd (extended-release), max 640 mg/day. Life-threatening arrhythmia: 1 mg IV q2min. Migraine prophylaxis: Start 40 mg PO bid or 80 mg PO qd (extended-release), max 240 mg/day. Beta1 and beta2 blocker. [Generic/Trade: Tabs, scored 10,20,40,60,80 (Generic only), 90 mg. Solution 20,40 mg/5 ml. Concentrate, 80 mg/mL. Trade: Caps, extended-release 60,80,120,160 mg.] ▶L ♀C ◗+ $$

timolol (***Blocadren***): HTN: Start 10 mg PO bid, max 60 mg/d. Beta1 and beta2 blocker. [Generic/Trade: Tabs, non-scored 5, scored 10,20 mg.] ▶LK ♀C ◗+ $$

Calcium Channel Blockers (CCBs) - Dihydropyridines

amlodipine (***Norvasc***): HTN: Start 2.5 to 5 mg PO qd, max 10 qd. [Trade: Tabs, non-scored 2.5,5,10 mg.] ▶L ♀C ◗? $$

bepridil (***Vascor***): Rarely indicated, consult cardiologist. Chronic stable angina: Start 200 mg PO qd, max dose 400 mg qd. [Trade: Tabs, scored 200, non-scored 300, 400 mg.] ▶L ♀C ◗- $$$

felodipine (***Plendil***, ✤***Renedil***): HTN: Start 2.5-5 mg PO qd, maximum 10 mg/day. [Trade: Tabs, extended-release, non-scored 2.5,5,10 mg.] ▶L ♀C ◗? $$

isradipine (***DynaCirc, DynaCirc CR***): HTN: Start 2.5 mg PO bid, max 20 mg/day (max 10 mg/day in elderly). Controlled-release: 5-10 mg PO qd. [Trade: Caps 2.5,5 mg; tab, controlled-release 5,10 mg.] ▶L ♀C ▶? $$$

nicardipine (***Cardene, Cardene SR***): HTN emergency: Begin IV infusion at 5 mg/h, titrate to effect, max 15 mg/h. HTN: Start 20 mg PO tid, max 120 mg/day. Sustained release: Start 30 mg PO bid, max 120 mg/day. [Generic/Trade: caps, immediate-release 20,30 mg. Trade only: caps, sustained-release 30,45,60 mg.] ▶L ♀C ▶? $$

nifedipine (***Procardia, Adalat, Procardia XL, Adalat CC***): HTN/angina: extended-release: 30-60 mg PO qd, max 120/d. Angina: immediate-release: Start 10 mg PO tid, max 120 mg/d. Avoid sublingual administration, may cause excessive hypotension, stroke. Do not use immediate-release caps for HTN. [Generic/Trade: Caps, 10,20 mg. Tabs, extended-release 30,60,90 mg.] ▶L ♀C ▶+ $$

nisoldipine (***Sular***): HTN: Start 20 mg PO qd, max 60 mg/day. [Trade: Tabs, extended-release 10,20,30,40 mg.] ▶L ♀C ▶? $$

Calcium Channel Blockers (CCBs) - Other

diltiazem (***Cardizem, Diltia XT, Tiazac, Dilacor, Tiamate***): Rapid atrial fibrillation: bolus 20 mg (0.25 mg/kg) IV over 2 min. Rebolus 15 min later (if needed) 25 mg (0.35 mg/kg). Infusion 5-15 mg/h. HTN: Once daily, extended-release: Start 120-240 mg PO qd, max 540 mg/day. Twice daily, sustained-release: Start 60-120 mg PO bid, max 360 mg/day. Angina: immediate-release, Start 30 mg PO qid, max 360 mg/day divided tid-qid; extended-release, Start 120-240 mg PO qd, max 540 mg/day. [Generic/Trade: tabs, immediate-release, non-scored (Cardizem) 30, scored 60,90,120 mg; caps, sustained-release (Cardizem SR q12h) 60,90,120 mg, extended-release (Cardizem CD qd) 120,180,240,300,360 mg. Trade only: tabs, ext'd-release (Tiamate qd) 120 mg, (Tiazac qd) 120,180,240,300,360,420 mg, (Dilacor XR, Diltia XT qd) 120,180,240 mg.] ▶L ♀C ▶+ $$

verapamil (***Isoptin, Calan, Covera-HS, Verelan PM***, ✤***Chronovera***): SVT: 5-10 mg IV over 2 min; peds (1-15 yo): 2-5 mg (0.1-0.3 mg/kg) IV, max dose 5 mg. Angina: immediate-release, start 40-80 mg PO tid-qid, max 480 mg/day; sustained-release, start 120-240 mg PO qd, max 480 mg/day (use bid dosing for doses > 240 mg/day with Isoptin SR and Calan SR); (Covera-HS) 180 mg PO qhs, max 480 mg/day. HTN: same as angina, except (Verelan PM) 100-200 mg PO qhs, max 400 mg/day; immediate-release Tabs should be avoided in treating HTN. [Generic/Trade: tabs, immediate-release, scored 40,80,120 mg; sustained-release, non-scored (Calan SR, Isoptin SR) 120, scored 180,240 mg; caps, sustained-release (Verelan) 120,180,240,360 mg. Trade only: tabs, extended-release (Covera HS) 180,240 mg; caps, extended-release (Verelan PM) 100,200,300 mg.] ▶L ♀C ▶+ $$

Diuretics - Carbonic Anhydrase Inhibitors

acetazolamide (***Diamox***): Acute mountain sickness: 125-250 mg PO bid-tid, beginning 1-2 days prior to ascent and continuing for ≥5 days at higher altitude. [Generic/Trade: Tabs, 125,250 mg; Trade only: cap, sustained-release 500 mg.] ▶LK ♀C ▶+ $

Diuretics - Loop

bumetanide (***Bumex***, ✤***Burinex***): Edema: 0.5-1 mg IV/IM; 0.5-2 mg PO qd. 1 mg bumetanide is roughly equivalent to 40 mg furosemide. [Generic/Trade: Tabs, scored 0.5,1,2 mg.] ▶K ♀C ▶? $

ethacrynic acid (***Edecrin***): Rarely used. Edema: 0.5-1.0 mg/kg IV, max 50 mg; 25-100 mg PO qd-bid. [Trade: Tabs, scored 25,50 mg (oral forms currently unavailable).] ▶K ♀B ▶? $$

furosemide (***Lasix***): Edema: Initial dose 20-80 mg IV/IM/PO, increase dose by 20-40 mg every 6-8h until desired response is achieved, max 600 mg/day. [Generic/Trade: Tabs, non-scored 20, scored 40,80 mg. Oral solution 10 mg/mL, 40 mg/5 ml.] ▶K ♀C ▶? $

torsemide (***Demadex***): Edema: 5-20 mg IV/PO qd. [Generic/Trade: Tabs, scored 5,10,20,100 mg.] ▶LK ♀B ▶? $

Diuretics - Potassium Sparing

amiloride (***Midamor***): Diuretic-induced hypokalemia: Start 5 mg PO qd, max 20 mg/day. [Generic/Trade: Tabs, non-scored 5 mg.] ▶LK ♀B ▶? $$

spironolactone (***Aldactone***): HTN/edema: 50-100 mg PO qd or divided bid. CHF: Start 12.5-25 mg PO qd, usual maintenance dose 25 mg qd, max dose 50 mg qd. [Generic/Trade: Tabs, non-scored 25; scored 50,100 mg.] ▶LK ♀D ▶+ $$

Diuretics - Thiazide Type

chlorothiazide (***Diuril***): HTN: 125-250 mg PO qd or divided bid, max 1000 mg/day divided bid. Edema: 500-2000 mg PO/IV qd or divided bid. [Generic/Trade: Tabs, scored 250,500 mg. Trade only: suspension, 250 mg/5 ml.] ▶L ♀D ▶+ $

chlorthalidone (***Hygroton, Thalitone***): HTN: 12.5-25 mg PO qd, max 50 mg/day. Edema: 50-100 mg PO qd, max 200 mg/day. [Trade only: Tabs, non-scored (Thalitone) 15 mg. Generic/Trade: Tabs, non-scored (Thalitone, Hygroton) 25,50, scored (Hygroton) 100 mg.] ▶L ♀D ▶+ $

hydrochlorothiazide (***HCTZ, Oretic, HydroDIURIL, Esidrix, Microzide***): HTN: 12.5-25 mg PO qd, max 50 mg/day. Edema: 25-100 mg PO qd, max 200 mg/day. [Generic/Trade: Tabs, scored 25,50,100 mg; cap, 12.5 mg; solution, 50 mg/5 ml, concentrate, 100 mg/mL.] ▶L ♀D ▶+ $

indapamide (***Lozol***, ***✤Lozide***): HTN: 1.25-5 mg PO qd, max 5 mg/day. Edema: 2.5-5 mg PO qam. [Generic/Trade: Tabs, non-scored 1.25, 2.5 mg.] ▶L ♀D ▶? $

metolazone (***Zaroxolyn, Mykrox***): Edema: 5-10 mg PO qd, max 10 mg/day in CHF, 20 mg/day in renal disease (Zaroxolyn). HTN: Start 0.5 mg PO qd, max 1 mg/day (Mykrox), 2.5-5 mg PO qd, max 10 mg/day (Zaroxolyn). [Trade: Tabs, non-scored (Mykrox) 0.5, (Zaroxolyn) 2.5,5,10 mg.] ▶L ♀D ▶? $$

Nitrates

isosorbide dinitrate (***Isordil, Sorbitrate, Dilatrate-SR***): Angina prophylaxis: 5-40 mg PO tid (7 am, noon, 5 pm), sustained-release: 40-80 mg PO bid (8 am, 2 pm). Acute angina, SL Tabs: 2.5-10 mg SL q5-10 min prn, up to 3 doses in 30 min. [Generic/Trade: Tabs, scored 5,10,20,30,40, chewable, scored 5,10, sustained-release, scored 40, sublingual Tabs, non-scored 2.5,5,10 mg. Trade only: cap, sustained-release (Dilatrate-SR, Isordil Tembids) 40 mg.] ▶L ♀C ▶? $

isosorbide mononitrate (***ISMO, Monoket, Imdur***): Angina: 20 mg PO bid (8 am and 3 pm). Extended-release: Start 30-60 mg PO qd, maximum 240 mg/day. [Generic/Trade: Tabs, non-scored (ISMO, bid dosing) 20, scored (Monoket, bid dosing) 10,20, extended-release, scored (Imdur, qd dosing) 30,60, non-scored 120 mg.] ▶L ♀C ▶? $$

nitroglycerin intravenous infusion (***Tridil, NitroBid IV***): Perioperative HTN, acute MI/CHF, acute angina: mix 50 mg in 250 mL D5W (200 mcg/mL), start at 10-20 mcg/min (3-6 mL/h), then titrate upward by 10-20 mcg/min prn. ▶L ♀C ▶? $

nitroglycerin ointment (***Nitrol, Nitro-bid***): Angina prophylaxis: Start 0.5 inch q8h, maintenance 1-2 inches q8h, maximum 4 inches q4-6h; 15 mg/inch. Allow for a nitrate-free period of 10-14 h to avoid nitrate tolerance. 1 inch ointment is approximately 15 mg. [Generic/Trade: Ointment, 2%.] ▶L ♀C ▶? $

nitroglycerin spray (***Nitrolingual***): Acute angina: 1-2 sprays under the tongue prn, max 3 sprays in 15 min. [Trade: Solution, 0.4 mg/spray (200 sprays/canister).] ▶L ♀C ▶? $$

nitroglycerin sublingual (***Nitrostat, NitroQuick***): Acute angina: 0.4 mg SL under tongue, repeat dose every 5 min as needed up to 3 doses in 15 min. [Generic/Trade: Sublingual tabs, non-scored 0.3,0.4,0.6 mg; in bottles of 100 or package of 4 bottles with 25 tabs each.] ▶L ♀C ▶? $

nitroglycerin sustained release (***Nitrong, Nitroglyn***): Angina prophylaxis: Start 2.5 or 2.6 mg PO bid-tid, then titrate upward prn. Allow for a nitrate-free period of 10-14 h to avoid nitrate tolerance. [Trade only: tabs, scored, extended-release (Nitrong) 2.6,6.5,9 mg. Generic/Trade: cap, extended-release (Nitroglyn) 2.5,6.5,9, 13 mg.] ▶L ♀C ▶? $

nitroglycerin transdermal (***Deponit, Minitran, Nitrodisc, Nitro-Dur, Transderm-Nitro, ✱Trinipatch***): Angina prophylaxis: 1 patch 12-14 h each day. Allow for a nitrate-free period of 10-14h each day to avoid tolerance. [Trade: Transdermal system, doses in mg/h: Nitro-Dur 0.1,0.2,0.3,0.4,0.6,0.8; Minitran 0.1,0.2,0.4,0.6; Nitrodisc 0.2,0.3,0.4; Deponit 0.2,0.4; Transderm-Nitro 0.1,0.2,0.4,0.6,0.8. Generic only: Transdermal system, doses in mg/h: 0.1,0.2,0.4,0.6.] ▶L ♀C ▶? $$

nitroglycerin transmucosal (***Nitroguard***): Acute angina and prophylaxis: 1-3 mg PO, between lip and gum or between cheek and gum, q 3-5 hours while awake. [Trade: Tabs, controlled-release, 1,2,3 mg.] ▶L ♀C ▶? $$$

CARDIAC PARAMETERS AND FORMULAS	*Normal*
Cardiac output (CO) = heart rate x stroke volume	4-8 l/min
Cardiac index (CI) = CO/BSA	2.8-4.2 l/min/m2
MAP (mean arterial press) = [(SBP - DBP)/3] + DBP	80-100 mmHg
SVR (systemic vasc resis) = (MAP - CVP)x(80)/CO	800-1200 dyne/sec/cm5
PVR (pulm vasc resis) = (PAM - PCWP)x(80)/CO	45-120 dyne/sec/cm5
QT_C = QT / square root of RR [calculate using both measures in sec]	≤0.44 sec
Right atrial pressure (central venous pressure)	0-8 mmHg
Pulmonary artery systolic pressure (PAS)	20-30 mmHg
Pulmonary artery diastolic pressure (PAD)	10-15 mmHg
Pulmonary capillary wedge pressure (PCWP)	8-12 mmHg (post-MI ~16 mmHg)

Pressors / Inotropes

dobutamine (***Dobutrex***): Inotropic support. 250 mg in 250 ml D5W (1 mg/mL) at 2-20 mcg/kg/min. 70 kg: 5 mcg/kg/min = 21 mL/h. ▶Plasma ♀D ▶- $

dopamine (***Intropin***): Pressor: 400 mg in 250 ml D5W (1600 mcg/mL) start at 5 mcg/kg/min, increase as needed by 5-10 mcg/kg/min increments at 10 min intervals, max 50 mcg/kg/min. 70 kg: 5 mcg/kg/min = 13 mL/h. Doses in mcg/kg/min: 2-4 = (traditional renal dose, apparently ineffective) dopaminergic receptors; 5-10 = (cardiac dose) dopaminergic and beta1 receptors; >10 = dopaminergic, beta1, and alpha1 receptors. ▶Plasma ♀C ▶- $

ephedrine: Pressor: 10-25 mg slow IV, repeat q5-10 min prn. [Generic: Caps, 25,50 mg.] ▶K ♀C ▶? $

epinephrine: Cardiac arrest: 1 mg IV. Anaphylaxis: 0.1-0.5 mg SC/IM, may repeat

SC dose q 10-15 minutes. IV Infusion: 1 mg in 250 mL D5W (4 mcg/mL) at 1-4 mcg/min (15-60 mL/h). ▶Plasma ♀C ▶- $

inamrinone (***Inocor***): CHF: 0.75 mg/kg bolus IV over 2-3 min, then infusion 100 mg in 100 mL NS (1 mg/mL) at 5-10 mcg/kg/min. 70 kg: 5 mcg/kg/min = 21 mL/h. ▶K ♀C ▶? $$$$$

midodrine (***ProAmatine***, ***♣Amatine***): Orthostatic hypotension: 10 mg PO tid while awake. [Trade: Tabs, scored 2.5,5 mg.] ▶LK ♀C ▶? $$$$$

milrinone (***Primacor***): CHF (NYHA class III,IV): Load 50 mcg/kg IV over 10 min, then begin IV infusion of 0.375-0.75 mcg/kg/min. ▶K ♀C ▶? $$$$$

norepinephrine (***Levophed***): Acute hypotension: 4 mg in 500 mL D5W (8 mcg/mL) start 8-12 mcg/min, adjust to maintain BP, average maintenance rate 2-4 mcg/min, ideally through central line. 3 mcg/min = 20 mL/h. ▶Plasma ♀C ▶? $

phenylephrine (***Neo-Synephrine***): Severe hypotension: 50 mcg boluses IV. Infusion: 20 mg in 250 ml D5W (80 mcg/mL), start 100-180 mcg/min (75-135 mL/h), usual dose once BP is stabilized 40-60 mcg/min. ▶Plasma ♀C ▶- $$$

THROMBOLYTIC THERAPY FOR ACUTE MI *Indications*:* Chest pain ≤12 hours; and either ST elevation ≥1 mm in 2 contiguous leads or left BBB obscuring ST-segment analysis. *Absolute contraindications*: Prior hemorrhagic stroke or any stroke within 6-12 months; brain neoplasm, suspected aortic dissection. *Relative contraindications* (weigh benefits against higher risk): Ready availability of high-volume interventional cath lab; major surgery or trauma in prior 14-21 days; bleeding diathesis or current warfarin with INR >2; prolonged CPR (>10 min); age ≥75 years, pregnancy; uncorrected GI bleeding within 3 months; severe uncontrolled HTN (>180/110) before or during treatment; venous/arterial puncture to noncompressible site (eg, internal jugular or subclavian); brain aneurysm or AVM; coma. Menses are NOT a contraindication. Streptokinase contraindicated if given in prior year.

**Circulation* 1999; 100:1016

Thrombolytics

alteplase (***t-PA, Activase, Cathflo***): Acute MI: 15 mg IV bolus, then 50 mg over 30 min, then 35 mg over the next 60 min; (patient ≤67 kg) 15 mg IV bolus, then 0.75 mg/kg (max 50 mg) over 30 min, then 0.5 mg/kg (max 35 mg) over the next 60 min. Concurrent heparin infusion. Acute ischemic stroke: 0.9 mg/kg up to 90 mg infused over 60 min, with 10% of dose as initial IV bolus over 1 minute; start within 3 h of symptom onset. Acute pulmonary embolism: 100 mg IV over 2h, then restart heparin when PTT ≤ twice normal. Occluded central venous access device: 2 mg/ml in catheter for 2 hr. May use second dose if needed. ▶L ♀C ▶? $$$$$

anistreplase (***APSAC, Eminase***): Acute MI: 30 units IV over 2-5 minutes. ▶L ♀C ▶? $$$$$

reteplase (***Retavase***): Acute MI: 10 units IV over 2 min; repeat in 30 minutes. ▶L ♀C ▶? $$$$$

streptokinase (***Streptase, Kabikinase***): Acute MI: 1.5 million units IV over 60 minutes. ▶L ♀C ▶? $$$$$

tenecteplase (***TNKase***): Acute MI: Single IV bolus dose over 5 seconds based on body weight; < 60 kg, 30 mg; 60-69 kg, 35 mg; 70-79 kg, 40 mg; 80-89 kg, 45 mg; ≥ 90kg, 50 mg. ▶L ♀C ▶? $$$$$

urokinase (***Abbokinase, Abbokinase Open -Cath***): PE: 4400 units/kg IV loading dose over 10 min, followed by IV infusion 4400 units/kg/h for 12 hours. Occluded IV catheter: 5000 units instilled into catheter, remove after 5 min. ▶L ♀B ▶? $$$$$

Volume Expanders

albumin (***Albuminar, Buminate, Albumarc, ♣Plasbumin***): Shock, burns: 500 mL of 5% solution IV infusion as rapidly as tolerated, repeat in 30 min if needed. ▶L ♀C ◗? $$$$

dextran (***Rheomacrodex, Gentran, Macrodex***): Shock/hypovolemia: 20 mL/kg up to 500 mL IV. ▶K ♀C ◗? $$$$

hetastarch (***Hespan, Hextend***): Shock/hypovolemia: 500-1000 mL IV 6% solution. ▶K ♀C ◗? $$

plasma protein fraction (***Plasmanate, Protenate, Plasmatein***): Shock/hypovolemia: 5% soln 250-500 ml IV prn. ▶L ♀C ◗? $$$$

Other

alprostadil (***Prostin VR Pediatric, prostaglandin E1***): Maintenance of patent ductus arteriosus in neonates: Start 0.1 mcg/kg/min IV infusion, max dose 0.4 mcg/kg/min. ▶Lung ♀- ◗- ?

cilostazol (***Pletal***): Claudication: 100 mg PO bid on empty stomach. 50 mg PO bid with cytochrome P450 3A4 inhibitors (like ketoconazole, itraconazole, erythromycin, diltiazem) or cytochrome P450 2C19 inhibitors (like omeprazole). Avoid grapefruit juice. [Trade: Tabs 50, 100 mg] ▶L ♀C ◗? $$$

indomethacin (***Indocin IV, ♣Indocid***): Closure of patent ductus arteriosus in neonates: Initial dose 0.2 mg/kg IV, if additional doses necessary, dose and frequency (q12h or q24h) based on neonate's age and urine output. ▶KL ♀- ◗- ?

nesiritide (***Natrecor***): Decompensated CHF: 2 mcg/kg IV bolus over 60 seconds, then 0.01 mcg/kg/min IV infusion for up to 48 hours. Do not initiate at higher doses. Limited experience with increased doses. 1.5 mg vial in 250mL D5W (6 mcg/mL). 70 kg: 2 mcg/kg bolus = 23.3 ml, 0.01 mcg/kg/min infusion = 7 mL/h. Symptomatic hypotension. ▶K, plasma ♀C ◗? $$$$$

pentoxifylline (***Trental***): 400 mg PO tid with meals. [Generic/Trade: Tabs 400 mg.] ▶L ♀C ◗? $$$

CONTRAST MEDIA

MRI Contrast

gadodiamide (***Omniscan***): Non-iodinated, non-ionic IV contrast for MRI. ▶K ♀C ◗? $$$$

gadopentetate (***Magnevist***): Non-iodinated IV contrast for MRI. ▶K ♀C ◗? $$$

Radiography Contrast

> **NOTE:** Beware of allergy/anaphylaxis. Avoid IV contrast in renal insufficiency or dehydration. Hold metformin (*Glucophage*) prior to or at the time of iodinated contrast dye use and for 48 h after procedure. Restart after procedure only if renal function is normal.

barium sulfate: Non-iodinated GI (eg, oral, rectal) contrast. ▶Not absorbed ♀? ◗+ $

diatrizoate (***Hypaque, Renografin, Gastrografin, MD-Gastroview, Cystografin***): Iodinated, ionic, high osmolality IV or GI contrast. ▶K ♀C ◗? $

iohexol (***Omnipaque***): Iodinated, non-ionic, low osmolality IV and oral/body cavity contrast. ▶K ♀B ◗? $$$

iopamidol (***Isovue***): Iodinated, non-ionic, low osmolality IV contrast. ▶K ♀? ◗? $$

iothalamate (***Conray***): Iodinated, ionic, high osmolality IV contrast. ▶K ♀B ◗- $

ioversol (***Optiray***): Iodinated, non-ionic, low osmolality IV contrast. ▶K ♀B ◗? $$

ioxaglate (***Hexabrix***): Iodinated, ionic, low osmolality IV contrast. ▶K ♀B ◗- $$$

DERMATOLOGY

Acne Preparations

adapalene (***Differin***): apply qhs. [Trade only: gel 0.1%, 15,45 g.] ▶Bile ♀C ▶? $$

azelaic acid (***Azelex***): apply bid. [Trade only: cream 20%, 30g.] ▶K ♀B ▶? $$$

BenzaClin (clindamycin + benzoyl peroxide): apply bid. [Trade only: gel clindamycin 1% + benzoyl peroxide 5%; 19.7 g.] ▶K ♀B ▶+ $$$

Benzamycin (erythromycin + benzoyl peroxide): apply bid. [Trade only: gel erythromycin 3% + benzoyl peroxide 5%; 23.3, 46.6 g.] ▶LK ♀B ▶? $$$

benzoyl peroxide (***Benzac, Desquam, Clearasil, ✤Acetoxyl, Solugel***): apply qd; increase to bid-tid if needed. [OTC and Rx generic: liquid 2.5,5,10%, bar 5,10%, mask 5%, lotion 5,5.5,10%, cream 5,10%, cleanser 10%, gel 2.5,4,5, 6,10,20%.] ▶LK ♀C ▶? $

clindamycin (***Cleocin T, ✤Dalacin T***): apply bid. [Generic/Trade: gel 10 mg/ml 7.5, 30g, lotion 10 mg/ml 60 ml, solution 10 mg/ml 30,60 ml.] ▶L ♀B ▶- $

doxycycline (***Vibramycin, Doryx***): Acne vulgaris: 100 mg PO bid. [Generic only: tabs 50 mg, caps 20,50 mg. Generic/Trade: Tabs 100 mg, caps 50,100 mg. Trade only: susp 25 mg/5 ml, syrup 50 mg/5 ml (contains sulfites).] ▶LK ♀D ▶+ $$

erythromycin (***Eryderm, Erycette, Erygel, A/T/S***): apply bid. [Generic: solution 1.5% 60 ml, 2% 60,120 ml, pads 2%, gel 2% 30,60 g, ointment 2% 25 g.] ▶L ♀B ▶? $$

isotretinoin (***Accutane***): 0.5-2 mg/kg/day PO divided bid for 15-20 weeks. Typical target dose is 1 mg/kg. Can only be prescribed by healthcare professionals who have undergone specific training. Potent teratogen; use extreme caution. May cause depression. Not for long-term use. [Trade only: caps 10,20,40 mg.] ▶LK ♀X ▶- $$$$$

sodium sulfacetamide (***Klaron***): apply bid. [Trade only: lotion 10% 59 ml.] ▶K ♀C ▶? $$

Sulfacet-R (sodium sulfacetamide + sulfur): apply 1-3 times daily. [Trade and generic: lotion (sodium sulfacetamide 10% & sulfur 5%) 25 g.] ▶K ♀C ▶? $$

tazarotene (***Tazorac***): Acne: apply 0.1% cream qhs. [Trade only: cream 0.05% 30,100g, 0.1% 30, 100g.] ▶L ♀X ▶? $$$

tretinoin (***Retin-A, Retin-A Micro, Renova, Retisol-A, ✤Stievaa***): Apply qhs. [Generic/Trade: cream 0.025% 20,45 g, 0.05% 20,45 g, 0.1% 20,45 g, gel 0.025% 15,45 g, 0.1% 15,45 g, liquid 0.05% 28 ml. Trade only: Renova cream 0.02%, 0.05% 40,60 g, Retin-A Micro gel 0.04%, 0.1% 20,45 g.] ▶LK ♀C ▶? $$

Actinic Keratosis Preparations

diclofenac (***Solaraze***): Actinic or solar keratoses: apply bid to lesions x 60-90 days. [Trade only: gel 3% 25, 50 g.] ▶L ♀B ▶? $$$$

fluorouracil (***5FU, Carac, Efudex, Fluoroplex***): Actinic keratoses: apply bid x 2-6 wks. Superficial basal cell carcinomas: apply 5% cream/solution bid. [Trade only: cream 5% 25 g (Efudex), 1% 30 g (Fluoroplex), solution 1% 30 ml (Fluoroplex), 2% 10 ml (Efudex), 5% 10 ml (Efudex).] ▶L ♀X ▶- $$$$$

masoprocol (***Actinex***): Actinic keratoses: apply bid. [Trade only: cream 10% 30 g.] ▶LK ♀B ▶? ?

Antibacterials

bacitracin: apply qd-tid. [OTC Generic/Trade: ointment 500 units/g 1,15,30g.] ▶Not absorbed ♀C ▶? $

gentamicin (***Garamycin***): apply tid-qid. [Generic/Trade: ointment 0.1% 15,30 g, cream 0.1% 15,30 g.] ▶K ♀D ▶? $

mafenide (***Sulfamylon***): Apply qd-bid. [Trade only: cream 37, 114, 411 g, 5% topical solution 50 g packets.] ▶LK ♀C ◗? $$$

metronidazole (***Noritate, Metrocream, MetroGel, MetroLotion***): Rosacea: apply bid. [Trade only: gel (MetroGel) 0.75% 29 g, cream (Noritate) 1% 30 g, lotion (MetroLotion) 0.75% 59 ml.] ▶KL ♀B(- in 1st trimester) ◗- $$$

mupirocin (***Bactroban***): Impetigo/infected wounds: apply tid. Nasal MRSA eradication: 0.5 g in each nostril bid x 5 days. [Trade only: cream/ointment 2% 15,30 g, nasal ointment 2% 1 g single-use tubes (for MRSA eradication).] ▶Not absorbed ♀B ◗? $$

Neosporin cream (neomycin + polymyxin): apply qd-tid. [OTC trade only: neomycin 3.5 mg/g + polymyxin 10,000 units/g 15 g and unit dose 0.94 g.] ▶K ♀C ◗? $

Neosporin ointment (bacitracin + neomycin + polymyxin): apply qd-tid. [OTC Generic/Trade: bacitracin 400 units/g + neomycin 3.5 mg/g + polymyxin 5,000 units/g 2.4,9.6,14.2,15, 30 g and unit dose 0.94 g.] ▶K ♀C ◗? $

Polysporin (bacitracin + polymyxin): apply ointment/aerosol/powder qd-tid. [OTC trade only: ointment 15,30 g and unit dose 0.9 g, powder 10 g, aerosol 90 g.] ▶K ♀C ◗? $

silver sulfadiazine (***Silvadene, ♣Dermazin, Flamazine***): apply qd-bid. [Generic/Trade: cream 1% 20,50,85,400,1000g.] ▶LK ♀B ◗- $

<u>***Antifungals***</u>

butenafine (***Lotrimin Ultra, Mentax***): apply qd-bid. [Trade only. Rx: cream 1% 15,30 g (Mentax). OTC: cream 1% (Lotrimin Ultra).] ▶L ♀B ◗? $$$

ciclopirox (***Loprox, Penlac***): Cream, lotion: apply bid. Nail solution: apply daily to affected nails; apply over previous coat; remove with alcohol every 7 days. [Trade only: cream (Loprox) 1% 15,30,90 g, lotion (Loprox) 1% 30,60 ml, nail solution (Penlac) 8%.] ▶K ♀B ◗? $$

clotrimazole (***Lotrimin, Mycelex, ♣Canesten***): apply bid. [Note that Lotrimin brand cream, lotion, solution are clotrimazole, while Lotrimin powders and liquid spray are miconazole. OTC & Rx generic/Trade: cream 1% 15, 30, 45, 90 g, solution 1% 10,30 ml. Trade only: lotion 1% 30 ml.] ▶L ♀B ◗? $

econazole (***Spectazole, ♣Ecostatin***): Tinea pedis, cruris, corporis, tinea versicolor: apply qd. Cutaneous candidiasis: apply bid. [Trade only: cream 1% 15,30,85g.] ▶Not absorbed ♀C ◗? $$

ketoconazole (***Nizoral***): Tinea/candidal infections: apply qd. Seborrheic dermatitis: apply cream qd-bid. Dandruff: apply 1% shampoo twice a week. Tinea versicolor: apply shampoo to affected area, leave on for 5 min, rinse. [Trade only: shampoo 1% (OTC), 2%, 120 ml. Trade/Generic: cream 2% 15,30,60 g.] ▶L ♀C ◗? $

miconazole (***Monistat-Derm, Micatin, Lotrimin***): Tinea, candida: apply bid. [Note that Lotrimin brand cream, lotion, solution are clotrimazole, while Lotrimin powders and liquid spray are miconazole. OTC generic: ointment 2% 29 g, spray 2% 105 ml, solution 2% 7.39, 30 ml. Generic/Trade: cream 2% 15,30,90 g, powder 2% 90 g, spray powder 2% 90,100 g, spray liquid 2% 105,113 ml.] ▶L ♀+ ◗? $

naftifine (***Naftin***): Tinea: apply qd (cream) or bid (gel). [Trade only: cream 1% 15,30,60 g, gel 1% 20,40, 60 g.] ▶LK ♀B ◗? $$

nystatin (***Mycostatin***): Candidiasis: apply bid-tid. [Generic/Trade: cream 100,000 units/g 15,30,240 g, ointment 100,000 units/g 15,30 g, powder 100,000 units/g 15 g.] ▶Not absorbed ♀C ◗? $

oxiconazole (***Oxistat, Oxizole***): Tinea pedis, cruris, and corporis: apply qd-bid. Tinea versicolor (cream only): apply qd. [Trade only: cream 1% 15,30,60 g, lotion 1% 30 ml.] ▶? ♀B ◗? $$

terbinafine (***Lamisil, Lamisil AT***): Tinea: apply qd-bid. [Trade only: cream 1% 15,30 g, gel 1% 5,15,30 g OTC: Trade only (Lamisil AT): cream 1% 12,24 g, spray pump solution 1% 30 ml.] ▶L ♀B ▶? $$$

tolnaftate (***Tinactin***): apply bid. [OTC Generic/Trade: cream 1% 15,30 g, solution 1% 10,15 ml, powder 1% 45,90 g, spray powder 1% 100,105,150 g, spray liquid 1% 60,120 ml. Trade only: gel 1% 15 g.] ▶? ♀? ▶? $

Antiparasitics (topical)

A-200 (pyrethrins + piperonyl butoxide, ♣***R&C***): Lice: Apply shampoo, wash after 10 min. Reapply in 5-7 days. [OTC Generic/Trade: shampoo (0.33% pyrethrins, 4% piperonyl butoxide) 60,120,240 ml.] ▶L ♀C ▶? $

crotamiton (***Eurax***): Scabies: apply cream/lotion topically from chin to feet, repeat in 24 hours, bathe 48 h later. Pruritus: massage prn. [Trade only: cream 10% 60 g, lotion 10% 60,480 ml.] ▶? ♀C ▶? $$

lindane: Other drugs preferred. Scabies: apply 30-60 ml of lotion, wash after 8-12h. Lice: 30-60 ml of shampoo, wash off after 4 min. Can cause seizures in epileptics or if overused/misused in children. Not for infants. [Generic/Trade: lotion 1% 30,60,480 ml, shampoo 1% 30,60,480 ml.] ▶L ♀B ▶? $

malathion (***Ovide***): apply to dry hair, let dry naturally, wash off in 8-12 hrs. [Trade only: lotion 0.5% 59 ml.] ▶? ♀B ▶? $$

permethrin (***Elimite, Acticin, Nix***, ♣***Kwellada-P***): Scabies: apply cream from head (avoid mouth/ nose/eyes) to soles of feet & wash after 8-14h. 30 g is typical adult dose. Lice: Saturate hair and scalp with 1% rinse, wash after 10 min. Do not use in children <2 months old. May repeat therapy in 7 days, as necessary. [Trade only: cream (Elimite, Acticin) 5% 60 g. OTC Trade/generic: liquid creme rinse (Nix) 1% 60 ml.] ▶L ♀B ▶? $$

RID (pyrethrins + piperonyl butoxide): Lice: Apply shampoo/mousse, wash after 10 min. Reapply in 5-10 days. [OTC Generic/Trade: shampoo 60,120,240 ml. Trade only: mousse 5.5 oz.] ▶L ♀C ▶? $

Antipsoriatics

acitretin (***Soriatane***): 25-50 mg PO qd. Avoid pregnancy during therapy and for 3 years after discontinuation. [Trade only: cap 10,25 mg.] ▶L ♀X ▶- $$$$$

anthralin (***Anthra-Derm, Drithocreme***, ♣***Anthrascalp***): Apply qd. Short contact periods (i.e. 15-20 minutes) followed by removal may be preferred. [Trade only: ointment 0.1% 42.5 g, 0.25% 42.5 g, 0.4% 60 g, 0.5% 42.5 g, 1% 42.5 g, cream 0.1% 50 g, 0.2% 50 g, 0.25% 50 g, 0.5% 50 g. Generic/Trade: cream 1% 50 g.] ▶? ♀C ▶- $$

calcipotriene (***Dovonex***): apply bid. [Trade only: ointment 0.005% 30,60,100 g, cream 0.005% 30,60,100 g, scalp solution 0.005% 60 ml.] ▶L ♀C ▶? $$$

tazarotene (***Tazorac***): Psoriasis: apply 0.05% cream qhs, increase to 0.1% prn. [Trade only: gel 0.05% 30,100 g, 0.1% 30, 100 g.] ▶L ♀X ▶? $$$

Antivirals (topical)

acyclovir (***Zovirax***): Herpes genitalis: apply q3h (6 times/d) x 7 days. [Trade only: ointment 5% 3,15 g.] ▶K ♀C ▶? $$$

docosanol (***Abreva***): oral-facial herpes simplex: apply 5x/day until healed. [OTC: Trade only: cream 10% 2 g.] ▶Not absorbed ♀B ▶? $

imiquimod (***Aldara***): Genital/perianal warts: apply 3 times weekly - put on at bedtime and wash off in 6-10 hours. [Trade only: cream 5% 250 mg single use packets.] ▶Not absorbed ♀B ▶? $$$$

penciclovir (***Denavir***): Herpes labialis: apply cream q2h while awake x 4 days. [Trade only: cream 1% 2 g tubes.] ▶Not absorbed ♀B ▶? $$$

podofilox (***Condylox***, ♣***Condyline***): External genital warts (gel and solution) and perianal warts (gel only): apply bid for 3 consecutive days of a week and repeat for up to 4 wks. [Trade only: gel 0.5% 3.5 g, solution 0.5% 3.5 ml.] ▶? ♀C ▶? $$$

podophyllin (***Podocon 25, Podofin, Podofilm***): Warts: apply by physician. Not to be dispensed to patients. [Not to be dispensed to patients. For hospital/clinic use; not intended for outpatient prescribing. Trade only: liquid 25% 15 ml.] ▶? ♀- ▶- $$

Atopic Dermatitis Preparations

pimecrolimus (***Elidel***): Atopic dermatitis: apply bid. [Trade: cream 1% 15, 30, 100 g.] ▶L ♀C ▶? $$$

tacrolimus (***Protopic***): Atopic dermatitis: apply bid. [Trade only: ointment 0.03% 30,60 g, 0.1% 30,60 g.] ▶Minimal absorption ♀C ▶? $$$$

CORTICOSTEROIDS – TOPICAL*

Agent	*Strength/Formulation**	*Frequency*	*Potency*
alclometasone dipropionate *(Aclovate)*	0.05% C O	bid-tid	Low
amcinonide *(Cyclocort)*	0.1% C L O	bid tid	High
betamethasone dipropionate *(Diprolene, Diprolene AF, Diprosone, Maxivate)*	0.05% CLO (non-*Diprolene*) 0.05% C G L O (*Diprolene*)	qd-bid qd-bid	High Very high
betamethasone valerate	0.1% CLO; 0.12% F (*Luxiq*)	qd-bid	Medium
clobetasol propionate (*Temovate, Cormax*)	0.05% C O S	bid	Very high
clocortolone pivalate (*Cloderm*)	0.1% C	tid	Low
desonide (*DesOwen, Tridesilon*)	0.05% C L O	bid-tid	Low
desoximetasone (*Topicort*)	0.05% C 0.05% G, 0.25% C O	bid bid	Medium High
diflorasone diacetate (*Maxiflor, Psorcon, Psorcon E*)	0.05% C O (non *Psorcon*) 0.05% C O (*Psorcon*)	bid qd-tid	High Very high
flucinolone acetonide (*Synalar*)	0.01% C S; 0.025% C O	bid-qid	Medium
fluocinonide (*Lidex*)	0.05% C G O S	bid-qid	High
flurandrenolide (*Cordran*)	0.025% C O; 0.05% CLO; T	bid-qid	Medium
fluticasone propionate (*Cutivate*)	0.005% O; 0.05% C	qd-bid	Medium
halcinonide (*Halog*)	0.1% C O S	bid-tid	High
halobetasol propionate (*Ultravate*)	0.05% C O	qd-bid	Very high
hydrocortisone (*Hytone, others*)	0.25% CL; 0.5% CLOS; 1% CLOS, 2% L; 2.5% CLOS	bid-qid	Low
hydrocortisone acetate (*Cortaid, Corticaine*)	0.5% C O, 1% C O	bid-qid	Low
hydrocortisone butyrate (*Locoid*)	0.1% C O	bid-tid	Medium
hydrocortisone valerate (*Westcort*)	0.2% C O	bid-tid	Medium
mometasone furoate (*Elocon*)	0.1% C L O	qd	Medium
triamcinolone acetonide (*Aristocort, Kenalog*)	0.025% C L O; 0.1% C L O 0.5% C	bid-tid bid-tid	Medium High

***C-cream, G-gel, L-lotion, O-ointment, S-solution, T=tape, F=foam**. Potency based on vasoconstrictive assays, which may not correlate with efficacy. Not all available products are listed, including those lacking potency ratings.

Corticosteroid / Antimicrobial Combinations

Cortisporin (neomycin + polymyxin + hydrocortisone): apply bid-qid. [Generic/Trade: cream 7.5 g, ointment 15 g.] ▶LK ♀C ▶? $

Lotrisone (clotrimazole + betamethasone, ♣***Lotriderm***): Apply bid. Do not use for diaper rash. [Trade/generic: cream (clotrimazole 1% + betamethasone 0.05%) 15,45 g.] ▶L ♀C ▶? $$$

Mycolog II (nystatin + triamcinolone): apply bid. [Generic/Trade: cream 15,30,60,120 g, ointment 15,30,60,120 g.] ▶L ♀C ▶? $

Hemorrhoid Care

dibucaine (***Nupercainal***): apply cream/ointment tid-qid prn. [OTC Generic/Trade: ointment 1% 30 g.] ▶L ♀? ▶? $

hydrocortisone (***Anusol HC***): apply cream tid-qid prn or supp bid. [Generic/Trade: cream 1% (Anusol HC-1), 2.5% 30 g (Anusol HC), suppository 25 mg (Anusol HC).] ▶L ♀? ▶? $

pramoxine (***Anusol Hemorrhoidal Ointment, Fleet Pain Relief, ProctoFoam NS***): ointment/pads/foam up to 5 times/day prn. [OTC Trade only: ointment (Anusol Hemorrhoidal Ointment), pads (Fleet Pain Relief), aerosol foam (ProctoFoam NS).] ▶Not absorbed ♀+ ▶+ $

starch (***Anusol Suppositories***): 1 suppository up to 6 times/day prn. [OTC Trade only: suppositories (51% topical starch; soy bean oil, tocopheryl acetate).] ▶Not absorbed ♀+ ▶+ $

witch hazel (***Tucks***): Apply to anus/perineum up to 6 times/day prn. [OTC Generic/Trade: pads,gel.] ▶? ♀+ ▶+ $

Other Dermatologic Agents

alitretinoin (***Panretin***): Apply bid-qid to cutaneous Kaposi's lesions [Trade only: gel 60 g.] ▶Not absorbed ♀D ▶- $$$$$

aminolevulinic acid (***Levulan Kerastick***): Apply solution to lesions on scalp or face; expose to special light source 14-18 h later. [Trade only: 20% solution single use ampules.] ▶Not absorbed ♀C ▶? $$$

becaplermin (***Regranex***): Diabetic ulcers: apply gel qd. [Trade only: gel 0.01% 2,7.5,15 g.] ▶Minimal absorption ♀C ▶? $$$$$

calamine: apply lotion tid-qid prn for poison ivy/oak or insect bite itching. [OTC Generic: lotion 120, 240, 480 ml.] ▶? ♀? ▶? $

capsaicin (***Zostrix, Zostrix-HP***): Arthritis, post-herpetic or diabetic neuralgia: apply cream up to tid-qid. [OTC Generic/Trade: cream 0.025%45,60 g, 0.075% 30,60 g, lotion 0.025% 59 ml, 0.075% 59 ml, gel 0.025% 15,30 g, 0.05% 43 g, roll-on 0.075% 60 ml.] ▶? ♀? ▶? $

coal tar (***Polytar, Tegrin***): apply shampoo at least twice a week, or for psoriasis apply qd-qid. [OTC Generic/Trade: shampoo, conditioner, cream, ointment, gel, lotion, soap, oil.] ▶? ♀? ▶? $

doxepin (***Zonalon***): Pruritus: apply qid for up to 8 days. [Trade only: cream 5% 30,45 g.] ▶L ♀B ▶- $

eflornithine (***Vaniqa***): Reduction of facial hair: apply to face bid. [Trade only: cream 13.9% 30 g.] ▶K ♀C ▶? $$

EMLA (lidocaine + prilocaine): Topical anesthesia: apply 2.5g cream or 1 disc to region at least 1 hour before procedure. Cover cream with an occlusive dressing. [Trade only: cream (2.5% lidocaine + 2.5% prilocaine) 5,30 g, disc 1 g.] ▶LK ♀B ▶? $$

finasteride (***Propecia***): Androgenetic alopecia in men: 1 mg PO qd. [Trade only: tab 1 mg.] ▶L ♀X ◗- $$

hydroquinone (***Eldopaque, Eldoquin, Esoterica, Lustra, Melanex, Solaquin***): Hyperpigmentation: apply to area bid. [OTC Generic/Trade: cream 1.5,2,4%, lotion 2%, solution 3%, gel 4%.] ▶? ♀C ◗? $$$

lactic acid (***Lac-Hydrin***): apply lotion/cream bid. [Trade only: cream 12% 140,385 g, lotion 12% 150,360 ml.] ▶? ♀? ◗? $$

lidocaine (***Xylocaine, Lidoderm, Numby Stuff, ELA-Max***): Apply prn. Dose varies with anesthetic procedure, degree of anesthesia required and individual patient response. Postherpetic neuralgia: apply up to 3 patches for up to 12h within a 24h period. Apply 30 min prior to painful procedure (ELA-Max 4%). Discomfort with anorectal disorders: apply prn (ELA-Max 5%) [For membranes of mouth and pharynx: spray 10%, ointment 5%, liquid 5%, solution 2,4%, dental patch. For urethral use: jelly 2%. Patch (Lidoderm) 5%. OTC: Trade: liposomal lidocaine 4%, 5% (ELA-Max).] ▶LK ♀B ◗? $$

minoxidil (***Rogaine, Rogaine Forte, Rogaine Extra Strength, Minoxidil for Men, ♣Minox***): Androgenetic alopecia in men or women: 1 ml to dry scalp bid. [OTC Trade only: solution 2%, 60 ml, 5%, 60 ml, 5% (Rogaine Extra Strength - for men only) 60 ml.] ▶K ♀C ◗- $$

oatmeal (***Aveeno***): Pruritus from poison ivy/oak, varicella: apply lotion qid prn. Also bathtub packets. [OTC Generic/Trade: lotion, packets.] ▶Not absorbed ♀?◗? $

selenium sulfide (***Selsun, Exsel, Versel***): Dandruff, seborrheic dermatitis: apply 5-10 ml lotion/shampoo twice weekly x 2 weeks then less frequently, thereafter. Tinea versicolor: Apply 2.5% lotion/shampoo to affected area qd x 7 days. [OTC Generic/Trade: lotion/shampoo 1% 120,210,240, 330 ml, 2.5% 120 ml. Rx generic/trade: lotion/shampoo 2.5% 120 ml.] ▶? ♀C ◗? $

Solag (mequinol + tretinoin): Apply to solar lentigines bid. [Trade only: soln 30 ml (mequinol 2% + tretinoin 0.01%).] ▶Not absorbed ♀X ◗? ?

Tri-Luma (fluocinolone + hydroquinone + tretinoin): Melasma of the face: apply qhs x 4-8 weeks. [Trade only: soln 30 g (fluocinolone 0.01% + hydroquinone 4% + tretinoin 0.05%).] ▶Minimal absorption ♀C ◗? $$$

ENDOCRINE & METABOLIC

Androgens / Anabolic Steroids (See OB/GYN section for other hormones)

fluoxymesterone (***Halotestin***): Inoperable breast cancer in women: 5-10 mg PO bid-qid x 1-3 months. Hypogonadism: 5-20 mg PO qd. [Trade: Tabs 2, 5 mg. Generic/Trade: Tabs 10 mg.] ▶L ♀X ◗? ©III $$$

methyltestosterone (***Android, Methitest, Testred, Virilon, ♣Metandren***): Inoperable breast cancer in women: 50-200 mg/day PO in divided doses. Hypogonadism: 10-50 mg PO qd. [Trade: Tabs 10 mg, Caps 10 mg. Generic/Trade: Tabs 25 mg.] ▶L ♀X ◗? ©III $$$

nandrolone decanoate (***Deca-Durabolin, Hybolin Decanoate***): Anemia of renal disease: women 50-100 mg IM q week, men 100-200 mg IM q week. [Generic/Trade: injection 100 mg/ml, 200 mg/ml. Trade only: injection 50 mg/ml.] ▶L ♀X ◗- ©III $$$

oxandrolone (***Oxandrin***): Weight gain: 2.5 mg PO bid-qid for 2-4 wks. [Trade: Tabs 2.5 mg.] ▶L ♀X ◗? ©III $$$$$

testosterone (***Androderm, Androgel, Testoderm, Testoderm TTS, Depo-Testosterone, Depotest, Testro-L.A., Virilon IM, Delatestryl, Everone, Testro AQ***):

Injectable enanthate or cypionate: 50-400 mg IM q2-4 wks. Transdermal – Androderm: 5 mg patch to nonscrotal skin hs; Testoderm TTS: one patch to arm/back/upper buttock qd. Testoderm: one patch to scrotal area qd. Androgel 1%: 1 gel pack (5 g) to shoulders/upper arms/abdomen. [Trade only: patch 5 mg (Testoderm TTS). patch 4, 6 mg (Testoderm). patch 2.5, 5 mg (Androderm). gel 1%-2.5, 5 g (Androgel). injection 200 mg/ml (enanthate). Generic/Trade: injection 100, 200 mg/ml (cypionate).] ▶L ♀X ▶? ©III $$$$

Bisphosphonates

alendronate (***Fosamax***): Postmenopausal osteoporosis prevention (5 mg PO qd or 35 mg PO weekly) & treatment (10 mg qd or 70 mg PO weekly). Glucocorticoid-induced osteoporosis: 5-10 mg PO qd. Increase bone mass in men with osteoporosis: 10 mg PO qd. Paget's disease: 40 mg PO qd x 6 mon. May cause esophagitis. [Trade: Tabs 5, 10, 35, 40, 70 mg.] ▶K ♀C ▶- $$$

etidronate (***Didronel***): Hypercalcemia: 7.5 mg/kg in 250 ml NS IV over ≥2h qd x 3d. Paget's disease: 5-10 mg/kg PO qd x 6 months or 11-20 mg/kg qd x 3 months. [Trade: Tabs 200, 400 mg.] ▶K ♀C ▶? $$$$

pamidronate (***Aredia***): Hypercalcemia: 60 mg IV over 4h or 90 mg IV over 24h. Wait ≥7 days before considering retreatment. ▶K ♀C ▶? $$$$$

risedronate (***Actonel***): Paget's disease: 30 mg PO qd x 2 months. Postmenopausal and glucocorticoid-induced osteoporosis prevention & treatment: 5 mg PO qd or 35 mg PO weekly. May cause esophagitis [Trade: Tabs 5, 30 mg.] ▶K ♀C ▶? $$$

tiludronate (***Skelid***): Paget's disease: 400 mg PO qd x 3 months. May cause esophagitis. [Trade: Tabs 200 mg.] ▶K ♀C ▶? $$$$$

zoledronic acid (***Zometa***): Hypercalcemia: 4 mg IV infusion over ≥15 min. Wait ≥7 days before considering retreatment. Multiple myeloma, metastatic bone lesions from solid tumors: 4 mg IV infusion over ≥15 min q3-4 weeks. ▶K ♀C ▶? $$$$$

Corticosteroids (See also dermatology, ophthalmology)

betamethasone (***Celestone***): 0.6-7.2 mg/day PO divided bid-qid; up to 9 mg/day IM. [Trade: Tabs 0.6 mg. syrup 0.6 mg/ 5 ml.] ▶L ♀C ▶- $$$$$

cortisone (***Cortone***): 25-300 mg PO qd. [Trade: Tabs 5, 10 mg. Generic/Trade: Tabs 25 mg.] ▶L ♀C ▶- $

dexamethasone (***Decadron, Dexone, ♣Dexasone, Hexadrol***): 0.5-9 mg/day PO/IV/IM, divided bid-qid. [Generic/Trade: Tabs 0.25, 0.5, 0.75, 1.0, 1.5, 2, 4, 6 mg. elixir/ solution 0.5 mg/5 ml. Trade only: oral solution 0.5 mg/ 0.5 ml. Decadron unipak (0.75 mg-12 tabs).] ▶L ♀C ▶- $

fludrocortisone (***Florinef***): Pure mineralocorticoid: 0.1 mg PO 3 times weekly to 0.2 mg PO qd. [Trade: Tabs 0.1 mg.] ▶L ♀C ▶? $

hydrocortisone (***Cortef, Solu-Cortef***): 100-500 mg IV/IM q2-10h as needed. 20-240 mg/day PO divided tid- qid. [Trade: Tabs 5, 10 mg. suspension 10 mg/ 5 ml. Generic/Trade: Tabs 20 mg.] ▶L ♀C ▶- $

methylprednisolone (***Solu-Medrol, Medrol, Depo-Medrol***): Parenteral: dose varies, 10-250 mg IV/IM. Oral (Medrol): dose varies, 4-48 mg PO qd. Peds: 0.5-2 mg/kg PO/IV/IM. Medrol Dosepak tapers 24 to 0 mg PO over 7 days. IM/Joints (Depo-Medrol): dose varies, 4-120 mg IM q1-2 weeks. [Trade only: Tabs 2, 8, 16, 24, 32 mg. Generic/Trade: Tabs 4 mg. Medrol Dosepak (4 mg-21 tabs).] ▶L ♀C ▶- $$$

prednisolone (***Prelone, Pediapred, Orapred***): 5-60 mg PO/IV/IM qd. [Generic/Trade: Tabs 5 mg. syrup 15 mg/ 5 ml (Prelone; wild cherry flavor). Trade only: solution 5 mg/5 ml (Pediapred; raspberry flavor); solution 15 mg/5 ml (Orapred; grape flavor).] ▶L ♀C ▶+ $$

CORTICOSTEROIDS	*Approximate equivalent dose (mg)*	*Relative anti-inflammatory potency*	*Relative mineralocorticoid potency*	*Biologic Half-life (hours)*
betamethasone	0.6-0.75	20-30	0	36-54
cortisone	25	0.8	2	8-12
dexamethasone	0.75	20-30	0	36-54
hydrocortisone	20	1	2	8-12
methylprednisolone	4	5	0	18-36
prednisolone	5	4	1	18-36
prednisone	5	4	1	18-36
triamcinolone	4	5	0	18-36

prednisone (***Deltasone, Meticorten, Pred-Pak, Sterapred***, ***✤Winpred, Metreton***): 1-2 mg/kg or 5-60 mg PO qd. [Generic/Trade: Tabs 1, 5, 10, 20, 50 mg. Trade only: Tabs 2.5 mg. Sterapred (5 mg tabs: tapers 30 to 5 mg PO over 6d or 30 to 10 mg over 12d), Sterapred DS (10 mg tabs: tapers 60 to 10 mg over 6d, or 60 to 20 mg PO over 12d) & Pred-Pak (5 mg 45 & 79 tabs) taper packs. solution 5 mg/5 ml & 5 mg/ml (Prednisone Intensol).] ▶L ♀C ▶+ $

triamcinolone (***Aristocort, Kenalog***, ***✤Aristospan***): 4-48 mg PO/IM qd. [Generic/Trade: Tabs 4 mg. Trade only: injection 10, 25, 40 mg/ml.] ▶L ♀C ▶- $$$$

Diabetes-Related - Alphaglucosidase Inhibitors

acarbose (***Precose***, ***✤Prandase***): Start 25 mg PO tid with meals, and gradually increase as tolerated to maintenance 50-100 mg tid. [Trade: Tabs 25, 50, 100 mg.] ▶Gut/K ♀B ▶- $$

miglitol (***Glyset***): Start 25 mg PO tid with meals, maintenance 50-100 tid. [Trade: Tabs 25, 50, 100 mg.] ▶K ♀B ▶- $$$

Diabetes-Related – Biguanides & Combinations

NOTE: metformin-containing products may cause lactic acidosis. Hold prior to IV contrast agents and for 48 h after. Avoid if ethanol abuse, heart failure (requiring treatment), renal or hepatic insufficiency.

Avandamet (rosiglitazone + metformin): 1 tablet PO bid. If inadequate control with metformin monotherapy, select tab strength based on adding 4 mg/day rosiglitazone to existing metformin dose. If inadequate control with rosiglitazone monotherapy, select tab strength based on adding 1000 mg/day metformin to existing rosiglitazone dose. Max 8/2000 mg/day. Monitor LFTs q2 months for first year. [Trade (rosiglitazone/metformin): Tabs 1/500, 2/500, 4/500 mg.] ▶LK ♀C ▶- ?

Glucovance (glyburide + metformin): Start 1.25/250 mg PO qd or bid with meals as initial therapy; max 10/2000 mg daily. Or start 2.5/500 or 5/500 mg PO bid with meals as second-line therapy; max 20/2000 mg daily. [Trade: Tabs 1.25/250, 2.5/500, 5/500 mg] ▶KL ♀B ▶? $$

metformin (***Glucophage, Glucophage XR***): Diabetes: Start 500 mg PO qd-bid with meals, gradually increase prn to max 2550 mg/day or 2000 mg/day (ext'd release). Polycystic ovary syndrome (unapproved): 500 mg PO tid. [Generic/ Trade: Tabs 500, 850, 1000 mg; extended release 500 mg.] ▶K ♀B ▶? $$$

Diabetes-Related - "Glitazones" (Thiazolidinediones)

pioglitazone (***Actos***): Start 15-30 mg PO qd, max 45 mg/day. Monitor LFTs. [Trade: Tabs 15, 30, 45 mg.] ▶L ♀C ▶- $$$

rosiglitazone (***Avandia***): Diabetes monotherapy or in combination with metformin or sulfonylurea: Start 4 mg PO qd or divided bid, max 8 mg/day monotherapy or in combination with metformin; there is no experience with doses greater than 4 mg/day in combination with sulfonylureas. Monitor LFTs q2 months for first year. [Trade: Tabs 2, 4, 8 mg.] ▶L ♀C ◗- $$$

DIABETES NUMBERS*		*Criteria for diagnosis of diabetes (repeat to confirm on subsequent day)*	
Self-monitoring glucose goals			
Preprandial	80-120 mg/dL	Fasting glucose	≥126 mg/dL
Bedtime	100-140 mg/dL	Random glucose with symptoms	≥200 mg/dL

Control	*A1c*
Normal	<6%
Goal	<7%
Action	>8%

Management schedule: Aspirin (75–325 mg/day) in all adults w/ macrovascular disease unless contraindicated.† *At every visit*: Measure weight and BP (goal <130/80mmHg; <125/75 mmHg if proteinuria >1 g/day†); foot exam for high-risk feet; review self-monitoring blood glucose record; review/adjust meds; review self-management skills, dietary needs, and physical activity; counsel on smoking cessation. *Twice a year*: A1c in patients meeting treatment goals with stable glycemia (quarterly if not). *Annually*: Fasting lipid profile (goal LDL <100 mg/dL†§), creatinine, UA for protein (check microalbumin if no overt proteinuria on UA); dilated eye exam; dental exam; flu vaccine; foot exam for low risk feet.

*See recommendations at the Diabetes Care website (care.diabetesjournals.org/)
†ADA. Diabetes Care 2002;25 (Suppl 1):S33-S49 §*JAMA* 2001;285:2486-2497.

Diabetes-Related - Meglitinides

nateglinide (***Starlix***): 120 mg PO tid 1-30 min before meals; use 60 mg PO tid in patients who are near goal A1c. [Trade: Tabs 60, 120 mg.] ▶L ♀C ◗? $$$

repaglinide (***Prandin***, ***✤Gluconorm***): Start 0.5- 2 mg PO tid before meals, maintenance 0.5-4 mg tid-qid, max 16 mg/day. [Trade: Tabs 0.5, 1, 2 mg] ▶L ♀C ◗? $$$

Diabetes-Related - Sulfonylureas - 1st Generation

chlorpropamide (***Diabinese***): Initiate 100-250 mg PO qd. Titrate after 5-7 days by increments of 50-125 mg every 3-5 days until optimal control. Max 750 mg/day. [Generic/Trade: Tabs 100, 250 mg.] ▶LK ♀C ◗- $

tolazamide (***Tolinase***): Initiate 100 mg PO qd if FBS < 200 mg/dl, and in patients who are malnourished, underweight, or elderly. Initiate 250 mg PO qd if FBS > 200 mg/dl. Give with breakfast. Doses > 500 mg/day, divide bid. Max 1,000 mg/day. [Generic/Trade: Tabs 100, 250, 500 mg.] ▶LK ♀C ◗? $

tolbutamide (***Orinase, Tol-Tab***): Initiate 1g PO qd. Maintenance 250-2000 mg PO qd or in divided doses, max 3 g/day. [Generic/Trade: tabs 500 mg.] ▶LK ♀C ◗+ $

Diabetes-Related - Sulfonylureas - 2nd Generation

glimepiride (***Amaryl***): Start 1-2 mg PO qd, usual 1-4 mg/day, max 8 mg/day. [Trade: Tabs 1, 2, 4 mg.] ▶LK ♀C ◗- $

INSULIN*	*Preparation*	*Onset (h)*	*Peak (h)*	*Duration (h)*
Rapid-acting:	Insulin aspart (*Novolog*)	¼	¾	3-5
	Insulin lispro (*Humalog*)	0-¼	½-1½	6-8
	Regular	½-1	2½-5	6-8
Intermediate-acting:	NPH	1-1½	4-12	24
	Lente	1-2½	7-15	24
Long-acting:	Ultralente	4-8	10-30	>36
	Insulin glargine (*Lantus*)	Slow, prolonged absorption†		

*These are general guidelines, as onset, peak, and duration of activity are affected by the site of injection, physical activity, body temperature, and blood supply.
†Relatively constant concentration/time profile over 24 h with no pronounced peak.

glipizide (***Glucotrol, Glucotrol XL***): Start 5 mg PO qd, usual 10-20 mg/day, max 40 mg/day (divide bid if >15 mg/day). Extended release: Start 5 mg PO qd, usual 5 to 10 mg/day, max 20 mg/day. [Generic/Trade: Tabs 5, 10 mg. Trade only: extended release Tabs (Glucotrol XL) 2.5, 5, 10 mg.] ▶LK ♀C ▶? $

glyburide (***Micronase, DiaBeta, Glynase PresTab***, ♣***Euglucon***): Start 1.25-5 mg PO qd, usual 1.25-20 mg qd or divided bid, max 20 mg/day. Micronized tabs: Start 1.5-3 mg PO qd, usual 0.75-12 mg/day divided bid, max 12 mg/d. [Generic/Trade: Tabs 1.25, 2.5, 5 mg. micronized Tabs 1.5, 3, 6 mg.] ▶LK ♀B ▶? $

Diabetes-Related Agents - Other

dextrose (***Glutose, B-D Glucose, Insta-Glucose***): Hypoglycemia: 0.5-1 g/kg (1-2 ml/kg) up to 25 g (50 ml) of 50% soln IV. Dilute to 25% for pediatric administration. [OTC/Trade only: chew Tabs 5 g. gel 40%.] ▶L ♀C ▶? $

diazoxide (***Proglycem***): Hypoglycemia: 3-8 mg/kg/day divided q8-12h, max 10- 15 mg/kg/day. [Trade: susp 50 mg/ ml.] ▶L ♀C ▶- $$$$$

glucagon (***Glucagon, GlucaGen***): Hypoglycemia: 1 mg IV/IM/SC, onset 5-20 min. [Trade: Injection 1 mg.] ▶LK ♀B ▶? $$$

glucose home testing (***Chemstrip bG, Dextrostix, Diascan, Glucometer, Glucostix, Clinistix, Clinitest, Diastix, Tes-Tape, GlucoWatch***): For home glucose monitoring. [Blood: Chemstrip bG, Dextrostix, Diascan, Glucometer, Glucostix; Urine: Clinistix, Clinitest, Diastix, Tes-Tape, GlucoWatch] ▶None ♀+ ▶+ $$

insulin (***Novolin, Novolog, Humulin, Humalog, Lantus***): Diabetes: 0.3-0.5 unit/kg/day SC in divided doses (Type 1), and 1-1.5 unit/kg/day SC divided doses (Type 2), but doses vary. Humalog/Novolog: 0.5-1 unit/kg/day SC, but doses vary. Lantus: Start 10 units SC qhs in insulin naïve patients, adjust to usual dose of 2-100 units/day. Other insulins are OTC and have no FDA-approved indications. Severe hyperkalemia: 5-10 units regular insulin plus concurrent dextrose IV. Profound hyperglycemia (eg, DKA): infusion 100 units regular in 100 ml NS (1 unit/ml), at 0.1 units/kg/hr. 70 kg. 7 units/h (7 ml/h). [Trade: injection NPH, regular, lente, ultralente, insulin lispro (Humalog), Insulin lispro protamine suspension/ insulin lispro (Humalog Mix 75/25), insulin glargine (Lantus), insulin aspart (Novolog), NPH and regular mixtures (70/30 or 50/50).] ▶LK ♀B/C ▶+ $$

Gout-Related

allopurinol (***Zyloprim***): 200-300 mg PO qd-bid, max 800 md/day. [Generic/Trade: Tabs 100, 300 mg.] ▶K ♀C ▶+ $

colchicine: Acute gouty arthritis: start 1-1.2 mg PO, then 0.5-1.2 mg PO q1-2h until pain relief or unacceptable side effects (eg, diarrhea, GI upset); or 2 mg IV over 2-5 minutes, followed by 0.5 mg IV q6h. Max 8 mg/day PO or 4 mg IV per treatment course. Gout prophylaxis: 0.5-1 mg PO qd-bid. [Generic/Trade: Tabs 0.5, 0.6 mg.] ▶L ♀C(oral), D(IV) ▶+ $

probenecid: Gout: 250 mg PO bid x 7 days, then 500 bid. Adjunct to penicillin injection: 1-2 g PO. [Generic: Tabs 500 mg.] ▶KL ♀B ▶? $

Minerals

calcium acetate (***PhosLo***): Hyperphosphatemia: Initially 2 tabs/caps PO with each meal. [Trade only: tab/cap 667 mg (169 mg elem Ca).] ▶K ♀+ ▶? $

calcium carbonate (***Tums, Os-Cal, Os-Cal+D, Caltrate***): 1-2 g elem Ca/day or more PO with meals divided bid-qid. [OTC Generic/Trade: tab 650,667,1250, 1500 mg, chew tab 750,1250 mg, cap 1250 mg, susp 1250 mg/5 ml.] ▶K ♀+ ▶+ $

calcium chloride: 500-1000 mg slow IV q1-3 days. [Generic: injectable 10% (1000 mg/10 ml) 10 ml ampules, vials, syringes.] ▶K ♀+ ▶+ $

calcium citrate (***Citracal***): 1-2 g elem Ca/day or more PO with meals divided bid-qid. [OTC: Trade (mg elem Ca): tab 200 mg, 250 mg with 125 units vitamin D, 315 mg with 200 units vitamin D, 250 mg with 62.5 units magnesium stearate vitamin D, effervescent tab 500 mg.] ▶K ♀+ ◗+ $

calcium gluconate: 2.25-14 mEq slow IV. 500-2000 mg PO bid-qid. [Generic: injectable 10% (1000 mg/10 ml, 4.65mEq/10 ml) 10,50,100,200 ml. OTC generic: tab 500,650,975,1000 mg.] ▶K ♀+ ◗+ $

ferrous gluconate (***Fergon***): 800-1600 mg ferrous gluconate PO divided tid. [OTC Generic/Trade: tab (ferrous gluconate) 240,300,324,325 mg.] ▶K ♀+ ◗+ $

ferrous polysaccharide (***Niferex***): 50-200 mg PO divided qd-tid. [OTC Generic/Trade: (elem iron): tab 50 mg, cap 150 mg, liquid 100 mg/5 ml.] ▶K ♀+ ◗+ $

ferrous sulfate (***Fer-in-Sol, FeoSol Tabs***): 500-1000 mg ferrous sulfate (100-200 mg elem iron) PO divided tid. Liquid: Adults 5-10 ml tid, non-infant children 2.5-5 ml tid. Many other available formulations. [OTC Generic/Trade (mg ferrous sulfate): tab 324,325 mg, liquid 220 mg/5 ml, drops 75 mg/0.6 ml.] ▶K ♀+ ◗+ $

fluoride (***Luride, ✤Flur-A-Day***):Adult dose: 10 ml of topical rinse swish and spit qd. Peds daily dose based on fluoride content of drinking water (table). [Generic: chew tab 0.5,1 mg, tab 1 mg, drops 0.125 mg, 0.25 mg, and 0.5 mg/dropperful, lozenges 1 mg, solution 0.2 mg/ml, gel 0.1%, 0.5%, 1.23%, rinse (sodium fluoride) 0.05,0.1,0.2%).] ▶K ♀? ◗? $

Peds qd dose is based on drinking water fluoride (shown in ppm)

Age (years)	*<0.3 ppm*	*0.3-0.6 ppm*	*>0.6 ppm*
0-0.5	none	none	none
0.5-3	0.25mg	none	none
3-6	0.5mg	0.25mg	none
6-16	1 mg	0.5 mg	none

iron dextran (***InFed, DexFerrum, ✤Dexiron***): 25-100 mg IM qd prn. Equations available to calculate IV dose based on weight and Hb. ▶KL ♀- ◗? $$$$

iron sucrose (***Venofer***): 5 ml (100 mg elem iron) IV over 5 min or diluted in 100 ml NS IV over ≥15 min. ▶KL ♀B ◗? $$$$$

magnesium gluconate (***Almore, Magtrate, Maganate***): 500-1000 mg PO divided tid. [OTC Generic: tab 500 mg, liquid 54 mg elem Mg/5 ml.] ▶K ♀A ◗+ $

magnesium oxide (***Mag-200, Mag-Ox 400***): 400-800 mg PO qd. [OTC Generic/Trade: cap 140,250,400,420,500 mg.] ▶K ♀A ◗+ $

magnesium sulfate: Hypomagnesemia: 1 g of 20% soln IM q6h x 4 doses, or 2 g IV over 1 h (monitor for hypotension). Peds: 25-50 mg/kg IV/IM q4-6h for 3-4 doses, max single dose 2g. ▶K ♀A ◗+ $

phosphorus (***Neutra-Phos, K-Phos***): 1 cap/packet PO qid. 1-2 tabs PO qid. Severe hypophosphatemia (eg, <1 mg/dl): 0.08-0.16 mmol/kg IV over 6h. [OTC: Trade: (Neutra-Phos, Neutra-Phos K) tab/cap/packet 250 mg (8 mmol) phosphorus. Rx: Trade: (K-Phos) tab 250 mg (8 mmol) phosphorus.] ▶K ♀C ◗? $

potassium: IV infusion 10 mEq/h (diluted). 20-40 mEq PO qd-bid. [Injectable, many different products in a variety of salt forms (i.e. chloride, bicarbonate, citrate, acetate, gluconate), available in tabs, caps, liquids, effervescent tabs, and packets. Potassium gluconate is available OTC.] ▶K ♀C ◗? $

sodium ferric gluconate complex (***Ferrlecit***): 125 mg elem iron IV over 10 min or diluted in 100 ml NS IV over 1 h. ▶KL ♀B ◗? $$$$$

PEDIATRIC REHYDRATION SOLUTIONS (ions in mEq/l)

Brand	*Glucose*	*Cal/l*	*Na*	*K*	*Cl*	*Citrate*	*Phos*	*Ca*	*Mg*
Lytren	20 g/l	80	50	25	45	30	0	0	0
Pedialyte	25 g/l	100	45	20	35	30	0	0	0
Rehydrate	25 g/l	100	75	20	65	30	0	0	0
Resol	20 g/l	80	50	20	50	34	5	4	4

POTASSIUM, oral forms

Liquids	Effervescent Tablets
20 mEq/15 ml: *Cena-K, Kaochlor 10%, Kay Ciel, Kaon*	25 mEq: *K-Lyte Cl, Klor-Con, K-Vescent*
40 mEq/15 ml: *Cena-K, Kaon-Cl 20%*	50 mEq: *K-Lyte DS, K-Lyte Cl 50*
Powders	**Tablets/Capsules**
20 mEq/pack: *Kay Ciel, K-Lor, Klor-Con EF, Klorvess*	8 mEq: *Klor-Con 8, Slow-K, Micro-K*
25 mEq/pack: *Klor-Con 25*	10 mEq: *Kaon-Cl 10, Klor-Con 10, Klotrix, K-Tab, K-Dur 10, Micro-K 10*
	20 mEq: *K-Dur 20*

Nutritionals

banana bag: Alcoholic malnutrition (one formula): Add thiamine 100 mg + magnesium sulfate 2g + IV multivitamins to 1 liter NS and infuse over 4h. "Banana bag" is jargon and not a valid drug order; specify individual components. ▶KL ♀+ ▶+ $

fat emulsion (***Intralipid, Liposyn***): dosage varies. ▶L ♀C ▶? $$$$$

formulas - infant (***Enfamil, Similac, Isomil, Nursoy, Prosobee, Soyalac, Alsoy***): Infant meals. [OTC: Milk-based (Enfamil, Silmilac, SMA) or soy-based (Isomil, Nursoy, Prosobee, Soyalac, Alsoy).] ▶L ♀I ▶+ $

levocarnitine (***Carnitor***): 10-20 mg/kg IV at each dialysis session. ▶KL ♀B ▶? $$$$$

omega-3-fatty acids (***Promega, Max EPA***): 1-2 caps PO tid w/meals. [OTC Generic /Trade: cap 600,1000,1200 mg (with varying ratios of EPA:DHA).] ▶L ♀- ▶? $

rally pack: Alcoholic malnutrition (one formula): Add thiamine 100 mg + magnesium sulfate 2g + IV multivitamins to 1 liter NS and infuse over 4h. "Rally pack" is jargon and not a valid drug order; specify individual components. ▶KL ♀C ▶- ?

INTRAVENOUS SOLUTIONS (ions in mEq/l)

Solution	*Dextrose*	*Cal/l*	*Na*	*K*	*Ca*	*Cl*	*Lactate*	*Osm*
0.9 NS	0 g/l	0	154	0	0	154	0	310
LR	0 g/l	9	130	4	3	109	28	273
D5 W	50 g/l	170	0	0	0	0	0	253
D5 0.2 NS	50 g/l	170	34	0	0	34	0	320
D5 0.45 NS	50 g/l	170	77	0	0	77	0	405
D5 0.9 NS	50 g/l	170	154	0	0	154	0	560
D5 LR	50 g/l	179	130	4	2.7	109	28	527

Thyroid Agents

levothyroxine (***T4, Synthroid, Levoxyl, Unithroid, Levothroid, L-thyroxine, Novothyrox, ✦Levotec, Eltroxin, Levo-T***): Start 100-200 mcg PO qd (healthy adults) or 12.5-50 mcg PO qd (elderly or CV disease), increase by 12.5-25 mcg/day at 3-8 week intervals. Usual maintenance dose 100-200 mcg/day, max 300 mcg/d. [Generic/Trade: Tabs 25, 50, 75, 100, 125, 150, 200, 300 mcg. Trade only: Tabs 88, 112, 137, 175 mcg.] ▶L ♀A ▶+ $

liothyronine (***T3, Cytomel***): Start 25 mcg PO qd, max 100 mcg/day. [Trade only: Tabs 5 mcg. Generic/Trade: Tabs 25, 50 mcg.] ▶L ♀A ▶? $

methimazole (***Tapazole***): Start 5-20 mg PO tid or 10-30 mg PO qd, then adjust. [Generic/Trade: Tabs 5, 10 mg.] ▶L ♀D ▶+ $$$

propylthiouracil (***PTU***): Start 100 mg PO tid, then adjust. Thyroid storm: 200-300 mg PO qid, then adjust. [Generic: Tabs 50 mg.] ▶L ♀D (but preferred over methimazole) ▶+ $

Vitamins

ascorbic acid (***vitamin C***): 70-1000 mg PO qd. [OTC: Generic: tab 25,50,100,250, 500,1000 mg, chew tab 100,250,500 mg, time released tab 500 mg, 1000,1500 mg, time released cap 500 mg, lozenge 60 mg, liquid 35 mg/0.6 ml, oral solution 100 mg/ml, syrup 500 mg/5 ml.] ▶K ♀C ▶? $

calcitriol (***Rocaltrol, Calcijex***): 0.25-2 mcg PO qd. [Trade only: cap 0.25,0.5 mcg, oral soln 1mcg/ml.] ▶L ♀C ▶? $$

cyanocobalamin (***vitamin B12, Nascobal***): Deficiency states: 100-200 mcg IM q month, 25-250 mcg/d PO or 500 mcg intranasal weekly. Some give 1000 mcg IM periodically. [OTC Generic: tab 25,50,100,250 mcg. Rx Trade only: nasal gel 500 mcg/0.1 ml.] ▶K ♀C ▶+ $

dihydrotachysterol (***vitamin D, DHT***): 0.2-1.75 mg PO qd. [Generic: tab 0.125,0.2, 0.4 mg, cap 0.125 mg, oral solution 0.2 mg/ml.] ▶L ♀C ▶? $$

doxercalciferol (***Hectorol***): Secondary hyperparathyroidism in dialysis: Initial dose 10 mcg PO or 4 mcg IV 3x/week. [Trade only: cap 2.5 mcg.] ▶L ♀C ▶? $$$$

folic acid (***folate, Folvite***): 0.4-1 mg IV/IM/PO/SC qd. [OTC Generic: tab 0.4,0.8 mg. Rx Generic 1 mg.] ▶K ♀A ▶+ $

Foltx (folic acid + cyanocobalamin + pyridoxine): 1 tab PO qd. [Brand: folic acid 2.5 mg/ cyanocobalamin 1 mg/ pyridoxine 25 mg tab.] ▶K ♀A ▶+ $

multivitamins (***MVI***): Dose varies with product. Tabs come with and without iron. [OTC & Rx: Many different brands and forms available with and without iron (tab, cap, chew tab, drops, liquid).] ▶LK ♀+ ▶+ $

niacin (***vitamin B3, Niacor, Slo-Niacin, Niaspan***): 10-500 mg PO qd. See cardiovascular section for lipid-lowering dose. [OTC: Generic: tab 50,100,250,500 mg, timed release cap 125,250,400 mg, timed release tab 250,500 mg, liquid 50 mg/5 ml. Trade: 250,500,750 mg (Slo-Niacin). Rx: Trade only: tab 500 mg (Niacor), timed release cap 500 mg, timed release tab 500,750,1000 mg (Niaspan, $$).] ▶K ♀C ▶? $

paricalcitol (***Zemplar***): CRF secondary hyperparathyroidism: 0.04-0.1 mcg/kg (2.8-7 mcg) IV 3x/wk at dialysis. Max dose 0.24 mcg/kg (16.8 mcg). ▶L ♀C ▶? $$$$$

phytonadione (***vitamin K, Mephyton, AquaMephyton***): Single dose of 0.5-1 mg IM within 1h after birth. High INR due to warfarin: dose varies based on INR and clinical situation. Adequate daily intake 120 mcg (males) and 90 mcg (females). [Trade only: tab 5 mg.] ▶L ♀C ▶+ $

pyridoxine (***vitamin B6***): 10-200 mg PO qd. INH overdose: 1 g IV/IM q 30 min, total dose of 1 g for each gram of INH ingested. [OTC Generic: tab 25,50,100 mg, timed release tab 100 mg.] ▶K ♀A ▶+ $

riboflavin (***vitamin B2***): 5-25 mg PO qd. [OTC Generic: tab 25,50,100 mg.] ▶K ♀A ▶+ $

thiamine (***vitamin B1***): 10-100 mg IV/IM/PO qd. [OTC Generic: tab 50,100,250,500 mg, enteric coated tab 20 mg.] ▶K ♀A ▶+ $

tocopherol (***vitamin E***): RDA is 22 units (natural, d-alpha-tochopherol) or 33 units (synthetic, d,l-alpha-tochopherol) or 15 mg (alpha-tocopherol). Max recommended 1000 mg (alpha-tocopherol). Antioxidant: 400-800 units PO qd. [OTC Generic: tab 200,400 units, cap 73.5, 100, 147, 165, 200, 330, 400, 500, 600, 1000 units, drops 50 mg/ml.] ▶L ♀A ▶? $

vitamin A: RDA: 900 mcg RE (retinol equivalents) (males), 700 mcg RE (females). Treatment of deficiency states: 100,000 units IM qd x 3 days, then 50,000 units IM qd for 2 weeks. 1 RE = 1 mcg retinol or 6 mcg beta-carotene. Max recommended daily dose 3000 mcg. [OTC: Generic: cap 10,000, 15,000 units. Trade: tab

5,000 units. Rx: Generic: 25,000 units. Trade: soln 50,000 units/ml.] ▶L ♀A (C if exceed RDA, X in high doses) ◗+ $

vitamin D (***vitamin D2, ergocalciferol, Calciferol, Drisdol***): Familial hypophosphatemia (Vitamin D Resistant Rickets): 12,000-500,000 units PO qd. Hypoparathyroidism: 50,000-200,000 units PO qd. Adequate daily intake adults: 19-50 yo: 5 mcg (200 units) ergocalciferol; 51-70 yo: 10 mcg (400 units); >70 yo: 15 mcg (600 units). [OTC: Trade: soln 8000 units/ml. Rx: Trade: cap 50,000 units, inj 500,000 units/ml.] ▶L ♀A (C if exceed RDA) ◗+ $

Other

bromocriptine (***Parlodel***): Start 1.25-2.5 mg PO qhs with food, usual effective dose 2.5-15 mg/day, max 40 mg/day (hyperprolactinemia) or 20-30 mg/day, max 100 mg/day (acromegaly). [Generic/Trade: Tabs 2.5 mg. Caps 5 mg.] ▶L ♀B ◗- $$$$

cabergoline (***Dostinex***): Hyperprolactinemia: 0.25-1 mg PO twice/wk. [Trade: Tabs 0.5 mg.] ▶L ♀B ◗- $$$$$

calcitonin-salmon (***Calcimar, Miacalcin***): Skin test before using injectable product: 1 unit intradermally and observe for local reaction. Osteoporosis: 100 units SC/IM or 200 units nasal spray qd (alternate nostrils). Paget's disease: 50-100 units SC/IM qd. [Trade: nasal spray 200 units/ activation in 2 ml bottle (minimum of 14 doses/bottle).] ▶Plasma ♀C ◗? $$$

cosyntropin (***Cortrosyn***, ***♣Synacthen***): Rapid screen for adrenocortical insufficiency: 0.25 mg (0.125 mg if <2 yo) IM/ IV over 2 min; measure serum cortisol before and 30-60 min after. ▶L ♀C ◗? $

desmopressin (***DDAVP, Stimate***): Diabetes insipidus: 10-40 mcg intranasally qd-tid, 0.05-1.2 mg/day PO or divided bid-tid, or 0.5-1 ml/day SC/IV in 2 divided doses. [Trade only: Tabs 0.1, 0.2 mg. nasal solution 1.5 mg/ml (150 mcg/ spray). Generic/Trade: nasal solution 0.1 mg/ml (10 mcg/ spray). Note difference in concentration of nasal solutions.] ▶LK ♀B ◗? $$$$

growth hormone human (***Protropin, Genotropin, Norditropin, Nutropin, Humatrope, Serostim, Saizen***): Dosages vary by indication. [Single dose vials (powder for injection with diluent).] ▶K ♀B/C ◗? $$$$$

raloxifene (***Evista***): Osteoporosis prevention/treatment: 60 mg PO qd. [Trade: Tabs 60 mg.] ▶L ♀X ◗- $$$

sevelamer (***Renagel***): Hyperphosphatemia: 800-1600 mg PO tid with meals. [Trade: Caps 403 mg. Tabs 400, 800 mg.] ▶Not absorbed ♀C ◗? $$$$

sodium polystyrene sulfonate (***Kayexalate***): Hyperkalemia: 1 g/kg up to 15-60 g PO or 30-50 g retention enema (in sorbitol) q6h prn. Irrigate with tap water after enema to prevent necrosis. [Generic: suspension 15 g/ 60 ml. Powdered rosin.] ▶Fecal excretion ♀C ◗? $$$$

spironolactone (***Aldactone***): Primary hyperaldosteronism, maintenance: 100-400 mg/day PO. [Generic/Trade: Tabs 25,50,100 mg.] ▶LK ♀D ◗? $

tamoxifen (***Nolvadex***): Breast cancer: 10-20 mg PO bid. [Generic/Trade: Tabs 10,20 mg.] ▶L ♀D ◗- $$$

vasopressin (***Pitressin***, ***♣Pressyn***): Diabetes insipidus: 5-10 units IM/SC bid-qid prn. ▶LK ♀C ◗? $$$$$

ENT

Antihistamines - Nonsedating

desloratadine (***Clarinex***): Adults & children ≥ 12 yo: 5 mg PO qd. [Trade: Tabs 5 mg. Fast-dissolve Reditabs 5 mg.] ▶LK ♀C ◗+ $$$

ENT COMBINATIONS *(selected)*	*Decon-gestant*	*Antihis-tamine*	*Anti-tussive*	*Typical Adult Doses*
OTC				
Actifed Cold & Allergy	PS	TR	-	1 tab or 10 ml q4-6h
Allerfrim, Aprodine	PS	TR	-	1 tab or 10 ml q4-6h
Dimetapp Cold & Allergy	PS	DBR	-	1 tab q12h
Robitussin CF	PS	-	GU, DM	10 ml q4h*
Robitussin DM, Mytussin DM	-	-	GU, DM	10 ml q4h*
Robitussin PE, Guaituss PE	PS	-	GU	10 ml q4h*
Drixoral Cold & Allergy	PS			1 tab q12h
Triaminic Cold & Allergy	PS	CH	-	20 ml q4-6h‡
Triaminic Cough	PS	-	DM	20 ml q4h‡
Rx Only				
Allegra-D	PS	FE	-	1 tab q12h
Bromfenex	PS	BR		1 cap q12h
Claritin-D 12 hour	PS	LO	-	1 tab q12h
Claritin-D 24 hour	PS	LO	-	1 tab qd
Deconamine	PS	CH	-	1 tab or 10 ml tid-qid
Deconamine SR, Chlordrine SR	PS	CH	-	1 tab q12h
Deconsal II	PS	-	GU	1-2 tabs q12h
Dimetane-DX	PS	BR	DM	10 ml PO q4h
Duratuss	PS	-	GU	1 tab q12h
Duratuss HD	PS		GU, HY	10ml q4-6h
Entex PSE, Guaifenex PSE 120	PS	-	GU	1tab q12h
Histussin D ©III	PS	-	HY	5 ml qid
Histussin HC ©III	PE	CH	HY	10 ml q4h
Humibid DM	-	-	GU, DM	1-2 tabs q12h
Hycotuss	-	-	GU, HY	5ml pc & qhs
Phenergan/Dextromethorphn	-	PR	DM	5 ml q4-6h
Phenergan VC	PE	PR	-	5 ml q4-6h
Phenergan VC w/codeine©V	PE	PR	CO	5 ml q4-6h
Polyhistine	-	PT/PY/PH	-	10ml q4h*
Robitussin AC ©V	-	-	GU, CO	10 ml q4h*
Robitussin DAC ©V	PS	-	GU, CO	10 ml q4h*
Rondec syrup	PS	CX	-	5 ml qid*
Rondec DM syrup	PS	CX	DM	5 ml qid*
Rondec Infant Drops	PS	CX	-	0.25 to 1 ml qid†
Rondec DM Infant drops	PS	CX	DM	0.25 to 1 ml qid†
Rynatan	PE	CH	-	1-2 tabs q12h
Rynatan-P Pediatric	PE	CH, PY		2.5-5ml q12h*
Semprex-D	PS	AC		1cap q4-6h
Tanafed	PS	CH	-	10-20ml q12h*
Triacin-C, Actifed w/codeine ©V	PS	TR	CO	10 ml q4-6h
Tussionex	-	CH	HY	5 ml q12h

AC=acrivastine	CX=carbinoxamine	HY=hydrocodone	PS=pseudoephedrine
AZ=azatadine	DM=dextromethorphan	LO=loratadine	PT=phenyltolaxamine
BR=brompheniramine	DBR=dexbrompheniramine	PE=phenylephrine	PY=pyrilamine
CH=chlorpheniramine	FE=fexofenadine	PH=pheniramine	TR=triprolidine
CO=codeine	GU=guaifenesin	PR=promethazine	

*5 ml/dose if 6-11 yo. 2.5 ml if 2-5yo. †1 ml/dose if 10-18 mo. ¾ ml if 7-9 mo. ½ ml if 4-6 mo. ¼ ml if 1-3 months old. ‡10 ml/dose if 6-11 yo. 5 ml if 2-5 yo. 2.5 ml if 13-23 mo. 1.25 ml if 4-12 mo.

fexofenadine (***Allegra***): 60 mg PO bid or 180 mg qd. 6-12 yo: 30 mg PO bid. [Trade: Tabs 30, 60, & 180 mg. Caps 60 mg.] ▶LK ♀C ◗+ $$$

loratadine (***Claritin***): Adults & children ≥ 6 yo: 10 mg PO qd. 2-5 yo: 5 mg PO qd. [Trade: Tabs 10 mg. Fast-dissolve Reditabs 10 mg. Syrup 1 mg/ml.] ▶LK ♀B ◗+ $$$

Antihistamines - Other

azatadine (***Optimine***): 1-2 mg PO bid. [Trade: Tabs 1 mg, scored.] ▶LK ♀B ◗- $$$

cetirizine (***Zyrtec***, ✤***Reactine***): Adults & children ≥6 yo: 5-10 mg PO qd. 2-5 yo: 2.5 mg PO qd-bid. [Trade: Tabs 5, 10 mg. Syrup 5 mg/5 ml.] ▶LK ♀B ◗- $$$

chlorpheniramine (***Chlor-Trimeton, Chlo-Amine, Aller-Chlor***): 4 mg PO q4-6h. Max 24 mg/day. [OTC: Trade: Tabs chew 2 mg. Generic/Trade: Tabs 4 mg. Syrup 2 mg/5 ml. Generic/Trade: Tabs, Timed-release 8 mg. Trade only: Tabs, Timed-release 12 mg.] ▶LK ♀B ◗- $

clemastine (***Tavist***): 1.34 mg PO bid. Max 8.04 mg/day. [OTC: Generic/Trade: Tabs 1.34 mg. Rx: Generic/Trade: Tabs 2.68 mg. Trade only: Syrup 0.67 mg/5 ml.] ▶LK ♀B ◗- $

cyproheptadine (***Periactin***). Start 4 mg PO tid. Max 32 mg/day. [Generic/Trade: Tabs 4 mg (trade scored). Syrup 2 mg/5 ml.] ▶LK ♀B ◗- $

dexchlorpheniramine maleate (***Polaramine***): 2 mg PO q4-6h. Timed release tabs: 4 or 6 mg PO at qhs or q8-10h. [Trade: Tabs, Immediate Release 2 mg. Syrup 2 mg/5 ml. Generic/Trade: Tabs, Timed Release: 4, 6 mg.] ▶LK ♀? ◗- $$$

diphenhydramine (***Benadryl***): 25-50 mg IV/IM/PO q4-6h. Peds: 5 mg/kg/day divided q4-6h. [OTC: Trade: Tabs 25, 50 mg, chew tabs 12.5 mg. OTC & Rx: Generic/Trade: Caps 25, 50 mg, softgel cap 25 mg. OTC: Generic/Trade: Liquid 6.25 mg/5 ml & 12.5 mg/5 ml.] ▶LK ♀B(- in 1st trimester) ◗- $

hydroxyzine (***Atarax, Vistaril***): 25-100 mg IM/PO qd-qid or prn. [Generic/Trade: Tabs 10, 25, 50. Trade only: 100 mg. Generic/Trade: Caps 25, 50, 100 mg. Syrup 10 mg/5 ml (Atarax). Trade: Suspension 25 mg/5 ml (Vistaril).] ▶L ♀C ◗- $

promethazine (***Phenergan***): Adults: 12.5-25 mg PO/IM/IV/PR qd-qid. Peds: 6.25-12.5 mg PO/IM/IV/PR qd-qid. [Trade: Tabs 12.5 mg scored. Generic/Trade: Tabs 25, 50 mg. Syrup 6.25 mg/5 ml. Trade only: Phenergan Fortis Syrup 25 mg/5 ml. Trade: Suppositories 12.5 & 25 mg. Generic/Trade: Suppositories 50 mg.] ▶LK ♀C ◗- $

Antitussives / Expectorants

benzonatate (***Tessalon, Tessalon Perles***): 100-200 mg PO tid. Swallow whole. Do not chew. Numbs mouth, possible choking hazard. [Generic/Trade: Softgel caps 100, 200 mg.] ▶L ♀C ◗? $

dextromethorphan (***Benylin, Delsym, Vick's***): 10-20 mg PO q4h or 30 mg PO q6-8h. Sustained action liquid 60 mg PO q12h. [OTC: Trade: Caps 30 mg. Lozenges 2.5, 5, 7.5, 15 mg. Liquid 3.5, 5, 7.5, 10, 12.5, 15 mg/5 ml; 10 & 15 mg/15 ml (Generic/Trade). Trade (Delsym): Sust'd action liquid 30 mg/5 ml.] ▶L ♀+ ◗+ $

guaifenesin (***Robitussin, Humibid LA, Hytuss, Guiatuss, Fenesin, Guaifenex LA***): 100-400 mg PO q4h. 600 -1200 mg PO q12h (extended release). 100-200 mg/dose if 6-11 yo. 50-100 mg/dose if 2-5 yo. [OTC: Trade: Tabs 100, 200 mg, Caps 200 mg. Syrup 100 & 200 mg/5 ml. Generic: Syrup 100 mg/5 ml. Rx: Trade: Tabs 200,1200 mg. Caps, sustained release 300 mg. Syrup 100 mg/5 ml. Generic/Trade: Tabs, extended release 600,1200 mg.] ▶L ♀C ◗+ $

Decongestants (See ENT - Nasal Preparations for nasal spray decongestants)

pseudoephedrine (***Sudafed, Sudafed 12 Hour, Efidac/24, PediaCare Infants' Decongestant Drops, Triaminic Oral Infant Drops***): Adult: 60 mg PO q4-6h. Peds: 30 mg/dose if 6-12 yo, 15 mg/dose if 2-5 yo. Ext rel tabs: 120 mg PO bid or 240 mg PO qd. Pediacare Infant Drops & Triaminic Infant Drops (7.5 mg/0.8 ml): Give PO q4-6h. Max 4 doses/day. 2-3 yo: 1.6 ml. 12-23 mo: 1.2 ml. 4-11 mo: 0.8 ml. 0-3 mo: 0.4 ml. [OTC: Generic/Trade: Tabs 30, 60 mg. Chewable tabs 15 mg. Trade only: Tabs, extended release 120, 240 mg. Trade only: Liquid 15 mg/5 ml. Generic/Trade: Liquid 30 mg/5 ml. Infant drops 7.5 mg/0.8 ml.] ▶L ♀C ▶+ $

Ear Preparations

Auralgan (benzocaine + antipyrine): 2-4 drops in ear(s) tid-qid prn. [Generic/Trade: Otic soln 10 & 15 ml.] ▶Not absorbed ♀C ▶? $

carbamide peroxide (***Debrox, Murine Ear***): 5-10 drops in ear(s) bid x 4 days. [OTC: Trade: Otic soln 6.5%, 15 or 30 ml bottle.] ▶Not absorbed ♀? ▶? $

Cipro HC Otic (ciprofloxacin + hydrocortisone): ≥1 yo to adult: 3 drops in ear(s) bid x 7 days. [Trade: Otic suspension 10 ml.] ▶Not absorbed ♀C ▶- $$$

Cortisporin Otic (hydrocortisone + polymyxin + neomycin): 4 drops in ear(s) tid-qid up to 10 days of soln or suspension (use suspension if TM perforation). Peds: 3 drops in ear(s) tid-qid up to 10 days. [Generic/Trade: Otic soln or suspension 7.5 & 10 ml.] ▶Not absorbed ♀? ▶? $$

Cortisporin TC Otic (hydrocortisone + neomycin + thonzonium + colistin): 4-5 drops in ear(s) tid-qid up to 10 days. [Trade: Otic suspension, 10 ml.] ▶Not absorbed ♀? ▶? $$$

docusate sodium (***Colace***): Cerumen removal: Instill 1 ml in affected ear. [Generic/Trade: Liquid 150 mg/15 ml.] ▶Not absorbed ♀+ ▶+ $

Domeboro Otic (acetic acid + alum. acetate): 4-6 drops in ear(s) q2-3h. Peds: 2-3 drops in ear(s) q3-4h. [Generic/Trade: Otic soln 60 ml.] ▶Not absorbed ♀? ▶? $

ofloxacin (***Floxin Otic***): >12 yo: 10 drops in ear(s) bid. 1-12 yo: 5 drops in ear(s) bid. [Trade: Otic soln 0.3% 5 ml.] ▶Not absorbed ♀C ▶- $$

Pediotic (hydrocortisone + polymyxin + neomycin): 3-4 drops in ear(s) tid-qid up to 10 days. [Trade: Otic suspension 7.5 ml.] ▶Not absorbed ♀? ▶? $$

Swim-Ear (isopropyl alcohol + anhydrous glycerins): 4-5 drops in ears after swimming. [OTC: Trade: Otic soln 30 ml.] ▶Not absorbed ♀? ▶? $

triethanolamine (***Cerumenex***): Fill ear canal x 15-30 mins to loosen cerumen, then flush. [Trade: Otic soln 6 & 12 ml with dropper.] ▶Not absorbed ♀C ▶- $$

VoSol otic (acetic acid + propylene glycol): 5 drops in ear(s) tid-qid. Peds > 3 yo: 3-4 drops in ear(s) tid-qid. VoSol HC adds hydrocortisone 1%. [Generic/Trade: Otic soln 2% 15 & 30 ml.] ▶Not absorbed ♀? ▶? $

Mouth & Lip Preparations

amlexanox (***Aphthasol***): Aphthous ulcers: Apply ¼ inch paste qid after oral hygiene. [Trade: Oral paste 5%, 5g tube.] ▶LK ♀B ▶? $

chlorhexidine gluconate (***Peridex, Periogard***): Rinse with 15 ml of undiluted soln for 30 seconds bid. Do not swallow. Spit after rinsing. [Trade: Oral rinse 0.12% 473-480 ml bottles.] ▶Fecal excretion ♀B ▶? $

clotrimazole (***Mycelex***): Oral troches dissolved slowly in mouth 5 times/day x 14 days. [Trade: Oral troches 10 mg.] ▶L ♀C ▶? $$$

docosanol (***Abreva***): Herpes labialis (cold sores): At 1st sign of infection apply 5x/day until healed. [OTC: Trade: 10% cream in 2g tube.] ▶? ♀B ▶? $

doxycycline (***Periostat***): Periodontitis, adjunct to scaling & root planing: 20 mg PO bid. [Trade: Caps 20 mg.] ▶L ♀D ◗- $$$

Gelclair (maltodextrin + propylene glycol): Aphthous ulcers, mucositis, stomatitis: Rinse mouth with 1 packet tid or prn. [Trade: 21 packets/box.] ▶Not absorbed ♀+ ◗+ $$$

lidocaine viscous (***Xylocaine***): Mouth or lip pain in adults only: 15-20 ml topically or swish & spit q3h. [Generic/Trade: soln 2%, 20 ml unit dose, 50, 100, 450 ml bottles.] ▶LK ♀B ◗+ $

magic mouthwash (Benadryl + Mylanta + Carafate): 5 ml PO swish & spit or swish & swallow tid before meals and prn. [Compounded suspension. A standard mixture is 30 ml diphenhydramine liquid (12.5 mg/5 ml) + 60 ml Mylanta or Maalox + 4g Carafate.] ▶LK ♀B(- in 1st trimester) ◗- $$$

nystatin (***Mycostatin***): Thrush: 5 ml PO swish & swallow qid. Infants: 2 ml/dose with 1 ml placed in each cheek. [Generic/Trade: Susp 100,000 units/ml 60 & 480 ml bottle. Trade: Oral lozenges (Pastilles) 200,000 units.] ▶Not absorbed ♀C ◗? $$

penciclovir (***Denavir***): Herpes labialis (cold sores): apply cream q2h while awake x 4 days. Start at first sign of symptoms. [Trade: Cream 1%, 1.5g tube.] ▶Not absorbed ♀B ◗- $

triamcinolone acetonide (***Kenalog In Orabase***): Apply paste bid-tid, ideally pc & qhs. [Generic/Trade: 0.1% oral paste 5 g tubes.] ▶L ♀C ◗? $

Nasal Preparations

azelastine (***Astelin***): Allergic/vasomotor rhinitis: 2 sprays/nostril bid. [Trade: Nasal spray, 100 sprays/bottle.] ▶L ♀C ◗? $$$

beclomethasone (***Vancenase, Vancenase AQ Double Strength, Beconase, Beconase AQ***): Vancenase, Beconase: 1 spray per nostril bid-qid. Beconase AQ: 1-2 spray(s) per nostril bid. Vancenase AQ Double Strength: 1-2 spray(s) per nostril qd. [Trade: Nasal inhalation aerosol (Beconase, Vancenase) 42 mcg/spray, 80 & 200 sprays/bottle. Nasal aqueous suspension (Beconase AQ) 42 mcg/spray, 200 sprays/bottle. Nasal aqueous suspension double strength (Vancenase AQ Double Strength) 84 mcg/spray, 120 sprays/bottle.] ▶L ♀C ◗? $$$

budesonide (***Rhinocort, Rhinocort Aqua***): 2 sprays per nostril bid or 4 sprays per nostril qd (Rhinocort). 1-4 sprays per nostril qd (Rhinocort Aqua). [Trade: (Rhinocort): Nasal inhaler 200 sprays/bottle. (Rhinocort Aqua): Nasal inhaler 120 sprays/bottle.] ▶L ♀C ◗? $$$

cromolyn (***NasalCrom, Children's NasalCrom***): 1 spray per nostril tid-qid. [OTC: Generic/Trade: Nasal inhaler 200 sprays/bottle. Trade: Children's NasalCrom w/special "child-friendly" applicator. 100 sprays/bottle.] ▶LK ♀B ◗+ $

flunisolide (***Nasalide, Nasarel, ✚Rhinalar***): Start 2 sprays/nostril bid. Max 8 sprays/nostril/day. [Generic/Trade: Nasal soln 0.025%, 200 sprays/bottle. Nasalide with pump unit. Nasarel with meter pump & nasal adapter.] ▶L ♀C ◗? $$

fluticasone (***Flonase***): 2 sprays per nostril qd. [Trade: Nasal spray 0.05%, 120 sprays/bottle.] ▶L ♀C ◗? $$$

ipratropium (***Atrovent Nasal Spray***): 2 sprays per nostril bid-qid. [Trade: Nasal spray 0.03%, 345 sprays/bottle & 0.06%, 165 sprays/bottle.] ▶L ♀B ◗? $$

mometasone (***Nasonex***): Adult: 2 sprays/nostril qd; Peds 2-11 yo: 1 spray/nostril qd. [Trade: Nasal spray, 120 sprays/bottle.] ▶L ♀C ◗? $$$

oxymetazoline (***Afrin, Dristan 12 Hr Nasal, Nostrilla***): 2-3 drops/sprays per nostril bid x 3 days. [OTC: Generic/Trade: Nasal spray 0.05%, 15 & 30 ml bottles. Nose drops 0.025% & 0.05%, 20 ml w/dropper.] ▶L ♀C ◗? $

phenylephrine (***Neo-Synephrine, Sinex, Nostril***): 2-3 sprays/drops per nostril q4h prn x 3 days. [OTC: Trade: Nasal drops 0.125, 0.16%. Generic/Trade: Nasal spray/drops 0.25, 0.5, 1%.] ▶L ♀C ▶? $

saline nasal spray (***SeaMist, Pretz, NaSal, Ocean***, ***♣HydraSense***): 1-3 sprays or drops per nostril prn. [Generic/Trade: Nasal spray 0.4, 0.5, 0.6, 0.65, 0.75%. Nasal drops 0.4, 0.65, & 0.75%.] ▶Not metabolized ♀A ▶+ $

triamcinolone (***Nasacort, Nasacort AQ***): Nasacort: 2 sprays per nostril qd-bid. Max 4 sprays/nostril/day. Nasacort AQ: 2 sprays per nostril qd. [Trade: Nasal inhaler 100 sprays/bottle. (Nasacort). Nasal pump 120 sprays/bottle (Nasacort AQ).] ▶L ♀C ▶- $$

triamcinolone acetonide (***Tri-Nasal***): 2-4 sprays per nostril qd. [Trade: 50 mcg/spray, 120 sprays/bottle.] ▶L ♀C ▶? $$

GASTROENTEROLOGY

Antidiarrheals

attapulgite (***Kaopectate, Diasorb, Donnagel***): 1200-1500 mg PO after each loose BM; max 9000 mg/day. Dose 600-1500 mg if 6-12 yo, 300-750 mg if 3-6 yo. [Generic/Trade: liquid 600 mg&750 mg/15 ml (Donnagel, Kaopectate), 750 mg/5 ml (Diasorb), tab 750, chew tab 300,600,750.] ▶Not absorbed ♀+ ▶+ $

bismuth subsalicylate (***Pepto-Bismol***): 2 tabs or 30 ml (262 mg/15 ml) PO q 30 min-1 h up to 8 doses/ day. Peds: 10 ml (262 mg/15 ml) or 2/3 tab if 6-9 yo, 5 ml (262 mg/15 ml) or 1/3 tab if 3-6 yo. Risk of Reye's syndrome in children. [OTC Generic/Trade: chew tab 262 mg, susp 262 & 524 mg/15 ml. Generic only: susp 130 mg/15 ml. Trade only: caplets 262 mg.] ▶K ♀D ▶? $

Imodium Advanced (loperamide + simethicone): 2 caplets PO initially, then 1 caplet PO after each unformed stool to a max of 4 caplets/24 h. Peds: 1 caplet PO initially, then ½ caplet PO after each unformed stool to a max of 2 caplets/day (if 6-8 yo or 48-59 lbs) or 3 caplets/day (if 9-11 yo or 60-95 lbs). [OTC: Trade: caplet 2 mg loperamide/125 mg simethicone.] ▶L ♀B ▶+ $

Lomotil (diphenoxylate + atropine): 2 tabs or 10 ml PO qid. [Generic/Trade: solution 2.5 mg diphenoxylate + 0.025 mg atropine per 5 ml, tab 2.5 mg diphenoxylate + 0.025 mg atropine per tab.] ▶L ♀C ▶- ©V $

loperamide (***Imodium, Imodium AD***, ***♣Loperacap***): 4 mg PO initially, then 2 mg PO after each unformed stool to a maximum of 16 mg/day. Peds: 2 mg PO tid if >30 kg, 2 mg bid if 20-30 kg, 1 mg tid if 13-20 kg. [Generic/Trade: cap 2 mg, tab 2 mg. OTC generic/trade: liquid 1 mg/5 ml.] ▶L ♀B ▶+ $

Motofen (difenoxin + atropine): 2 tabs PO initially, then 1 after each loose stool q3-4 h prn. Maximum of 8 tabs in a 24h period. [Trade only: tab difenoxin 1 mg + atropine 0.025 mg.] ▶L ♀C ▶- ©IV $

opium (***opium tincture, paregoric***): 5-10 ml paregoric PO qd-qid or 0.3-0.6 ml PO opium tincture qid. [Trade: opium tincture 10% (deodorized opium tincture). Generic: paregoric (camphorated opium tincture, 2 mg morphine equiv./5 ml).] ▶L ♀B (D with long-term use) ▶? ©II (opium tincture), III (paregoric) $

Antiemetics - 5-HT3 Receptor Antagonists

dolasetron (***Anzemet***): Nausea with chemo: 1.8 mg/kg up to 100 mg IV/PO single dose. Post-op nausea: 12.5 mg IV in adults and 0.35 mg/kg IV in children as single dose. Alternative for prevention 100 mg (adults) or 1.2 mg/kg (children) PO 2 h before surgery. [Trade only: tab 50,100 mg.] ▶LK ♀B ▶? $$$

granisetron (***Kytril***): Nausea with chemo: 10 mcg/kg IV over 5 minutes, 30 minutes prior to chemo. Oral: 1 mg PO bid x 1 day only. Radiation induced nausea and vomiting: 2 mg PO 1 hr before first irradiation fraction of each day. [Trade only: tab 1 mg, oral soln 2 mg/10 ml.] ▶L ♀B ▶? $$$

ondansetron (***Zofran***): Nausea with chemo: 32 mg IV over 15 min, or 0.15 mg/kg doses 30 min prior to chemo and repeated at 4 & 8 hrs after first dose. Oral dose if ≥12 yo: 8 mg PO bid. If 4-11 yo: 4 mg PO tid. Post-op nausea: 4 mg IV over 2-5 min or 4 mg IM or 16 mg PO 1 hr before anesthesia. If 2-12 yo: 0.1 mg/kg IV over 2-5 min x 1 if ≤40 kg; 4 mg IV over 2-5 min x 1 if >40 kg. Prevention of N/V associated with radiotherapy: 8 mg PO tid. [Trade only: tab 4,8,24 mg,orally disintegrating tab 4, 8 mg, solution 4 mg/5 ml.] ▶L ♀B ▶? $$$

Antiemetics - Other

dimenhydrinate (***Dramamine***, ***♣Gravol***): 50-100 mg PO/IM/IV q4-6h prn. [OTC: Generic/Trade: tab/cap 50 mg, liquid 12.5 mg/4 ml. Trade only: chew tab 50 mg, liquid 12.5 mg/ 4 ml (Children's Dramamine), 12 mg/5 ml. Rx: Generic/Trade: liquid 15.62 mg/5 ml.] ▶LK ♀B ▶- $

doxylamine (***Unisom Nighttime Sleep Aid, others***): 12.5 mg PO bid; often used in combination with pyridoxine. [OTC Trade/Generic: tab 25 mg.] ▶L ♀A ▶? $

dronabinol (***Marinol***): Nausea with chemo: 5 mg/m2 1-3 h before chemo then 5 mg/m2/dose q2-4h after chemo for 4-6 doses/day. Anorexia associated with AIDS: Initially 2.5 mg PO bid before lunch and dinner. [Trade only: cap 2.5,5,10 mg.] ▶L ♀C ▶- ©III $$$$$

droperidol (***Inapsine***): 0.625-2.5 mg IV or 2.5-10 mg IM. May cause fatal QT prolongation, even in patients with no risk factors. Monitor ECG before, during and after administration. ▶L ♀C ▶? $

meclizine (***Antivert, Bonine, Medivert, Meclicot, Meni-D***): Motion sickness: 25-50 mg PO 1 hr before travel. May repeat q24h prn. [Rx/OTC/Generic/Trade: Tabs 12.5, 25 mg chew Tabs 25 mg. Rx/Trade only: Tabs 30, 50 mg. Caps 25 mg.] ▶L ♀B ▶? $

metoclopramide (***Reglan***, ***♣Maxeran***): 10 mg IV/IM q2-3h prn. 10-15 mg PO qid, 30 min before meals and qhs. [Generic/Trade: tabs 5,10 mg, liquid 5 mg/5 ml.] ▶K ♀B ▶? $$

phosphorated carbohydrates (***Emetrol***): 15-30 ml PO q15min prn, max 5 doses. Peds: 5-10 ml. [OTC Generic/Trade: Solution containing dextrose and fructose.] ▶L ♀A ▶+ $

prochlorperazine (***Compazine***, ***♣Stemetil***): 5-10 mg IV over at least 2 min. 5-10 mg PO/IM tid-qid. 25 mg PR q12h. Sustained release: 15 mg PO qam or 10 mg PO q12h. Peds: 0.1 mg/kg/dose PO/PR tid-qid or 0.1-0.15 mg/kg/dose IM tid-qid. [Generic/Trade: tabs 5,10,25 mg, supp 25 mg. Trade only: extended release caps (Compazine Spansules) 10,15,30 mg, supp 2.5,5 mg, liquid 5 mg/5 ml.] ▶LK ♀C ▶? $

promethazine (***Phenergan***): Adults: 12.5-25 mg PO/IM/PR q4-6h. Peds: 0.25-0.5 mg/kg PO/IM/PR q4-6h. IV use common but not approved. [Generic/Trade: tab 25,50 mg, syrup 6.25 mg/5 ml, supp 50 mg. Trade only: tab 12.5 mg, syrup 25 mg/5 ml, supp 12.5,25 mg.] ▶LK ♀C ▶- $

scopolamine (***Transderm Scop***, ***♣Transderm-V***): Motion sickness: Apply 1 disc (1.5 mg) behind ear 4h prior to event; replace q3 days. [Trade only: topical disc 1.5 mg/72h, box of 4.] ▶L ♀C ▶+ $

thiethylperazine (***Torecan***): 10 mg PO/IM 1-3 times/day. [Trade only: tab 10 mg.] ▶L ♀? ▶? $

trimethobenzamide (***Tigan***): 250 mg PO q6-8h, 200 mg IM/PR q6-8h. Peds: 100-200 mg/dose PO/PR q6-8h if 13.6-40.9 kg; 100 mg PR q6-8h if <13.6kg (not newborns). [Trade only: cap 100 mg. Generic only: cap 300 mg. Generic/Trade: cap 250 mg, supp 100,200 mg.] ▶LK ♀C but + ▶? $

Antiulcer - Antacids

aluminum hydroxide (***Alternagel, Amphojel, Alu-tab***): 5-10 ml or 1-2 tabs PO up to 6 times daily. Constipating. [OTC Generic/Trade: tabs 300,475,500,600 mg, susp 320,450,600,675 mg/5 ml.] ▶K ♀+ (? 1st trimester) ▶? $

calcium carbonate (***Tums, Mylanta Children's, Titralac, Rolaids Calcium Rich, Surpass***): 1000-3000 mg PO q2h prn or 1-2 pieces gum chewed prn, max 8000 mg/day. [OTC Generic/Trade: tabs 350,400,420,500,550,650,750,850,1000 mg, susp 400,1250 mg/5 ml, gum (Surpass) 300, 450 mg.] ▶K ♀+ (? 1st trimest.) ▶? $

Maalox (aluminum & magnesium hydroxide): 10-20 ml or 1-4 tab PO prn. [OTC Generic/Trade: chew tabs, susp.] ▶K ♀+ (? 1st trimester) ▶? $

magaldrate (***Riopan***): 5-10 ml PO prn. [OTC Generic/Trade: susp 540 mg/5 ml. (Riopan Plus available as susp 540, 1080 mg/5 ml, chew tab 480, 1080).] ▶K ♀+ (? 1st trimester) ▶? $

Mylanta suspension (aluminum & magnesium hydroxide + simethicone): 2-4 tab or 10-45 ml PO prn. [OTC Generic/Trade: Liquid, double strength liquid, tab, double strength tab.] ▶K ♀+ (? 1st trimester) ▶? $

Antiulcer - H2 Antagonists

cimetidine (***Tagamet, Tagamet HB***): 300 mg IV/IM/PO q6-8h, 400 mg PO bid, or 400-800 mg PO qhs. Erosive esophagitis: 800mg PO bid or 400 mg PO qid. Continuous IV infusion 37.5-50 mg/h (900-1200 mg/day). [Generic/Trade: tab 200,300,400,800 mg, liquid 300 mg/5 ml. OTC, trade only: tab 100 mg, susp 200 mg/20 ml.] ▶LK ♀B ▶+ $$$

famotidine (***Pepcid, Pepcid RPD, Pepcid AC***): 20 mg IV q12h. 20-40 mg PO qhs, or 20 mg PO bid. [Generic/Trade: tab 10 mg (OTC, Pepcid AC Acid Controller), 20, 30, 40 mg. Trade only: orally disintegrating tab (Pepcid RPD) 20, 40 mg, suspension 40 mg/5 ml.] ▶LK ♀B ▶? $$$$

nizatadine (***Axid, Axid AR***): 150-300 mg PO qhs, or 150 mg PO bid. [Trade only: tabs 75 mg (OTC, Axid AR). Generic/Trade: cap 150,300 mg.] ▶K ♀B ▶? $$$$

Pepcid Complete (famotidine + calcium carbonate + magnesium hydroxide): Treatment of heartburn: 1 tab PO prn. Max 2 tabs/day. [OTC: Trade only: chew tab famotidine 10 mg with Ca carb 800 mg & Mg hydroxide 165 mg.] ▶LK ♀B ▶? $

ranitidine (***Zantac, Zantac 75, Peptic Relief***): 150 mg PO bid or 300 mg PO qhs. 50 mg IV/IM q8h, or continuous infusion 6.25 mg/h (150 mg/d). [Generic/Trade: tabs 75 mg (OTC, Zantac 75), 150,300 mg, syrup 75 mg/5 ml. Trade only: effervescent tab 150 mg, caps 150,300 mg, granules 150 mg.] ▶K ♀B ▶? $$$

Antiulcer - Helicobacter pylori Treatment

Helidac (bismuth subsalicylate + metronidazole + tetracycline): 1 dose PO qid for 2 weeks. To be given with an H2 antagonist. [Trade only: Each dose: bismuth subsalicylate 524 (2x262 mg) + metronidazole 250 mg + tetracycline 500 mg.] ▶LK ♀D ▶- $$$$

PrevPac (lansoprazole + amoxicillin + clarithromycin, ✤***Hp-Pac***): 1 dose PO bid x 10 days. [Trade only: lansoprazole 30 mg x 2 + amoxicillin 1 g (2x500 mg) x 2, clarithromycin 500 mg x 2.] ▶LK ♀C ▶? $$$$$

GASTROENTEROLOGY: Antiulcer - Helicobacter pylori Treatment		
*Regimen**	*Dosing*	*Eradication*
lansoprazole, and clarithromycin, and amoxicillin *(PrevPac)*	30 mg PO bid x 14 days 500 mg PO bid x 14 days 1g PO bid x 14 days EQUALS 1 *Prevpac* dose PO bid x 2 wks	86%
omeprazole, and clarithromycin, and amoxicillin	20 mg PO bid x 14 days 500 mg PO bid x 14 days 1 g PO bid x 14 days	80-86%
lansoprazole, <u>or</u> omeprazole, and clarithromycin, and metronidazole	30 mg PO bid x 14 days <u>or</u> 20 mg PO bid x 14 days 500 mg PO bid x 14 days 500 mg PO bid x 14 days	≥ 80%
lansoprazole, <u>or</u> omeprazole, and BSS, and metronidazole and tetracycline	30 mg PO qd x 14 days <u>or</u> 20 mg PO qd x 14 days 525mg PO qid x 14 days 500 mg PO tid x 14 days 500 mg PO qid x 14 days	83-95%
famotidine, <u>or</u> ranitidine, <u>or</u> nizatidine, and BSS, and metronidazole, and tetracycline**	40 mg/d PO qd/bid x 28 days <u>or</u> 300 mg/day PO qd/bid x 28 days <u>or</u> 300 mg/day PO qd/bid x 28 days 525 mg PO qid x initial14 days 250 mg PO qid x initial14 days 500 mg PO qid x initial14 days	≥ 80%

**American College of Gastroenterology Guidelines (Am J Gastroenterol 1998; 93:2330). BSS = bismuth subsalicylate (Pepto-Bismol) **BSS,metronidazole, tetracycline available as Helidac.*

Antiulcer - Other

dicyclomine (***Bentyl, Bentylol***): 10-20 mg PO/IM qid up to 40 mg PO qid. [Generic/Trade: tab 20 mg, cap 10 mg, syrup 10 mg/5 ml. Generic only: cap 20 mg.] ▶LK ♀B ▶- $$

Donnatal (phenobarbital + atropine + hyoscyamine + scopolamine): 1-2 tabs/caps or 5-10 ml PO tid-qid. 1 extended release tab PO q8-12h. [Generic/Trade: Phenobarbital 16.2 mg + hyoscyamine 0.1 mg + atropine 0.02 mg + scopolamine 6.5 mcg in each tab, cap or 5 ml. Each extended release tab has phenobarbital 48.6 mg + hyoscyamine 0.3111 mg + atropine 0.0582 mg + scopolamine 0.0195 mg.] ▶LK ♀C ▶- $

GI cocktail (***green goddess***): Acute GI upset: mixture of Maalox/Mylanta 30 ml + viscous lidocaine (2%) 10 ml + Donnatal 10 ml administered PO in a single dose. ▶LK ♀See individual ▶See individual $

hyoscyamine (***Levsin, NuLev***): 0.125-0.25 mg PO/SL q4h prn. Sustained release: 0.375-0.75 mg PO q12h. [Generic/Trade: tab 0.125,0.15 mg, SL tab 0.125 mg, solution 0.125 mg/ml. Trade only: extended release tab/cap 0.375 mg, orally disintegrating tab 0.125 mg (NuLev), elixir 0.125 mg/5 ml.] ▶LK ♀C ▶- $

misoprostol (***Cytotec***): Prevention of NSAID-induced gastric ulcers: Start 100 mcg PO bid, then titrate as tolerated up to 200 mcg PO qid. Abortifacient. Diarrhea in 13-40%, abdominal pain in 7-20%. [Trade/generic : tab 100,200 mcg.] ▶LK ♀X ▶- $$$$

propantheline (***Pro-Banthine***): 7.5-15 mg PO 30 min ac & qhs. [Generic/Trade: tab 15 mg. Trade only: tab 7.5 mg.] ▶LK ♀C ▶- $$$

simethicone (***Mylicon, Gas-X, Phazyme***): 40-160 mg PO qid prn. Infants: 20 mg PO qid prn [OTC: Generic/Trade: tab 60,95 mg, chew tab 40,80,125 mg, cap 125 mg, drops 40 mg/0.6 ml.] ▶Not absorbed ♀C but + ▶? $

sucralfate (***Carafate***, ***✤Sulcrate***): 1 g PO 1h before meals (2h before other medications) and qhs. [Generic/Trade: tab 1 g. Trade only: susp 1 g/10 ml.] ▶Not absorbed ♀B ▶? $$$

Antiulcer - Proton Pump Inhibitors

esomeprazole (***Nexium***): Erosive esophagitis: 20-40 mg PO qd x 4-8 weeks. Maintenance of erosive esophagitis: 20 mg PO qd. GERD: 20 mg PO qd x 4 weeks. H pylori eradication: 40 mg PO qd x 10 days with amoxicillin & clarithromycin. [Trade only: delayed release cap 20, 40 mg.] ▶L ♀B ▶? $$$$

lansoprazole (***Prevacid***): Duodenal ulcer or maintenance therapy after healing of duodenal ulcer, or erosive esophagitis, NSAID-induced gastric ulcer: 30 mg PO qd x 8 weeks (treatment), 15 mg PO qd for up to 12 weeks (prevention). GERD: 15 mg PO qd. Erosive esophagitis or gastric ulcer: 30 mg PO qd. [Trade only: cap 15,30 mg. Susp 15,30 mg packets.] ▶L ♀B ▶? $$$$

omeprazole (***Prilosec, Losec***): Duodenal ulcer or erosive esophagitis: 20 mg PO qd. Gastric ulcer: 40 mg PO qd. Hypersecretory conditions: 60 mg PO qd. [Trade only: cap 10,20,40 mg.] ▶L ♀C ▶? $$$$

pantoprazole (***Protonix, Pantoloc***): GERD: 40 mg PO qd, or 40 mg IV qd x 7-10 days until taking PO. Zollinger-Ellison syndrome: 80 mg IV q8-12h x 6 days until taking PO. [Trade only: tab 40 mg.] ▶L ♀B ▶? $$$

rabeprazole (***Aciphex***): 20 mg PO qd. [Trade only: tab 20 mg.] ▶L ♀B ▶? $$$$

Laxatives

bisacodyl (***Correctol, Dulcolax, Feen-a-Mint***): 10-15 mg PO prn, 10 mg PR prn, 5-10 mg PR prn if 2-11 yo. [OTC Generic/Trade: tab 5 mg, supp 10 mg.] ▶L♀+▶? $

cascara: 325 mg PO qhs prn or 5 ml of aromatic fluid extract PO qhs prn. [OTC Generic: tab 325 mg, liquid aromatic fluid extract.] ▶L ♀C ▶+ $

castor oil (***Purge, Fleet Flavored Castor Oil***): 15-30 ml of castor oil or 30-60 ml emulsified castor oil PO qhs, 5-15 ml/dose of castor oil PO or 7.5-30 ml emulsified castor oil PO for child. [OTC Generic/Trade: liquid 30,60,120,480 ml, emulsified suspension 45,60,90,120 ml.] ▶Not absorbed ♀- ▶? $

docusate calcium (***Surfak***): 240 mg PO qd. Peds: 50-150 mg/d. [OTC Generic/Trade: cap 240 mg. Trade only: cap 50 mg.] ▶L ♀+ ▶? $

docusate sodium (***Colace***): 50-400 mg/day PO divided in 1-4 doses. Peds: 10-40 mg/d if <3 yo, 20-60 mg/d if 3-6 yo, 40-150 mg/d if 6-12 yo. [OTC Generic/Trade: cap 50,100,240,250 mg, tab 50,100 mg, liquid 10 & 50 mg/5 ml, syrup 16.75 & 20 mg/5 ml.] ▶L ♀+ ▶? $

glycerin: one adult or infant suppository PR prn. [OTC Generic/Trade: supp infant & adult, solution (Fleet Babylax) 4 ml/applicator.] ▶Not absorbed ♀C ▶? $

lactulose (***Chronulac, Cephulac, Kristalose***, ***✤Acilac***): Constipation: 15-30 ml (syrup) or 10-20 g (powder for oral solution) PO qday. Hepatic encephalopathy: 30-45 ml (syrup) PO tid-qid, or 300 ml retention enema. [Generic/Trade: syrup 10 g/15 ml. Trade only (Kristalose): 10, 20 g packets for oral solution.] ▶Not absorbed ♀B ▶? $$

magnesium citrate: 150- 300 ml PO divided qd-bid. Children < 6 yo: 2-4 ml/kg/24h. [OTC Generic: solution 300 ml/bottle.] ▶K ♀+ ▶? $

magnesium hydroxide (***Milk of Magnesia***): Laxative: 30-60 ml regular strength liquid PO. Antacid: 5-15 ml regular strength liquid or 622-1244 mg PO qid prn. [OTC

Generic/Trade: liquid 400 & 800 (concentrated) mg/5 ml, chew tab 311 mg.] ▶K ♀+ ▶? $

methylcellulose (***Citrucel***): 1 heaping tablespoon in 8 oz. water PO qd-tid. [OTC Trade only: Packets, multiple use canisters.] ▶Not absorbed ♀+ ▶? $

mineral oil (***Agoral, Kondremul, Fleet Mineral Oil Enema***): 15-45 ml PO. Peds: 5-20 ml/dose PO. Mineral oil enema: 120 ml PR. Peds 30-60 ml PR. [OTC Generic/Trade: plain mineral oil, mineral oil emulsion (Agoral, Kondremul).] ▶Not absorbed ♀C ▶? $

Peri-Colace (docusate + casanthranol): 1-2 caps (100+30) PO qhs prn, 15-30 ml liquid (60+30 per 15 ml) PO qhs prn. Peds: 5-15 ml PO qhs prn. [OTC Generic/Trade: cap 100 mg docusate + 30 mg casanthranolol/cap, syrup 60 mg docusate + 30 mg casanthranolol/15 ml.] ▶L ♀C ▶? $

polycarbophil (***FiberCon, Fiberall, Konsyl Fiber, Equalactin***): Laxative: 1 g PO qid prn. Diarrhea: 1 g PO q30 min. Max daily dose 6 g. [OTC Generic/Trade: tab 500,625 mg, chew tab 500,1000 mg.] ▶Not absorbed ♀+ ▶? $

polyethylene glycol (***Miralax***): 17 g (1 heaping tablespoon) in 8 oz water PO qd. [Trade only: powder for oral solution (with bottle cap marked to measure 17 g).] ▶Not absorbed ♀C ▶? $

polyethylene glycol with electrolytes (***GoLytely, CoLyte, ✤Klean-Prep, Lyteprep***): Bowel prep: 240 ml q10 min PO or 20-30 ml/min per NG until 4L is consumed. [Generic/Trade: powder for oral solution.] ▶Not absorbed ♀C ▶? $

psyllium (***Metamucil, Fiberall, Konsyl, Hydrocil***): 1 tsp in liquid, 1 packet in liquid or 1-2 wafers with liquid PO qd-tid. [OTC: Generic/Trade: powder, granules, wafers, including various flavors and various amounts of psyllium.] ▶Not absorbed ♀+ ▶? $

senna (***Senokot, SenokotXTRA, Ex-Lax, Fletcher's Castoria***): 2 tabs or 1 tsp granules or 10-15 ml syrup PO. Max 8 tabs, 4 tsp granules, 30 ml syrup per day. Take granules with full glass of water. [OTC Generic/Trade: granules 15mg/tsp, syrup 8.8 mg/5 ml, liquid 33.3 mg/ml senna concentrate, 25 mg/15 ml, tab 6, 8.6, 15, 17, 25 mg.] ▶L ♀C ▶+ $

Senokot-S (senna + docusate): 2 tabs PO qd. [OTC Trade: tab 8.6 mg senna concentrate/50 mg docusate.] ▶L ♀C ▶+ $

sodium phosphate (***Fleet enema, Fleet Phospho-Soda, Visicol***): 1 adult or pediatric enema PR or 20-30 ml of oral soln PO prn (max 45 ml/24 h). Visicol: Evening before colonoscopy: 3 tabs with 8 oz clear liquid q15 min until 20 tabs are consumed. Day of colonoscopy: starting 3-5 h before procedure, 3 tabs with 8 oz clear liquid q15 min until 20 tabs are consumed. [OTC Trade only. pediatric & adult enema, oral solution. Visicol tab (trade $$): 1.5 g.] ▶Not absorbed ♀C ▶? $

sorbitol: 30-150 ml (of 70% solution) PO or 120 ml (of 25-30% solution) PR as a single dose. [Generic: solution 70%.] ▶Not absorbed ♀+ ▶? $

Other GI Agents

alosetron (***Lotronex***): Diarrhea-predominant IBS in women who have failed conventional therapy: 1 mg PO bid. [Trade: tab 1 mg.] ▶L ♀B ▶? $$$$

balsalazide (***Colazal***): 2.25 g PO tid x 8-12 weeks. [Trade: cap 750 mg.] ▶Minimal absorption ♀B ▶? $$$$$

budesonide (***Entocort EC***): 9 mg PO qd. [Trade: cap 3 mg.] ▶L ♀C ▶? $$$$$

cisapride (***Propulsid, ✤Prepulsid***): 10 mg PO qid, at least 15 min before meals and qhs. Available only through limited-access protocol through manufacturer. Can cause potentially fatal cardiac arrhythmias. Many drug and disease interactions. [Trade: Tab 10,20 mg, susp 1 mg/1 ml.] ▶LK ♀C ▶? $

glycopyrrolate (***Robinul, Robinul Forte***): 0.1 mg/kg PO bid-tid, max 8 mg/day. [Trade: tab 1, 2 mg.] ▶K ♀B ▶? $$$

infliximab (***Remicade***): 5 mg/kg IV infusion. May be repeated at 2 & 6 weeks, then every 8 weeks for fistulizing Crohn's disease. Serious, life-threatening infections, including sepsis & disseminated TB have been reported. Monitor for signs and symptoms of CHF. Hypersensitivity reactions may occur. ▶Serum ♀C ▶? $$$$$

lactase (***Lactaid***): Swallow or chew 3 caplets (Original strength), 2 caplets (Extra strength), 1 caplet (Ultra) with first bite of dairy foods. Adjust dose based on response. [OTC Trade/generic: caplets, chew tab.] ▶Not absorbed ♀+ ▶+ $

Librax (clidinium + chlordiazepoxide): 1 cap PO tid-qid. [Generic/Trade: cap clidinium 2.5 mg + chlordiazepoxide 5 mg.] ▶K ♀D ▶- $

mercaptopurine (***Purinethol***): Inflammatory bowel disease: 0.5-1.5 mg/kg PO qd. [Trade: tab 50 mg.] ▶L ♀D ▶? $$$

mesalamine (**5-aminosalicylic acid, 5-ASA,** ***Asacol, Pentasa, Rowasa, Canasa, ✤Mesasal***): Asacol: 800 mg PO tid. Pentasa: 1000 mg PO qid. Rowasa: 500 mg PR bid or 4 g enema qhs. Canasa: 500 mg PR bid-tid. [Trade only: delayed release tab 400 mg (Asacol), controlled release cap 250 mg (Pentasa), supp 500 mg (Rowasa), rectal susp 4 g/60 ml (Rowasa).] ▶Gut ♀B ▶? $$$$

neomycin (***Mycifradin***): Hepatic encephalopathy: 4-12 g/day PO divided q6-8h. Peds: 50-100 mg/kg/day PO divided q6-8h. [Generic/Trade: tab 500 mg, solution 125 mg/5 ml.] ▶Minimally absorbed ♀D ▶? $$$

octreotide (***Sandostatin***): Variceal bleeding: Bolus 25-50 mcg IV followed by infusion 25-50 mcg/hr. AIDS diarrhea: 100-500 mcg SC tid. Other indications with varying doses. [Trade only: vials for injection 0.05,0.1,0.2,0.5,1 mg.] ▶LK ♀B ▶? $$$$$

olsalazine (***Dipentum***): Ulcerative colitis: 500 mg PO bid. [Trade only: cap 250 mg.] ▶L ♀C ▶- $$$$

orlistat (***Xenical***): Weight loss: 120 mg PO tid with meals. [Trade only: cap 120 mg.] ▶Gut ♀B ▶? $$$$

pancreatin (***Creon, Donnazyme, Ku-Zyme***, ***✤Entozyme***): 8,000-24,000 units lipase (1-2 tab/cap) PO with meals and snacks. [Tab, cap with varying amounts of pancreatin, lipase, amylase and protease.] ▶Gut ♀C ▶? $$$

pancrelipase (***Viokase, Pancrease, Cotazym, Ku-Zyme HP***): 4,000-33,000 units lipase (1-3 tab/cap) PO with meals and snacks. [Tab, cap, powder with varying amounts of lipase, amylase and protease.] ▶Gut ♀C ▶? $$$

sibutramine (***Meridia***): 10 mg PO qd; can increase to 15 mg qd after 4 weeks. [Trade only: cap 5,10,15 mg.] ▶L ♀C ▶- ©IV $$$

sulfasalazine (***Azulfidine, Azulfidine EN-tabs***, ***✤Salazopyrin, Salazopyrin EN***): 500-1000 mg PO qid. Peds: 30-60 mg/kg/daydivided q4-6h. [Generic/Trade: tab 500 mg.] ▶K ♀- ▶? $$

tegaserod (***Zelnorm***): Constipation-predominant IBS in women: 6 mg PO bid before meals for 4-6 weeks. [Trade: tab 2, 6 mg.] ▶stomach/L ♀B ▶? $$$$

ursodiol (***Actigall, Ursofalk, Urso***): Gallstone dissolution (Actigall); 8-10 mg/kg/day PO divided bid-tid. . Prevention of gallstones associated with rapid weight loss (Actigall): 300 mg PO bid. Primary biliary cirrhosis (Urso): 13-15 mg/kg/day PO divided in 4 doses. [Trade/generic: cap 300 mg. Trade only: Tab 250 mg (Urso).] ▶Bile ♀B ▶? $$$$

vasopressin (***Pitressin, ADH***, ***✤Pressyn***): Variceal bleeding: 0.2-0.4 units/min initially (max 0.9 units/min). ▶LK ♀C ▶? $$$$$

HEMATOLOGY (See cardiovascular sectionfor antiplatelet drugs and thrombolytics)

Anticoagulants - Low-Molecular-Weight Heparins & Heparinoids

dalteparin (***Fragmin***): DVT prophylaxis, abdominal surgery: 2,500 units SC 1-2 h preop & qd postop x 5-10d. DVT prophylaxis, abdominal surgery in patients with malignancy: 5,000 units SC evening before surgery and qd postop x 5-10 days. DVT prophylaxis, hip replacement: Give SC for up to 14 days. Pre-op start: 2,500 units given 2 h preop and 4-8h postop, then 5,000 units qd starting ≥6h after second dose. Postop start: 2,500 units 4-8h postop, then 5,000 units qd starting ≥6h after first dose. Unstable angina or non-Q-wave MI: 120 units/kg up to 10,000 units SC q12h with aspirin (75-165 mg/day PO) until clinically stable. [Trade: Single-dose syringes 2,500 & 5,000 anti-Xa units/0.2 ml; multi-dose vial 10,000 units/ml, 9.5 ml.] ▶KL ♀B ▶+ $$$$

danaparoid (***Orgaran***): DVT prophylaxis, hip replacement: 750 units SC q12h starting 1-4 h preop x 7-10 days. Second dose not <2 h postop. [Trade: Ampules & pre-filled syringes 750 anti-Xa units/0.6 ml.] ▶K ♀B ▶? $$$$$

enoxaparin (***Lovenox***): DVT prophylaxis, hip/knee replacement: 30 mg SC q12h starting 12-24 h postop. Alternative for hip replacement: 40 mg SC qd starting 12h preop. Abdominal surgery: 40 mg SC qd starting 2 h preop. Outpatient treatment of DVT without pulmonary embolus: 1 mg/kg SC q12h until PO anticoagulation established. Inpatient treatment of DVT with/without pulmonary embolus: 1 mg/kg SC q12h or 1.5 mg/kg SC q24h. Unstable angina or non-Q-wave MI: 1 mg/kg SC q12h with aspirin (100-325 mg PO qd) for ≥2 days and until clinically stable. [Trade: Syringes 30,40 mg; graduated syringes 60,80,100,120,150 mg; ampules 30 mg. Concentration is 100 mg/mL except for 120,150 mg which are 150 mg/mL.] ▶KL ♀B ▶+ $$$$$

fondaparinux (***Arixtra***): DVT prophylaxis, hip/knee replacement or hip fracture surgery: 2.5 mg SC qd starting 6-8 h post-op. [Trade: Pre-filled syringes 2.5 mg/0.5 mL.] ▶K ♀B ▶? $$$$$

tinzaparin (***Innohep***): DVT with/without pulmonary embolus: 175 units/kg SC qd for ≥6 days and until adequate anticoagulation with warfarin. [Trade: 20,000 anti-Xa units/ml, 2 ml multi-dose vial.] ▶K ♀B ▶+ $$$$$

Anticoagulants - Other

aprotinin (***Trasylol***): To reduce blood loss during CABG: 1 ml IV test dose ≥10 min before loading dose. Regimen A: 200 ml loading dose, then 200 ml pump prime dose, then 50 ml/h. Regimen B: 100 ml loading dose, then 100 ml pump prime dose, then 25 ml/h. May cause anaphylaxis. ▶lysosomes & K ♀B ▶? $$$$$

argatroban: Start 2 mcg/kg/min IV infusion. Get PTT at baseline and 2 h after starting infusion. Adjust dose (not >10 mcg/kg/min) until PTT is 1.5-3 times baseline (not >100 seconds). ▶L ♀B ▶- $$$$$

bivalirudin (***Angiomax***): 1 mg/kg IV bolus just prior to PTCA, then infuse 2.5 mg/kg/h for 4 h. Can additionally infuse 0.2 mg/kg/h for up to 20 h more. ▶proteolysis/K ♀B ▶? $$$$$

heparin: DVT/PE treatment: Load 80 units/kg IV, then mix 25,000 units in 250 ml D5W (100 units/ml) and infuse at 18 units/kg/h. 63 kg adult: Load 5,000 units, then infuse at 11 ml/h. Adjust based on coagulation testing (APTT). DVT prophylaxis: 5,000 units SC q8-12h. Peds: Load 50 units/kg IV, then infuse 25 units/kg/h. [Generic: 1000, 2500, 5000, 7500, 10,000, 20,000 units/ml in various vial and syringe sizes.] ▶Reticuloendothelial system ♀C but + ▶+ $

lepirudin (***Refludan***): Thromboembolism in heparin-induced thrombocytopenia: Bolus 0.4 mg/kg up to 44 mg IV over 15-20 seconds, then infuse 0.15 mg/kg/h up to 16.5 mg/h. ▶K ♀B ◗? $$$$$

warfarin (***Coumadin***): Start 5 mg PO qd x 2-4 days, then adjust dose to PT/INR. Higher loading doses no longer recommended. [Generic/Trade: Tabs 1, 2, 2.5, 3, 4, 5, 6, 7.5, 10 mg.] ▶L ♀X ◗+ $

WEIGHT-BASED HEPARIN DOSING*

Initial dose: 80 units/kg IV bolus, then 18 units/kg/h. Check APTT in 6 h.
APTT <35 sec (<1.2 x control): 80 units/kg IV bolus, then ↑ infusion rate by 4 units/kg/h.
APTT 35-45 sec (1.2-1.5 x control): 40 units/kg IV bolus, then ↑ infusion by 2 units/kg/h.
APTT 46-70 seconds (1.5-2.3 x control): No change.
APTT 71-90 seconds (2.3-3 x control): ↓ infusion rate by 2 units/kg/h.
APTT >90 sec (>3 x control): Hold infusion for 1 h, then ↓ infusion rate by 3 units/kg/h.

*APTT = Activated partial thromboplastin time. Monitor APTT q6h during first 24h of therapy and 6h after each heparin dosage adjustment. The frequency of APTT monitoring can be reduced to q morning when APTT is stable within therapeutic range. Check platelet count between days 3 to 5. Can begin warfarin on first day of heparin; continue heparin for at least ≥4 to 5 days of combined therapy. Adapted from *Ann Intern Med* 1993;119:874; *Chest* 2001:119:69S, and *Circulation* 2001; 103:2994.

Other Hematological Agents (See endocrine section for vitamins and minerals)

aminocaproic acid (***Amicar***): 4-5 g PO/IV over 1h, then 1 g/h as needed. [Generic/Trade: Syrup 250 mg/ml, tabs 500 mg.] ▶K ♀D ◗? $$

anagrelide (***Agrylin***): Thrombocythemia due to myeloproliferative disorders: Start 0.5 mg PO qid or 1 mg PO bid, then after 1 week adjust to lowest effective dose. Max 10 mg/d. [Trade: Caps, 0.5,1 mg.] ▶LK ♀C ◗? $$$$$

darbepoetin alfa (***Aranesp, NESP***): Anemia: 0.45 mcg/kg IV/SC once weekly. [Trade: Single-dose vials 25,40,60,100,200 mcg/1 ml.] ▶sialidase,L ♀C ◗? $$$$$

desmopressin (***DDAVP, Stimate***): Hemophilia A, von Willebrand's disease: 0.3 mcg/kg IV over 15-30 min, or 150-300 mcg intranasally. [Trade: Stimate nasal spray 150 mcg/0.1 ml (1 spray), 2.5 ml bottle (25 sprays). Generic/Trade (DDAVP nasal spray): 10 mcg/0.1 ml (1 spray), 5 ml bottle (50 sprays). Note difference in concentration of nasal solutions.] ▶LK ♀B ◗? $$$$$

erythropoietin (***Epogen, Procrit, epoetin alfa***, ***✤Eprex***): Anemia: 1 dose IV/SC 3 times/week. Initial dose if renal failure = 50-100 units/kg, AZT = 100 units/kg, or chemo = 150 units/kg. [Trade: Single-dose 1 ml vials 2,000, 3,000, 4,000, 10,000, 20,000 40,000 units/ml. Multi-dose vials 10,000 units/ml 2 ml & 20,000 units/ml 1 ml.] ▶L ♀C ◗? $$$$$

factor VIII, factor IX: specialized dosing. ▶L ♀C ◗? $$$$$

filgrastim (***G-CSF, Neupogen***): Neutropenia: 5 mcg/kg SC/IV qd. [Trade: Single-dose vials 300 mcg/1 ml, 480 mcg/1.6 ml. Single-dose syringes 300 mcg/0.5 ml, 480 mcg/0.8 ml.] ▶L ♀C ◗? $$$$$

oprelvekin (***Neumega***): Chemotherapy-induced thrombocytopenia in adults: 50 mcg/kg SC qd. [Trade: 5 mg single-dose vials with diluent.] ▶K ♀C ◗? $$$$$

pegfilgrastim (***Neulasta***): 6 mg SC once each chemo cycle. [Trade: Single-dose syringes 6 mg/0.6 ml.] ▶Plasma ♀C ◗? $$$$$

protamine: Reversal of heparin: 1 mg antagonizes ~100 units heparin. May cause allergy/anaphylaxis. ▶Plasma ♀C ◗? $

sargramostim (***GM-CSF, Leukine***): Specialized dosing for marrow transplant. ▶L ♀C ◗? $$$$$

HERBAL & ALTERNATIVE THERAPIES

NOTE: Not by prescription. In the US, herbal and alternative therapy products are regulated as dietary supplements, not drugs. Premarketing evaluation and FDA approval is not required unless specific therapeutic claims are made. Since these products are not required to demonstrate efficacy, it is unclear whether many of them have health benefits. In addition, there may be considerable variability from lot to lot or between products.

aristolochic acid (**Aristolochia, Asarum, Bragantia**): Nephrotoxic & carcinogenic; do not use. ▶? ♀- ◗- $

arnica (**Arnica montana, leopard's bane, wolf's bane**): Do not take by mouth. Topical promoted for treatment of skin wounds, but efficacy unproven. Do not use on open wounds. ▶? ♀- ◗- $

bilberry (**Vaccinium myrtillus, huckleberry**): Cataracts, macular degeneration (efficacy unproven): 160 mg PO bid of 25% antocyanosides extract. ▶? ♀- ◗- $

bitter orange (**Citrus aurantium,** ***Acutrim Natural AM, Dexatrim Natural Ephedrine Free***): Similar to ephedra; safety and efficacy not established. Do not use with MAOIs. ▶K ♀- ◗- $

black cohosh (**Cimicifuga racemosa,** ***Remifemin***): Menopausal symptoms (possibly effective): 20 mg PO bid of Remifemin. Ineffective for symptoms induced by breast cancer treatment. ▶? ♀- ◗- $

chaparral (**Larrea divaricata, creosote bush**): Hepatotoxic; do not use. ▶? ♀- ◗ $

chasteberry (**Vitex agnus castus fruit extract,** ***Femaprin***): Premenstrual syndrome: 20 mg PO qd of extract ZE 440. ▶? ♀- ◗- $

chondroitin: Osteoarthritis (possibly effective): 200-400 mg PO bid-tid or 1200 mg PO qd. ▶? ♀? ◗? $

coenzyme Q10 (**CoQ-10, ubiquinone**): Heart failure, hypertension (possibly effective): 50-150 mg PO qd. Does not improve athletic performance or hyperglycemia in diabetes. ▶? ♀- ◗- $

comfrey (**Symphytum officinale**): May cause hepatic cancer; don't use. ▶? ♀- ◗- $

creatine: Promoted to enhance athletic performance. Does not benefit endurance exercise, but has modest benefit for intense anerobic tasks lasting <30 seconds. Usually taken as loading dose of 20 g/day PO x 5 days, then 2-5 g/day taken bid. ▶L,K ♀ ◗- $

dong quai (**Angelica sinensis**): Ineffective for postmenopausal symptoms. Increased INR with warfarin. ▶? ♀- ◗- $

echinacea (**E. purpurae, E. angustifolia, E. pallida, cone flower**): Efficacy unproven for prevention or treatment of upper respiratory infections. ▶? ♀- ◗- $

ephedra (**Ephedra sinica, ma huang,** ***Metabolife 356, Biolean***): Efficacy unproven for short-term weight loss. Avoid in patients with cardiovascular disease. Per FDA, not >8 mg PO q6h or 24 mg/day for ≤7 days. ▶? ♀- ◗- $

evening primrose oil (**Oenothera biennis**): Ineffective for premenstrual syndrome or postmenopausal symptoms. ▶? ♀? ◗? $

garcinia (**Garcinia cambogia,** ***CitriLean***): Inadequate evidence of efficacy for weight loss. ▶? ♀- ◗- $

garlic supplements (**Allium sativum,** ***Kwai, Kyolic***): Questionable long-term benefit for hyperlipidemia, no benefit for HTN, DM. Cytochrome P450 3A4 inducer. Significantly decreases saquinavir levels. Reports of ↑ INR with warfarin. ▶? ♀ ◗- $

ginger (**Zingiber officinale**): Prevention of motion sickness: 500-1000 mg powdered rhizome PO single dose 1 h before exposure. Hyperemesis gravidarum (possibly effective, but safety unclear): 1 g PO qd. Ineffective for postop nausea & vomiting. ▶? ♀? ◗? $

ginkgo biloba (**EGb 761, *Ginkgold, Ginkoba, Quanterra Mental Sharpness***): Dementia (possibly effective): 40 mg PO tid of standardized extract containing 24% ginkgo flavone glycosides and 6% terpene lactones. Benefit may be delayed for up to 4 weeks. Possibly effective for intermittent claudication, prevention of acute altitude sickness. ▸? ♀- ▸- $

ginseng, Asian (**Panax ginseng, *Ginsana, Ginsai, G115***): Promoted to improve vitality and wellbeing: 200 mg PO qd. Ginsana: 2 caps PO qd or 1 cap PO bid. Ginsana Sport: 1 cap PO qd. Does not appear to benefit physical or psychomotor performance, diabetes, herpes simplex infections, cognitive or immune function, postmenopasual hot flashes (American College of Obstetrics and Gynecologists recommends against use). ▸? ♀- ▸- $

glucosamine (***Aflexa, Cosamin DS, Flextend, Promotion***): Osteoarthritis: 500 mg PO tid. ▸? ♀- ▸- $

horse chestnut seed extract (**Aesculus hippocastanum, *HCE50, Venastat***): Varicose veins, chronic venous insuffiency: 1 cap Venastat (16% aescin standardized extract) PO bid with water before meals. ▸? ♀- ▸- $

kava kava (**Piper methysticum, *One-a-day Bedtime & Rest, Sleep-Tite***): Promoted as anxiolytic or sedative. Do not use due to hepatotoxicity. ▸? ♀- ▸- $

kombucha tea (**Manchurian or Kargasok tea**): Recommend against use; has no proven benefit for any indication; may cause severe acidosis. Avoid. ▸? ♀- ▸- $

methylsulfomethane (***MSM, dimethyl sulfone, crystaline DMSO2***): Efficacy of oral and topical for arthritis pain is unproven. Bladder infusion has been used for interstitial cystitis. ▸? ♀- ▸- $

milk thistle (**Silybum marianum, *Legalon,* silymarin**): Hepatic cirrhosis (possibly effective): 100-200 mg PO tid of standardized extract with 70-80% silymarin. ▸? ♀- ▸- $

probiotics (**acidophilus, Bifidobacteria, Lactobacillus, *Culturelle, Lactinex, Probiotica***): Culturelle. Prevention of antibiotic-induced diarrhea: 1 cap PO bid during & for 1 week after antibiotic therapy. Give 2 h before/after antibiotic. Prevention of travelers' diarrhea: 1 cap PO bid from 2-3 days before until end of trip. Probiotica: 1 chew tab PO qd. [Not by prescription. Culturelle contains Lactobacillus GG 10 billion cells/cap. Probiotica contains Lactobacillus reuteri 100 million cells/chew tab.] ▸? ♀+ ▸+ $

pygeum africanum (**African plum tree, *Prostata, Prostatonin, Provol***): Benign prostatic hypertrophy (may have modest efficacy): 50-100 mg PO bid or 100 mg PO qd of standardized extract containing 14% triterpenes. Prostatonin (also contains Urtica dioca): 1 cap PO bid with meals; up to 6 weeks for full response. ▸? ♀- ▸- $

saw palmetto (***Serona repens, One-a-day Prostate Health, Prostata, Quanterra***): Benign prostatic hypertrophy: 160 mg PO bid or 320 mg PO qd of standardized liposterolic extract. Take with food. ▸? ♀- ▸- $

shark cartilage (***Benefin, Cancenex, Cartilade***): Ineffective for palliative care of advanced cancer. ▸? ♀- ▸- $$$$$

silver, colloidal (***mild & strong silver protein; silver ion***): Promoted as antimicrobial; unsafe and ineffective for any use. Silver accumulates in skin (leads to grey tint), conjunctiva, and internal organs with chronic use. [Not by prescription. May come as silver chloride, cyanide, iodide, oxide, or phosphate.] ▸? ♀- ▸- $

St Johns wort (***Alterra,* Hypericum perforatum, *Kira, Movana, One-a-day Tension & Mood, LI-160***): Mild depression: 300 mg PO tid of standardized extract (0.3% hypericin). Ineffective for moderate major depression. May decrease efficacy of many drugs (eg, oral contraceptives) by inducing liver metabolism. Serotonin syndrome with SSRIs, MAOIs. ▶? ♀- ◗- $

valerian (**Valeriana officinalis, *Alluna, One-a-day Bedtime & Rest, Sleep-Tite***): Insomnia (efficacy unproven): 400-900 mg of standardized extract PO 30 minutes before bedtime. Alluna: 2 tabs PO 1 h before bedtime. ▶? ♀- ◗- $

yohimbe (**Pausinystalia yohimbe, Corynanthe yohimbe**): Nonprescription yohimbe promoted for impotence and as aphrodisiac, but these products rarely contain much yohimbine. FDA considers yohimbe bark in herbal remedies an unsafe herb. ▶? ♀- ◗- $

IMMUNOLOGY

Immunizations (For vaccine info see CDC website www.cdc.gov)

BCG vaccine (***Tice BCG***): 0.2-0.3 ml percutaneously. ▶? ♀C ◗? $$$$

Comvax (haemophilus b + hepatitis B vaccine): 0.5 ml IM. ▶L ♀C ◗? $$$

diphtheria tetanus & acellular pertussis vaccine (***DTaP, Tripedia, Infanrix, Daptacel***): 0.5 ml IM. ▶L ♀C ◗- $

diphtheria-tetanus toxoid (***Td, DT***): 0.5 ml IM. [Injection DT (pediatric: 6 weeks- 6 yo). Td (adult and children: ≥7 years).] ▶L ♀C ◗? $

haemophilus b vaccine (***ActHIB, HibTITER, PedvaxHIB***): 0.5 ml IM. ▶L ♀C ◗? $

hepatitis A vaccine (***Havrix, Vaqta***): Adult formulation 1 ml IM, repeat in 6-12 months. Peds: 0.5 ml IM, repeat 6-18 months later. [Single dose vial (specify pediatric or adult).] ▶L ♀C ◗+ $$$

hepatitis B vaccine (***Engerix-B, Recombivax HB***): Adults: 1 ml IM, repeat in 1 and 6 months. Separate pediatric formulations and dosing. ▶L ♀C ◗+ $$$

influenza vaccine (***Fluzone, Fluvirin, FluShield, ✤Fluviral***): 0.5 ml IM. ▶L ♀C ◗+ $

Japanese encephalitis vaccine (***JE-Vax***): 1.0 ml SC x 3 doses on days 0, 7, and 30. ▶? ♀C ◗? $$$$$

measles mumps & rubella vaccine (***M-M-R II***): 0.5 ml (1 vial) SC. ▶L ♀C ◗+ $$

meningococcal polysaccharide vaccine (***Menomune-A/C/Y/W-135***): 0.5 ml SC. ▶? ♀C ◗? $$$

plague vaccine (***Plague vaccine***): Age 18-61 yo: 1 ml IM x 1 dose, then 0.2 ml IM 1-3 months after the 1st injection, then 0.2 ml IM 5-6 months after the 2nd injection. ▶? ♀C ◗+ $

CHILDHOOD IMMUNIZATION SCHEDULE*						*Months*				*Years*		
Age	*Birth*	*1*	*2*	*4*	*6*	*12*	*15*	*18*	*24*	*4-6*	*11-12*	*14-16*
Hepatitis B	HB-1	← only if mother HbsAg(-)										
		HB-2			HB-3							
DPT†			DTP	DTP	DTP		DTP			DTP	Td	
H influenza b			Hib	Hib	Hib	Hib						
Pneumococci			PCV	PCV	PCV	PCV						
Polio§			IPV	IPV	IPV					IPV		
MMR						MMR				MMR		
Varicella						Varicella						
Hepatitis A¶									HA (some areas)			

*2002 schedule from the CDC, ACIP, AAP, & AAFP, see CDC website (www.cdc.gov). Annual influenza vaccine recommended for children >6 months old with risk factors such as asthma, cardiac disease, sickle cell diseases, HIV, diabetes. †Acellular form preferred for all DTP doses. §Inactivated form (IPV) preferred for all doses in the US. ¶Recommended for selected high-risk areas, consult local public health authorities.

pneumococcal 23-valent vaccine (***Pneumovax, Pnu-Imune, *Pneumo 23***): 0.5 ml IM/SC. ▶L ♀C ▶+ $

pneumococcal 7-valent conjugate vaccine (***Prevnar***): 0.5 ml IM x 3 doses 6-8 weeks apart starting at 2-6 months of age, followed by a fourth dose at 12-15 months. ▶L ♀C ▶? $$$

poliovirus vaccine (***Orimune (Sabin), IPOL (inactivated)***): An all-IPV schedule is recommended. Inactivated (IPOL): 0.5 ml SC. ▶L ♀C ▶? $$

rabies vaccine (***RabAvert, Imovax Rabies, BioRab, Rabies Vaccine Adsorbed***): 1 ml IM in deltoid region on days 0, 3, 7, 14, 28. ▶L ♀C ▶? $$$$$

tetanus toxoid: 0.5 ml IM/SC. ▶L ♀C ▶+ $

TriHibit (haemophilus b + DTaP): 4th dose only, 15-18 mos: 0.5 ml IM. ▶L ♀C▶- $$

Twinrix (hepatitis A inactivated + hepatitis B recombinant vaccines): Adults: 1 ml IM in deltoid, repeat in 1 & 6 months. ▶L ♀C ▶? $$$

typhoid vaccine (***Vivotif Berna, Typhim Vi, Typhoid Vaccine***): 0.5 ml IM x 1 dose (Typhim Vi); 0.5 ml SC x 2 doses (Typhoid Vaccine, USP); 1 cap qod x 4 doses (Vivotif Berna). May revaccinate q2-5 yrs in high risk patients. [Trade only: Caps] ▶? ♀C ▶? $$

varicella vaccine (***Varivax***): Children 1 to 12 yo: 0.5 ml SC x 1 dose. Age ≥13: 0.5 ml SC, repeat 4-8 weeks later. ▶L ♀C ▶+ $$$

yellow fever vaccine (***YF-Vax***): 0.5 ml SC ▶? ♀C ▶+ $$$

Immunoglobulins

antivenin - crotalidae immune Fab ovine polyvalent (***CroFab***): Rattlesnake envenomation: Give 4-6 vials IV infusion over 60 minutes, <6 hours of bite if possible. Administer 4-6 additional vials if no initial control of envenomation syndrome, then 2 vials q6h for up to 18 hours (3 doses) after initial control has been established. ▶? ♀C ▶? $$$$$

hepatitis B immune globulin (***H-BIG, BayHep B, NABI-HB***): 0.06 ml/kg IM within 24 h of needlestick, ocular, or mucosal exposure, repeat in 1 month. ▶L ♀C ▶? $$$

immune globulin (***Gamimune, Polygam, Sandoglobulin, Gammagard, Gammar, Venoglobulin, Baygam***): IV dosage varies by indication. IM form (Baygam): Hepatitis A protection: 0.02-0.06 ml/kg IM depending on length of stay. Measles (within 6 days post-exposure): 0.2-0.25 ml/kg IM. ▶L ♀C ▶? $$$$$

rabies immune globulin human (***Imogam, BayRab***): 20 units/kg, as much as possible infiltrated around bite, the rest IM. ▶L ♀C ▶? $$$$$

RHO immune globulin (***RhoGAM, MICRhoGAM, BayRho-D, WinRho SDF***): 1 vial IM within 72h if mother Rh-. Microdose (MICRhoGAM) OK if spontaneous abortion <12 weeks gestation. ▶L ♀C ▶? $$$$

RSV immune globulin (***RespiGam***): IV infusion for pediatric RSV. ▶Plasma ♀C ▶? $$$$$

tetanus immune globulin (***BayTet***): Prophylaxis: 250 units IM. ▶L ♀C ▶? $$$$

varicella-zoster immune globulin (***VZIG***): Specialized dosing. ▶L ♀C ▶? $$$$$

Immunosuppression

basiliximab (***Simulect***): Specialized dosing for organ transplantation. ▶Plasma ♀B ▶? $$$$$

cyclosporine (***Sandimmune, Neoral, Gengraf***): Specialized dosing for organ transplantation. [Generic/Trade: microemulsion Caps 25, 100 mg. Trade only: Caps (Sandimmune) 25, 100 mg. Solution (Sandimmune) 100 mg/ml. Microemulsion solution (Neoral, Gengraf) 100 mg/ml.] ▶L ♀C ▶- $$$$$

daclizumab (***Zenapax***): Specialized dosing for organ transplantation. ▶L ♀C ▶? $$$$$

mycophenolate mofetil (***Cellcept***): Specialized dosing for organ transplantation. [Trade only: Caps 250 mg. Tabs 500 mg. Oral susp 200 mg/ml.] ▶? ♀C ▶? $$$$$

sirolimus (***Rapamune***): Specialized dosing for organ transplantation. [Trade: oral solution 1 mg/ml.] ▶L ♀C ▶- $$$$$

tacrolimus (***Prograf, FK 506***): Specialized dosing for organ transplantation. [Trade only: Caps 1,5 mg.] ▶L ♀C ▶- $$$$$

Other

tuberculin PPD (***Aplisol, Tubersol, Mantoux, PPD***). 5 TU (0.1 ml) intradermally, read 48-72h later. ▶L ♀C ▶+ $

TETANUS WOUND MANAGEMENT

www.cdc.gov/nip/publications/pink/tetanus.pdf

Prior tetanus immunizations	*Non tetanus prone wound**	*Tetanus prone wound**
Uncertain or less than 3	Td§	Td§, TIG†
3 or more	Td if >10y since last dose	Td if >5y since last dose

* Non-tetanus prone are clean & minor. Tetanus prone include those with dirt or other contamination, punctures, or crush components. † Tetanus immune glob 250 units IM at site other than dT. § DT if <7 yo.

NEUROLOGY

Alzheimer's Dementia

donepezil (***Aricept***): Start 5 mg PO qhs. May increase to 10 mg PO qhs in 4-6 wks. [Trade; Tabs 5, 10 mg.] ▶LK ♀C ▶? $$$$

galantamine (***Reminyl***): Start 4 mg PO bid, increase to 8 mg bid after 4 weeks, then 12 mg bid after 4 weeks. Usual dose 16-24 mg/day. [Trade: tabs 4,8,12 mg. Oral solution 4 mg/ml.] ▶K ♀B ▶? $$$$

rivastigmine (***Exelon***): Start 1.5 mg PO bid, increase to 3 mg bid after 2 weeks. Max 12 mg/day. [Trade: Caps 1.5, 3, 4.5, 6 mg. Oral soln 2 mg/ml.] ▶L ♀B ▶? $$$$

tacrine (***Cognex***): 10 mg PO qid for 4 weeks (monitor LFT's q2 weeks), then increase to 20 mg qid. Titrate to higher doses q4 weeks based on tolerability. Hepatotoxicity. [Trade: Caps 10, 20, 30, 40 mg.] ▶L ♀C ▶? $$$$

Anticonvulsants

carbamazepine (***Tegretol, Tegretol XR, Carbatrol, Atretol, Epitol***): 200-400 mg PO bid-qid. Extended release: 200 mg PO bid. Age 6-12 yo: 100 mg PO bid or 50 mg PO qid, increase by 100 mg/day at weekly intervals divided tid-qid (regular release) or bid (extended release). Age < 6 yo: 10- 20 mg/kg/day PO bid-qid. Aplastic anemia. [Trade: Tabs 200 mg (Tegretol, Epitol, Atretol) chew tabs 100 mg (Tegretol) Susp 100 mg/5 ml (Tegretol) extended release tabs 100, 200 mg, 400 mg (Tegretol XR) extended release caps 200, 300 mg (Carbatrol). Generic: Tabs 200 mg. chew tabs 100 mg. susp 100 mg/5 ml.] ▶LK ♀D ▶+ $

clonazepam (***Klonopin, ✤Clonapam, Rivotril***): Start 0.5 mg PO tid, max 20 mg/d. [Generic/Trade: Tabs 0.5, 1, 2 mg.] ▶LK ♀D ▶? ©IV $$$

diazepam (***Valium, Diastat, ✤Vivol, E Pam***): Active seizing: 0.2-0.4 mg/kg up to 5-30 mg IV, or 0.2-0.5 mg/kg rectal gel PR. [Generic/Trade: Tabs 2, 5, 10 mg. solution 5 mg/ 5 ml. Trade only: concentrated solution (Intensol) 5 mg/ml. rectal gel (Diastat) 2.5, 5, 10, 15, 20 mg.] ▶LK ♀D ▶- ©IV $

MOTOR FUNCTION BY NERVE ROOTS

Level	Motor function
C4	Spontaneous breathing
C5	Shoulder shrug / deltoid
C6	Biceps / wrist extension
C7	Triceps / wrist flexion
C8/T1	finger flexion
T1-T12	Intercostal / abd muscles

Level	Motor function
T12	cremasteric reflex
L1/L2	hip flexion
L2/L3/L4	hip adduction / quads
L5	great toe dorsiflexion
S1/S2	foot plantarflexion
S2-S4	rectal tone

ethosuximide (***Zarontin***): 250 mg PO qd or divided bid if 3-6 yo, 500 mg PO qd or divided bid if >6 yo. [Trade only: Caps 250 mg. Generic/Trade: syrup 250 mg/ 5 ml.] ▶LK ♀C ▶+ $$$$

felbamate (***Felbatol***): Start 400 mg PO tid, max 3600 mg/day. Peds: Start 15 mg/kg/day PO, max 45 mg/kg/day. Aplastic anemia, hepatotoxicity. [Trade: Tabs 400, 600 mg. suspension 600 mg/ 5 ml.] ▶KL ♀C ▶- $$$$

fosphenytoin (***Cerebyx***): Load 15-20 mg "phenytoin equivalents" (PE) per kg either IM, or IV no faster than 100-150 mg/min. ▶L ♀D ▶+ $$$$$

gabapentin (***Neurontin***): Start 300 mg PO qhs, and increase over a few days to 300-600 mg PO tid, max 3600 mg/day. Postherpetic neuralgia: Start 300 mg PO on day 1, 300 mg bid on day 2, 300 mg tid day 3, max 1,800 mg per day. [Trade: Caps 100, 300, 400 mg. Tabs 600, 800 mg. soln 50 mg/ml.] ▶K ♀C ▶? $$$$

lamotrigine (***Lamictal, Lamictal CD***): Start 50 mg PO qd x 2 weeks, then 50 mg bid x 2 weeks, then maintenance 150-250 mg PO bid. Life-threatening rashes in 1:1000 adults and 1:50 children. Drug interaction with valproic acid (see product information for dosing guidelines). [Trade: Tabs 25, 100, 150, 200 mg. chew Tabs 5, 25 mg.] ▶LK ♀C ▶- $$$$

levetiracetam (***Keppra***): Start 500 mg PO bid, titrate to maximum dose of 3000 mg/day. [Trade: Tabs 250, 500, 750 mg.] ▶LK ♀C ▶? $$$$$

lorazepam (***Ativan***): status epilepticus (unapproved): 0.05-0.1 mg/kg IV over 2-5 min. ▶LK ♀D ▶- ©IV $$$

oxcarbazepine (***Trileptal***): Start 300 mg PO bid, titrate to 1200 mg/day (adjunctive) or 1200- 2400 mg/day (monotherapy). Peds age 4-16 yo: start 8- 10 mg/kg/day divided bid (adjunctive). [Trade: Tabs 150, 300, 600 mg. Oral suspension 300 mg/5 ml.] ▶L ♀C ▶- $$$$

phenobarbital (***Luminal***): Load 200- 600 mg IV at rate ≤60 mg/min up to total dose of 20 mg/kg. Maintenance 100-300 mg/day PO, peds 3-5 mg/kg/day PO divided bid-tid. Multiple drug interactions. [Generic/Trade: Tabs 15, 16, 30, 32, 60, 65, 100 mg. elixir 20 mg/5 ml.] ▶L ♀D ▶- ©IV $

phenytoin (***Dilantin***): Load 10-20 mg/kg (1000 mg in typical adult) IV no faster than 50 mg/min. Oral load: 400 mg PO initially, then 300 mg in 2h and 4h. Maintenance: 5 mg/kg or 300 mg PO qd or divided tid. QD dosing only recommended with extended release caps. [Generic/Trade: Caps 100 mg. Suspension 125 mg/5 ml. Extended release Caps 100 mg. Trade only: Extended release Caps 30 mg. chew Tabs 50 mg.] ▶L ♀D ▶+ $

primidone (***Mysoline***): Start 100-125 mg PO qhs, increase over 10d to 250 mg tid/ qid. Metabolized to phenobarbital. [Trade only: Tabs 50 mg. suspension 250 mg/ 5 ml. Generic/Trade: Tabs 250 mg.] ▶LK ♀D ▶- $

tiagabine (***Gabitril***): Start 4 mg PO qd, and gradually increase by 4-8 mg/week to max 32 mg/day (children) or 56 mg/d (adults) divided bid-qid. [Trade: Tabs 2, 4, 12, 16, 20 mg.] ▶LK ♀C ▶- $$$$

topiramate (***Topamax***): Start 25-50 mg PO qhs, then increase by 25-50 mg/d (divided doses) once weekly to usual effective dose of 200 mg bid. [Trade only: Tabs 25, 100, 200 mg. sprinkle Caps 15, 25 mg.] ▶K ♀C ▶? $$$$$

valproic acid (***Depakene, Depakote, Depakote ER, Depacon, ✦Epiject, Epival, Deproic***): Seizures: 10- 15 mg/kg/day PO/IV divided bid-qid, titrate to max 60 mg/kg/day. Mania/ Migraine prophylaxis: 250 mg PO bid-tid or 500-1000 mg PO qd (ext'd release). Parenteral (Depacon): ≤ 20 mg/min IV. Hepatotoxicity, drug interactions, reduce dose in elderly. [Trade only: Tabs, delayed release (Depakote) 125, 250, 500 mg. Tabs, extended release (Depakote ER) 500 mg. Caps, sprinkle (Depakote) 125 mg. Generic/Trade: syrup (Depakene) 250 mg/ 5 ml. Caps (Depakene) 250 mg.] ▶L ♀D ▶+ $$$$

DERMATOMES

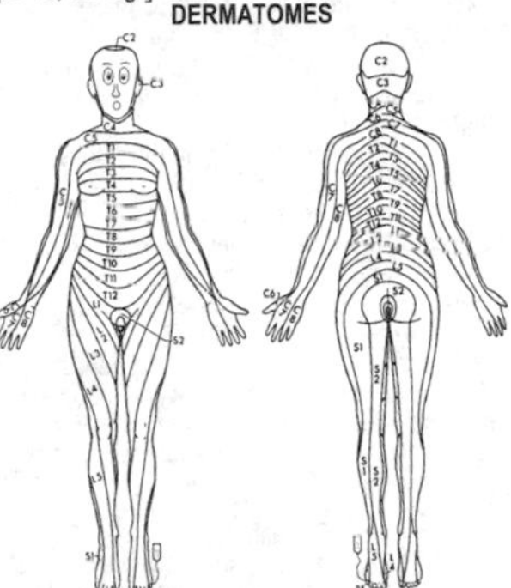

zonisamide (***Zonegran***): Start 100 mg PO qd, titrate q2 weeks up to 300-400 mg/day qd or divided bid. Max 600 mg/day. Contraindicated in patients allergic to sulfonamides. [Trade: Caps 100 mg.] ▶LK ♀C ▶- $$$$

Migraine Therapy - Triptans (5-HT1 Receptor Agonists)

almotriptan (***Axert***): 6.25-12.5 mg PO, may repeat in 2h, max dose 25 mg/day. [Trade: tabs 6.25, 12.5 mg.] ▶LK ♀C ▶? $

frovatriptan (***Frova***): 2.5 mg PO, may repeat in 2h, max 7.5 mg/24 hours. [Trade: Tabs 2.5 mg.] ▶LK ♀C ▶? ?

naratriptan (***Amerge***): 1-2.5 mg PO, may repeat in 4h for maximum daily dose of 5 mg. [Trade: Tabs 1, 2.5 mg.] ▶KL ♀C ▶? $$

rizatriptan (***Maxalt, Maxalt MLT***): 5-10 mg PO, may repeat in 2h, max dose 30 mg/24h. MLT form dissolves on tongue without liquids. [Trade: Tabs 5, 10 mg. orally disintegrating Tabs (MLT) 5, 10 mg.] ▶LK ♀C ▶? $$

sumatriptan (***Imitrex***): 6 mg SC, may repeat after 1h, max 12 mg/day. 25 mg PO, may repeat q2h with 25-100 mg doses to max of 200-300 mg/day. 5-20 mg intranasal spray q2h to max 40 mg/day. [Trade: Tabs 25, 50 mg. nasal spray 5, 20 mg/ spray. injection 6 mg/0.5 ml.] ▶K ♀C ▶+ $$

zolmitriptan (***Zomig, Zomig ZMT***): 1.25-2.5 mg PO q2h, max 10 mg/24 hours. Orally disintegrating tabs (ZMT) 2.5 mg PO, may repeat in 2h up to max of 10 mg/24h. [Trade: Tabs 2.5, 5 mg. Orally disintegrating tabs $$$ (ZMT) 2.5, 5 mg.] ▶L ♀C ▶? $$

LUMBOSACRAL NERVE ROOT COMPRESSION	Root	Motor	Sensory	Reflex
	L4	quadriceps	medial foot	knee-jerk
	L5	dorsiflexors	dorsum of foot	medial hamstring
	S1	plantarflexors	lateral foot	ankle-jerk

Migraine Therapy - Other

Cafergot (ergotamine + caffeine): 2 tabs (1/100 mg each) PO at onset, then 1 q30 min up to 6 tabs/attack. Suppositories (2/100 mg): up to 2 per attack. [Trade: Tabs 1 mg ergotamine/100 mg caffeine. Supp 2 mg ergot/100 mg caf] ▶L ♀X ◗- $

dihydroergotamine (***DHE 45, Migranal***): 1 mg IV/IM/SC, repeat in 1h prn; max 2 mg (IV) or 3 mg (IM/SC) per day. Nasal spray (Migranal): 1 spray in each nostril, repeat 15 minutes later. Max 6 sprays/24h and 8 sprays/wk. [Trade: nasal spray 0.5 mg/ spray.] ▶L ♀X ◗- $$

Excedrin Migraine (acetaminophen + aspirin + caffeine): 2 Tabs PO q6h, max 8 tabs/d. [OTC/Generic/Trade: Tabs acetaminophen 250 mg/ aspirin 250 mg/ caffeine 65 mg.] ▶LK ♀D ◗? $

methysergide (***Sansert***): Initiate 2 mg PO qd, titrate to 4-8 mg/day PO in divided doses. Requires drug-free interval of 3-4 weeks after each 6-month course of therapy. Wean over 2-3 weeks to avoid rebound headache. [Trade: Tabs 2 mg.] ▶L ♀D ◗- $$$$

Midrin (isometheptene + dichloralphenazone + acetaminophen, Duradrin): 2 tabs PO followed by 1 per hour until relief, up to 5 per 12-hour period. [Trade: Caps 65 mg isometh/ 100 mg dichloralphen/ 325 mg acetaminophen.] ▶L ♀? ◗? ©IV $

valproic acid (***Depakene, Depakote, Depakote ER***, ***♣Epiject, Epival, Deproic***): Migraine prophylaxis: 250 mg PO bid, or 500-1000 mg PO qd (ext'd release). Hepatotoxicity, drug interactions, reduce dose in elderly. [Trade only: Tabs, delayed release (Depakote) 125, 250, 500 mg. Tabs, extended release (Depakote ER) 500 mg. Caps, sprinkle (Depakote) 125 mg. Generic/Trade: syrup (Depakene) 250 mg/ 5 ml. Caps (Depakene) 250 mg.] ▶L ♀D ◗+ $$

Parkinsonian Agents - Anticholinergics

benztropine mesylate (***Cogentin***, ***♣Bensylate***): 0.5-2 mg IM/PO/IV qd-bid. [Generic/Trade: Tabs 0.5, 1, 2 mg.] ▶LK ♀C ◗? $

biperiden (***Akineton***): 2 mg PO tid-qid or 2 mg IV/IM q30 min prn. [Trade: Tabs 2 mg] ▶LK ♀C ◗? $$

trihexyphenidyl (***Artane***): Start 1 mg/day PO, then increase slowly to 6-10 mg/day, divided tid. Max 15 mg/day. [Generic/Trade: Tabs 2, 5 mg. elixir 2 mg/ 5 ml.] ▶LK ♀C ◗? $

Parkinsonian Agents - COMT Inhibitors

entacapone (***Comtan***): Start 200 mg PO as adjunct to levodopa/carbidopa, max 8 times/day (1600 mg). [Trade: Tabs 200 mg.] ▶L ♀C ◗? $$$$

tolcapone (***Tasmar***): Start 100 mg PO tid, only as an adjunct to levodopa/carbidopa. Max 600 mg/day. Hepatotoxicity, monitor LFTs. [Trade: Tabs 100, 200 mg.] ▶LK ♀C ◗? $$$$

Parkinsonian Agents - Dopaminergic Agents

amantadine (***Symmetrel***, ***♣Endantadine***): 100 mg PO bid. [Trade only: Tabs 100 mg. Generic: Caps 100 mg. Generic/Trade: syrup 50 mg/ 5 ml.] ▶K ♀C ◗- $

Atamet (carbidopa + levodopa): Start 1 tab PO tid, then increase q1-4 days as needed to max 200 mg/day carbidopa. [Generic/Trade: Tabs 25/100, 25/250.] ▶L ♀C ◗- $$$

bromocriptine (***Parlodel***): Start 1.25 mg PO bid, usual effective dose 10-40 mg/day, max 100 mg/day. [Generic/Trade: Tabs 2.5 mg. Caps 5 mg.] ▶L ♀B ◗- $$$$

levodopa (***Laradopa***): Start 250-500 mg PO bid, max 8g/day. [Trade: Tabs 100, 250, 500 mg.] ▶L ♀- ◗- $$

pergolide (***Permax***): Start 0.05 mg PO qd, then gradually increase to 1 mg PO tid. Maximum 5 mg/day. [Trade: Tabs 0.05, 0.25, 1 mg.] ▶K ♀B ▶? $$$$$

pramipexole (***Mirapex***): Start 0.125 mg PO tid, then gradually increase to 0.5-1.5 mg PO tid. [Trade: Tabs 0.125, 0.25, 0.5, 1, 1.5 mg.] ▶K ♀C ▶? $$$$

ropinirole (***Requip***): Start 0.25 mg PO tid, then gradually increase to 1 mg PO tid. Maximum 24 mg/day. [Trade: Tabs 0.25, 0.5, 1, 2, 4, 5 mg.] ▶L ♀C ▶? $$$

selegiline (***Eldepryl, Atapryl, Carbex, Selpak***): 5 mg PO q am and q noon. [Generic/Trade: Caps 5 mg. Tabs 5 mg.] ▶LK ♀C ▶? $$$

Sinemet (carbidopa + levodopa): Start 1 tab PO tid, then increase q1-4 days as needed to max 200 mg/day carbidopa. Sustained release: Start 1 tab PO bid, increase as needed. [Generic/Trade: Tabs 10/100, 25/100, 25/250. Tabs, sustained release 25/100, 50/200.] ▶L ♀C ▶- $$$

Other Agents

Aggrenox (aspirin + dipyridamole): One cap PO bid [Trade: Caps 25 mg aspirin/ 200 mg extended-release dipyridamole.] ▶LK ♀D ▶? $$$

alteplase (***t-PA, Activase***): Thrombolysis for acute CVA with symptoms ≤3h: 0.9 mg/ kg up to 90 mg, 10% of total dose IV bolus and remainder IV over 60 min. Multiple exclusion criteria. ▶L ♀C ▶? $$$$$

dexamethasone (***Decadron***, ***✱Dexasone***): Cerebral edema. Load 10- 20 mg IV/IM, then 4 mg IV/IM q6h or 1-3 mg PO tid. Bacterial meningitis: 0.15 mg/kg IV/IM q6h. [Generic/Trade: Tabs 0.25, 0.5, 0.75, 1.0, 1.5, 2, 4, 6 mg. elixir/ solution 0.5 mg/5 ml. Trade only: solution concentrate 0.5 mg/ 0.5 ml (Intensol)] ▶L ♀C ▶- $$$

edrophonium (***Tensilon, Enlon, Reversol***): Evaluation for myasthenia gravis: 2 mg test IV, then 8 mg more after 45 sec while on cardiac monitor. Duration 5-10 min. ▶Plasma ♀C ▶? $

glatiramer (***Copaxone***): Multiple sclerosis: 20 mg SC qd. [Trade: injection 20 mg single dose vial.] ▶Serum ♀D ▶? $$$$$

interferon beta-1A (***Avonex, Rebif***): Multiple sclerosis: Avonex- 30 mcg (6 million units) IM q wk. Rebif start 8.8 mcg SC tiw and titrate to 44 mcg tiw over 4 weeks. [Trade: Avonex: injection 33 mcg (6.6 million units) single dose vial. Rebif- starter kit 20 mcg pre-filled syringes, 44 mcg prefilled syringes.] ▶L ♀C ▶? $$$$$

interferon beta-1B (***Betaseron***): Multiple sclerosis: 0.25 mg (8 million units) SC qod. [Trade: injection 0.3 mg (9.6 million units) single dose vial.] ▶L ♀C ▶? $$$$$

mannitol (***Osmitrol, Resectisol***): Intracranial HTN: 0.25-2 g/kg IV over 30-60 min. ▶K ♀C ▶? $$$

meclizine (***Antivert, Bonine, Medivert, Meclicot, Meni-D, ✱Bonamine***): Vertigo: 25 mg PO q6h prn. [Rx/OTC Generic/Trade: Tabs 12.5, 25 mg. chew Tabs 25 mg. Rx/Trade only: Tabs 30, 50 mg. Caps 25 mg.] ▶L ♀B ▶? $

methylprednisolone (***Solu-Medrol, Medrol, Depo-Medrol***): Spinal cord injury: 30 mg/kg IV over 15 min, followed in 45 min by 5.4 mg/kg/h IV infusion x 23-47h. ▶L ♀C ▶- $$$$$

neostigmine (***Prostigmin***): 0.5 mg IM/SC. 15-375 mg/d PO divided. [Trade: Tabs 15 mg.] ▶L ♀C ▶? $$$

GLASGOW COMA SCALE

Eye Opening	*Verbal Activity*	*Motor Activity*
		6. Obeys commands
	5. Oriented	5. Localizes pain
4. Spontaneous	4. Confused	4. Withdraws to pain
3. To command	3. Inappropriate	3. Flexion to pain
2. To pain	2. Incomprehensible	2. Extension to pain
1. None	1. None	1. None

nimodipine (***Nimotop***): Subarachnoid hemorrhage: 60 mg PO q4h for 21 days. [Trade: Caps 30 mg.] ▶L ♀C ▶- $$$$$

pyridostigmine (***Mestinon, Regonal***): Myasthenia gravis: 60-200 mg PO tid or 180 mg (ext release) PO qd-bid. [Trade: Tabs 60 mg. extended release Tabs 180 mg. syrup 60 mg/ 5 ml.] ▶L ♀C ▶+ $$$

riluzole (***Rilutek***): ALS: 50 mg PO q12h. [Trade: Tabs 50 mg.] ▶LK ♀C ▶- $$$$$

OB/GYN

Estrogens (See also Vaginal Preparations, Hormone Replacement Combinations)

NOTE: Unopposed estrogens increase the risk of endometrial cancer in postmenopausal women. In women with an intact uterus, a progestin may be administered daily throughout the month or for the last 10-12 days of the month. May increase the risk of DVT/PE.

esterified estrogens (***Menest, Estratab***): HRT: 0.3 to 1.25 mg PO qd. [Trade: Tabs 0.3, 0.625, 1.25, 2.5 mg.] ▶L ♀X ▶- $

estradiol (***Estrace, Estradiol***): HRT: 1-2 mg PO qd. [Generic/Trade: Tabs, micronized 0.5, 1, 2 mg, scored.] ▶L ♀X ▶- $

estradiol cypionate (***depGynogen, Depo-Estradiol Cypionate, DepoGen***): HRT: 1-5 mg IM q 3-4 weeks. ▶L ♀X ▶- $

estradiol transdermal system (***Alora, Climara, Esclim, Estraderm, FemPatch, Vivelle, Vivelle Dot***): HRT: Apply one patch weekly (Climara, FemPatch, Estradiol) or twice per week (Esclim, Estraderm, Vivelle, Vivelle Dot, Alora). [Trade: Transdermal patches doses in mg/day: Climara (q week) 0.025,0.05, 0.075, 0.1. FemPatch (q week) 0.025. Esclim (twice/week) 0.025, 0.0375, 0.05, 0.075, 0.1. Vivelle, Vivelle Dot (twice/week) 0.025, 0.0375, 0.05, 0.075, 0.1. Estraderm (twice/week) 0.05, & 0.1. Alora (twice/week) 0.025, 0.05, 0.075, 0.1. Generic: Estradiol transdermal patches: (q week) 0.05 & 0.1.] ▶L ♀X ▶- $$

estradiol valerate (***Delestrogen, Gynogen L.A. 20, Valergen 20, Estra-L 40, Valergen 40***): HRT: 10-20 mg IM q4 weeks. ▶L ♀X ▶- $

estrogens conjugated (***Premarin, C.E.S., Congest***): HRT: 0.3 to 1.25 mg PO qd. Abnormal uterine bleeding: 25 mg IV/IM. Repeat in 6-12h if needed. [Trade: Tabs 0.3, 0.625, 0.9, 1.25, 2.5 mg.] ▶L ♀X ▶- $

estrogens synthetic conjugated (***Cenestin***): HRT: 0.3 to 1.25 mg PO qd. [Trade: Tabs 0.3, 0.625, 0.9, 1.25 mg.] ▶L ♀X ▶- $

estrone (***Kestrone 5, EstraGyn 5***): HRT 0.1-1 mg IM q week, up to 2 mg weekly. ▶L ♀X ▶- $

estropipate (***Ogen, Ortho-Est***): HRT: 0.625 to 5 mg PO qd. [Generic/Trade: Tabs 0.625, 1.25, 2.5, 5 mg.] ▶L ♀X ▶- $

ethinyl estradiol (***Estinyl***): HRT: 0.02-0.05 mg PO qd. [Trade: Tabs 0.02, 0.05 mg.] ▶L ♀X ▶- $

GnRH Agents

cetrorelix acetate (***Cetrotide***): Infertility: 0.25mg SC qd during the early to mid follicular phase or 3 mg SC x 1 usually on stimulation day 7. [Trade: Injection 0.25 mg in 1 & 7-dose kits. 3 mg in 1 dose kit.] ▶Plasma ♀X ▶- $$$$$

ganirelix acetate (***Follistim-Antagon Kit***): Infertility: 250 mcg SC qd during the early to mid follicular phase. Continue until hCG administration [Trade: Injection 250 mcg/0.5 ml in pre-filled, disposable syringes with 3 vials follitropin beta.] ▶Plasma ♀X ▶? $$$$$

ORAL CONTRACEPTIVES* ▸L ♀X	Estrogen (mcg)	Progestin (mg)
Monophasic		
Norinyl 1+50, Ortho-Novum 1/50, Necon 1/50	50 mestranol	1 norethindrone
Ovcon-50	50 ethinyl estradiol	
Demulen 1/50, Zovia 1/50E		1 ethynodiol
Ovral, Ogestrel		0.5 norgestrel
Norinyl 1+35, Ortho-Novum 1/35, Necon 1/35, Nortrel 1/35	35 ethinyl estradiol	1 norethindrone
Brevicon, Modicon, Necon 0.5/35, Nortrel 0.5/35		0.5 norethindrone
Ovcon-35		0.4 norethindrone
Ortho-Cyclen		0.25 norgestimate
Demulen 1/35, Zovia 1/35E		1 ethynodiol
Loestrin 21 1.5/30, Loestrin Fe 1.5/30, Microgestin Fe 1.5/30	30 ethinyl estradiol	1.5 norethindrone
Lo/Ovral, Low-Ogestrel		0.3 norgestrel
Apri, Desogen, Ortho-Cept		0.15 desogestrel
Levlen, Levora, Nordette, Portia		0.15 levonorgestrel
Yasmin		3 drospirenone
Loestrin 21 1/20, Loestrin Fe 1/20, Microgestin Fe 1/20	20 ethinyl estradiol	1 norethindrone
Alesse, Aviane, Lessina, Levlite		0.1 levonorgestrel
Progestin-only		
Micronor, Nor-Q.D.	none	0.35 norethindrone
Ovrette		0.075 norgestrel
Biphasic *(estrogen & progestin contents vary)*		
Kariva, Mircette	20/10 eth estrad	0.15/0 desogestrel
Ortho Novum 10/11, Necon 10/11	35 ethinyl estrad	0.5/1 norethindrone
Triphasic *(estrogen & progestin contents vary)*		
Cyclessa	25 ethinyl estradiol	0.100/0.125/0.150 desogestrel
Ortho-Novum 7/7/7	35 ethinyl estradiol	0.5/0.75/1 norethindrone
Tri-Norinyl		0.5/1/0.5 norethindrone
Enpresse, Tri-Levlen, Triphasil, Trivora-28	30/40/30 ethinyl estradiol	0.5/0.75/0.125 levonorgestrel
Ortho Tri-Cyclen Lo	25 ethin estradiol	0.18/0.215/0.25 norgestimate
Ortho Tri-Cyclen	35 ethin estradiol	
Estrostep Fe	20/30/35 eth estr	1 norethindrone

*__All__: Not recommended in smokers. Increase risk of thromboembolism, stroke, MI, hepatic neoplasia & gallbladder disease. Nausea, breast tenderness, & breakthrough bleeding are common transient side effects. Effectiveness reduced by hepatic enzyme-inducing drugs such as certain anticonvulsants and barbiturates,rifampin, rifabutin, griseofulvin, & protease inhibitors. Coadministration with antibiotics or St. John's wort may decrease efficacy. Consider an additional form of birth control in above circumstances. See product insert for instructions on missing doses. Most available in 21 and 28 day packs. **__Progestin only__**. Must be taken at the same time every day. Because much of the literature regarding adverse effects associated with oral contraceptives pertains mainly to combination products containing estrogen and progestins, the extent to which progestin-only contraceptives cause these effects is unclear. No significant interaction has been found with broad-spectrum antibiotics. The effect of St. John's wort is unclear. No placebo days, start new pack immediately after finishing current one. Available in 28 day packs. Readers may find the following website useful: www.managingcontraception.com.

EMERGENCY CONTRACEPTION within 72 hours of unprotected sex: Take first dose ASAP, then identical dose 12h later. Each dose is either 2 pills of *Ovral or Ogestrel*, 4 pills of *Cryselle, Levlen, Levora, Lo/Ovral, Nordette, Tri-Levlen*, Triphasil*, Trivora*, or Low Ogestrel*, or 5 pills of *Alesse, Aviane,* or *Levlite*. If vomiting occurs within 1 hour of taking either dose of medication, consider whether or not to repeat that dose and give an antiemetic 1h prior. *Preven* kit includes patient info booklet, urine pregnancy test, & blister pack of 4 tablets containing levonorgestrel 0.25mg & ethinyl estradiol 0.05mg. Each dose is 2 pills. *Plan B* kit contains two levonorgestrel 0.75mg tablets. Each dose is 1 pill. The progestin-only method causes less nausea & may be more effective.
Use 0.125 mg levonorgestrel/30 mcg ethinyl estradiol tabs.

Readers may find the following website useful: www.not-2-late.com.

goserelin (***Zoladex***): Endometriosis: 3.6 mg implant SC q28 days or 10.8 mg implant q12 weeks x 6 months. ▶LK ♀X ▶- $$$$$

leuprolide (***Lupron***): Endometriosis/fibroid-associated anemia: 3.75 mg IM q month or 11.25 mg IM q3 months, for total therapy of 6 months (endometriosis) or 3 months (fibroids). Concurrent iron for fibroid-associated anemia. ▶L ♀X ▶- $$$$$

nafarelin (***Synarel***): Endometriosis: 200-400 mcg intranasal bid x 6 months. [Trade: Nasal soln 2 mg/ml in 8 ml bottle (200 mcg per spray) about 80 sprays/bottle.] ▶L ♀X ▶- $$$$$

Hormone Replacement Combinations (See also vaginal preparations & estrogens)

NOTE:. Unopposed estrogens increase the risk of endometrial cancer in postmenopausal women. In women with an intact uterus, a progestin may be administered daily throughout the month or for the last 10-12 days of the month. May increase the risk of DVT/PE, gallbladder disease. Interactions with oral anticoagulants, phenytoin, rifampin, barbiturates, corticosteroids and St. John's wort. In the Women's Health Initiative, the combination of conjugated equine estrogens and medroxyprogesterone acetate (*Prempro*) caused a small, but statistically significant increase in the risk of breast cancer, CHD, CVA, & DVT/PE. Absolute numbers were small, however, and should be interpreted carefully. As always, patients should be counseled regarding the risks/benefits of HRT.

Activella (estradiol + norethindrone): HRT: 1 tab PO qd. [Trade: Tab 1 mg estradiol/0.5 mg norethindrone acetate in calendar dial pack dispenser.] ▶L ♀X ▶- $$

CombiPatch (estradiol + norethindrone): HRT: 1 patch twice weekly. [Trade: Transdermal patch 0.05 estradiol/ 0.14 norethindrone & 0.05 estradiol/0.25 norethindrone in mg/day, 8 patches/box.] ▶L ♀X ▶- $$

Estratest (esterified estrogens + methyltestosterone): HRT: 1 tab PO qd. [Trade: Tabs 1.25 mg esterified estrogens/2.5 mg methyltestosterone.] ▶L ♀X ▶- $$

Estratest H.S. (esterified estrogens + methyltestosterone): HRT: 1 tab PO qd. [Trade: Tabs 0.625 mg esterified estrogens/1.25 mg methyltest.] ▶L ♀X ▶- $$

FemHRT 1/5 (ethinyl estradiol + norethindrone): HRT: 1 tab PO qd. [Trade: Tabs 5 mcg ethinyl estradiol/1 mg norethindrone, 28/blister card.] ▶L ♀X ▶- $$

Ortho-Prefest (estradiol + norgestimate): HRT: 1 pink tab PO qd x 3 days followed by 1 white tab PO qd x 3 days, sequentially throughout the month. [Trade: Tabs in 30-day blister packs 1 mg estradiol (15 pink) & 1 mg estadiol/0.09 mg norgestimate (15 white).] ▶L ♀X ▶- $$

Premphase (conjugated estrogens + medroxyprogesterone): HRT: 1 tab PO qd. [Trade: Tabs in 28-day EZ-Dial dispensers: 0.625 mg conjugated estrogens (14) & 0.625 mg/5 mg conjugated estrogens/medroxyprogesterone (14).] ▶L ♀X ▶- $$

Prempro (conjugated estrogens + medroxyprogesterone): HRT: 1 tab PO qd. [Trade: Tabs in 28-day EZ-Dial dispensers: 0.625 mg/5 mg or 0.625 mg/2.5 mg conjugated estrogens/medroxyprogesterone.] ▶L ♀X ▶- $$

Labor Induction / Cervical Ripening

dinoprostone (**PGE2, *Prepidil, Cervidil***): Cervical ripening: One syringe of gel placed directly into the cervical os for cervical ripening or one insert in the posterior fornix of the vagina. [Trade: Gel (Prepidil) 0.5 mg/3 g syringe. Vaginal insert (Cervidil) 10 mg.] ▶Lung ♀C ◗? $$$$

misoprostol (**PGE1, *Cytotec***). Cervical ripening: 25-100 mcg intravaginally q3-4h to max 500 mcg/24h. [Generic/Trade: Oral tabs 100 & 200 mcg.] ▶LK ♀X ◗- $

oxytocin (***Pitocin***): Labor induction: 10 units in 1000 ml NS (10 milliunits/ml), start at 6-12 ml/h (1-2 milliunits/min). ▶LK ♀? ◗- $

Ovulation Stimulants

clomiphene (***Clomid, Serophene***): Specialized dosing for ovulation induction. [Generic/Trade: Tabs 50 mg, scored.] ▶L ♀D ◗? $$

gonadotropins (**menotropins, FSH/LH, *Pergonal, Humegon, Repronex*, *✦Propasi HP***): Specialized dosing for ovulation induction. [Trade: Powder or pellet for injection, 75 IU & 150 IU FSH activity.] ▶L ♀X ◗? $$$$$

DRUGS GENERALLY ACCEPTED AS SAFE IN PREGNANCY (selected)

<u>Analgesics:</u> acetaminophen, codeine*, meperidine*, methadone*. <u>Antimicrobials:</u> penicillins, cephalosporins, erythromycins (not estolate), azithromycin, nystatin, clotrimazole, metronidazole**, nitrofurantoin***, *Nix*. Antivirals:acyclovir, valacyclovir, famciclovir. <u>CV:</u> labetalol, methyldopa, hydralazine. <u>Derm:</u> erythromycin, clindamycin, benzoyl peroxide. <u>Endo</u>: insulin, liothyronine, levothyroxine. <u>ENT:</u> chlorpheniramine, diphenhydramine**, dimenhydrinate, dextromethorphan, guaifenesin, nasal steroids, nasal cromolyn. <u>GI:</u> trimethobenzamide, antacids*, simethicone, cimetidine, famotidine, ranitidine, nizatidine, psyllium, metoclopramide, bisacodyl, docusate, doxylamine, meclizine. <u>Psych:</u> fluoxetine, desipramine, doxepin. <u>Pulmonary:</u> short-acting inhaled beta-2 agonists, cromolyn, nedocromil, beclomethasone, budesonide, theophylline, prednisone**. <u>Other</u> - heparin.

**Except if used long-term or in high does at term*
***Except 1st trimester.* ****Contraindicated at term and during labor and delivery.*

Progestins

hydroxyprogesterone caproate (***Hylutin***): Amenorrhea, dysfunctional uterine bleeding, metrorrhagia: 375 mg IM. Production of secretory endometrium & desquamation: 125-250 mg IM on 10th day of the cycle, repeat q7days until suppression no longer desired. ▶L ♀X ◗? $

medroxyprogesterone acetate (***Provera, Cycrin, Amen, Curretab***): HRT: 10 mg PO qd for last 10-12 days of month, or 2.5-5 mg PO qd daily. Secondary amenorrhea, abnormal uterine bleeding: 5-10 mg PO qd x 5-10 days. Endometrial hyperplasia: 10-30 mg PO qd. [Generic/Trade: Tabs 2.5,5,10 mg, scored.] ▶L ♀X ◗+ $

medroxyprogesterone acetate (injectable contraceptive) (***Depo-Provera***): Contraception: 150 mg IM in deltoid or gluteus maximus q13 weeks. ▶L ♀X ◗+ $

megestrol (***Megace***): Endometrial hyperplasia: 40-160 mg PO qd x 3-4 mo. AIDS anorexia: 800 mg (20 ml) susp PO qd. [Generic/Trade: Tabs 20 & 40 mg. Suspension 40 mg/ml in 237 ml.] ▶L ♀D ◗? $$$$$

norethindrone (***Aygestin, Norlutate***): Amenorrhea, abnormal uterine bleeding: 2.5-10 mg PO qd x 5-10 days during the second half of the menstrual cycle. Endometriosis: 5 mg PO qd x 2 weeks. Increase by 2.5 mg q 2 weeks to 15 mg. [Generic/trade: Tabs 5 mg, scored.] ▶L ♀D ◗? $

progesterone micronized (***Prometrium***): HRT: 200 mg PO qhs 10-12 days per month or 100 mg qhs daily. Secondary amenorrhea: 400 mg PO qhs x 10 days. Contraindicated in patients allergic to peanuts since caps contain peanut oil. [Caps 100 & 200 mg.] ▶L ♀B ◗+ $

Selective Estrogen Receptor Modulators

raloxifene (***Evista***): Osteoporosis prevention/treatment: 60 mg PO qd. [Trade: Tabs 60 mg.] ▶L ♀X ◗- $$$

tamoxifen (***Nolvadex, Tamone***): Breast cancer prevention: 20 mg PO qd x 5 years. [Generic/Trade: Tabs 10 & 20 mg.] ▶L ♀D ◗- $$$

APGAR SCORE				
	Heart rate	0. Absent	1. <100	2. >100
	Respirations	0. Absent	1. Slow/irreg	2. Good/crying
	Muscle tone	0. Limp	1. Some flexion	2. Active motion
	Reflex irritability	0. No response	1. Grimace	2. Cough/sneeze
	Color	0. Blue	1. Blue extremities	2. Pink

Tocolytics

indomethacin (***Indocin, Indocid***): Preterm labor: initial 50-100 mg PO/PR followed by 25 mg PO/PR q6-12h up to 48 hrs. [Generic/Trade: Immediate release caps 25 & 50 mg. Trade: Oral suspension 25 mg/5 ml. Suppositories 50 mg.] ▶L ♀? ◗- $

magnesium sulfate: Eclampsia: 4-6 g IV over 30min, then 2 g/h. Drip: 5 g in 250 ml D5W (20 mg/ml), 2 g/h = 100 ml/h. Preterm labor: 6 g IV over 20 minutes, then 2-3 g/h titrated to decrease contractions. Monitor respirations & reflexes. If needed, may reverse hypocalcemic effects with calcium gluconate 1 g IV. ▶K ♀A ◗+ $$

nifedipine (***Procardia, Adalat, Procardia XL, Adalat CC***): Preterm labor: loading dose: 10 mg PO q20-30 min if contractions persist, up to 40 mg within the first hour. Maintenance dose: 10-20 mg PO q4-6h or 60-160 mg extended release PO qd. [Generic/Trade: immediate release caps 10 & 20 mg. Extended release tabs 30, 60, 90 mg.] ▶L ♀C ◗+ $

terbutaline (***Brethine, Bricanyl***): Preterm labor: 0.25 mg SC q30 min up to 1 mg in four hrs. Infusion: 2.5-10 mcg/min IV, gradually increased to effective max doses of 17.5-30 mcg/minute. Maintenance: 2.5-5 mg PO q4-6h until term. Tachycardia common. [Tabs 2.5, 5 mg.] ▶L ♀B ◗+ $$$$

Uterotonics

carboprost (**Hemabate, 15-methyl-prostaglandin F2 alpha**): Refractory postpartum uterine bleeding: 250 mcg deep IM. ▶LK ♀C ◗? $$$

methylergonovine (***Methergine***): Refractory postpartum uterine bleeding: 0.2 mg IM/PO tid-qid prn. [Trade: Tabs 0.2 mg.] ▶LK ♀C ◗? $

oxytocin (***Pitocin***): Uterine contractions/postpartum bleeding: 10 units IM or 10-40 units in 1000 ml NS IV, infuse 20-40 milliunits/minute. ▶LK ♀? ◗? $

Vaginal Preparations (See also STD/vaginitis table in antimicrobial section)

butoconazole (***Gynazole-1, Mycelex 3***): Vulvovaginal candidiasis: Femstat 3: 1 applicatorful qhs x 3-6 days. Gynazole-1: 1 applicatorful intravaginally qhs x 1. [OTC: Trade (Mycelex 3): 2% vaginal cream in 5 g pre-filled applicators (3s) & 20 g tube with applicators. Rx: Trade (Gynazole-1): 2% vaginal cream in 5 g pre-filled applicator.] ▶LK ♀C ◗? $(OTC)

clindamycin phosphate (***Cleocin***, ✤***Dalacin***): Bacterial vaginosis: 1 applicatorful cream qhs x 7d or one vaginal supp qhs x 3d. [Trade: 2% vaginal cream in 40 g tube with 7 disposable applicators. Vag supp (Ovules) 100 mg (3) w/applicator.] ▶L ♀B ▶+ $$

clotrimazole (***Mycelex 7, Gyne-Lotrimin***, ✤***Canestin***): Vulvovaginal candidiasis: 1 applicatorful 1% cream qhs x 7 days. 1 applicatorful 2% cream qhs x 3 days. 1 vag tab 100 mg qhs x 7days. 1 vag tab 200 mg qhs x 3days. [OTC: Generic/Trade: 1% vaginal cream with applicator (some pre-filled). 2% vaginal cream with applicator. Vaginal tablets 100 mg (7) & 200 mg (3) with applicators. 1% topical cream in some combination packs.] ▶LK ♀B ▶? $

estradiol vaginal ring (***Estring***): Menopausal atrophic vaginitis: Insert & replace after 90 days. [Trade: 2 mg ring single pack.] ▶L ♀X ▶- $$

estradiol vaginal tab (***Vagifem***): Menopausal atrophic vaginitis: one tablet vaginally qd x 2 weeks, then one tablet vaginally 2x/week. [Trade: Vaginal tab: 25 mcg in disposable single-use applicators, 15/pack.] ▶L ♀X ▶- $-$$

estrogen cream (***Premarin, Estrace, Ogen***): Atrophic vaginitis: Premarin: 0.5-2 g qd. Estrace: 2-4 g qd x 2 weeks, then reduce. Ogen: 2-4 g qd. [Trade: Vaginal cream. Premarin: 0.625 mg conjugated estrogens/g in 42.5 g with or w/o calibrated applicator. Estrace: 0.1 mg estradiol/g in 42.5 g w/calibrated applicator. Ogen: 1.5 mg estropipate/g in 42.5 g with calibrated applicator.] ▶L ♀X ▶? $$-$$$

metronidazole (***MetroGel-Vaginal***): Bacterial vaginosis: 1 applicatorful qhs or bid x 5 days. [Trade: 0.75% gel in 70 g tube with applicator.] ▶LK ♀B ▶? $$

miconazole (***Monistat-1, Monistat-3, Monistat-7, Femizol-M, M-Zole, Micozole, Monazole***): Vulvovaginal candidiasis: 1 applicatorful qhs x 3 or 7 days. 100 mg vag supp qhs x 7 days. 400 mg vag supp qhs x 3 days. [OTC: Generic/Trade: 2% vaginal cream in 45 g with 1 applicator or 7 disposable applicators. Vaginal suppositories 100 mg (7) OTC: Trade: 400 mg (3) with applicator. 4% vaginal cream in 25 g tubes or 3 prefilled applicators. Some in combination packs with 2% miconazole cream for external use.] ▶LK ♀+ ▶? $

nystatin (***Mycostatin***): Vulvovaginal candidiasis: 1 vag tab qhs x 14 days. [Generic/Trade: Vaginal Tabs 100,000 units in 15s & 30s with or without applicator(s).] ▶Not metabolized ♀A ▶? $$

terconazole (***Terazol***): Vulvovaginal candidiasis: 1 applicatorful of 0.4% cream qhs x 7 days. 1 applicatorful of 0.8% cream qhs x 3 days. 80 mg vaginal supp qhs x 3 days. [Trade: Vaginal cream 0.4% in 45 g tube with applicator. Vaginal cream 0.8% in 20 g tube with applicator. Vaginal suppositories 80 mg (3) with applicator.] ▶LK ♀C ▶- $$

tioconazole (***Monistat 1-Day, Vagistat-1***, ✤***Gynecure***): Vulvovaginal candidiasis: 1 applicatorful of 6.5% ointment intravaginally qhs single-dose. [OTC: Trade: Vaginal ointment: 6.5% (300 mg) in 4.6 g prefilled single-dose applicator.] ▶Not absorbed ♀C ▶- $

Other OB/GYN Agents

betamethasone sodium phosphate (***Celestone***): Fetal lung maturation, maternal antepartum: 12 mg IM q24h x 2 doses. ▶L ♀C ▶- $$

clonidine (***Catapres, Catapres-TTS***): Menopausal flushing: 0.1-0.4 mg/day PO divided bid-tid. Transdermal system q week: 0.1 mg/day. [Generic/Trade: Tabs 0.1, 0.2,0.3 mg. Trade: Transdermal weekly patch: 0.1,0.2,0.3 mg/day.] ▶KL ♀C ▶? $

danazol (***Danocrine***, ✤***Cyclomen***): Endometriosis: Start 400 mg PO bid, then titrate downward to maintain amenorrhea x 3-6 months. Fibrocystic breast disease: 100-200 mg PO bid x 4-6 months. [Generic/Trade: Caps 50, 100, 200 mg.] ▶L ♀X ▶- $$$$$

dexamethasone (***Decadron***): Fetal lung maturation, maternal antepartum: 6 mg IM q12h x 4 doses. ▶L ♀C ▶- $

fluconazole (***Diflucan***): Vaginal candidiasis: 150 mg PO single dose. [Trade: Tabs 50, 100, 150, & 200 mg; Suspension 10 mg/ml & 40 mg/ml.] ▶K ♀C ▶- $

levonorgestrel (***Plan B***): Emergency contraception: 1 tab PO ASAP but within 72h of intercourse. 2nd tab 12h later. [Trade: Kit has two 0.75 mg tabs.] ▶L ♀X ▶- $

Lunelle (medroxyprogesterone + estradiol): Contraception: 0.5 ml IM q month. ▶L ♀X ▶- $$

mifepristone (***Mifeprex, RU-486***): 600 mg PO x 1 followed by 400 mcg misoprostol on day 3, if abortion not confirmed. [Trade: Tabs 200 mg.] ▶L ♀X ▶? $$$$$

Ortho Evra (norelgestromin + ethinyl estradiol): Contraception: 1 patch q week x 3 weeks, then 1 week patch-free. [Trade: Transdermal patch: 150 mcg norelgestromin + 20 mcg ethinyl estradiol/day. 1 and 3 patches/box.] ▶L ♀X ▶- $$

Premesis-Rx (B6 + folic acid + B12 + calcium carbonate): Pregnancy-induced nausea: 1 tab PO qd. [Trade: Tabs 75 mg vitamin B6 (pyridoxine), sustained-release, 12 mcg vitamin B12 (cyanocobalamin), 1 mg folic acid, and 200 mg calcium carbonate.] ▶L ♀A ▶+ $

Preven (levonorgestrel + ethinyl estradiol): Emergency contraception: 2 tabs PO ASAP but within 72h of intercourse. 2 tabs 12h later. [Trade: Kit contains patient info booklet, pregnancy test, & 4 tabs 0.25mg levonorgestrel/50 mcg ethinyl estradiol.] ▶L ♀X ▶- $

RHO immune globulin (***RhoGAM, BayRho-D, WinRho SDF, MICRhoGAM, BayRho-D Mini Dose***): 1 vial (300 mcg) IM within 72h if mother Rh-. Microdose (50 mcg) (MICRhoGAM) OK if spontaneous abortion <12 weeks gestation. ▶L ♀C ▶? $$$$

ONCOLOGY

Variable dosages. **Alkylating agents:** altretamine (*Hexalen*), busulfan (*Myleran, Busulfex*), carboplatin (*Paraplatin*), carmustine (*BCNU, BiCNU, Gliadel*), chlorambucil (*Leukeran*), cisplatin (*Platinol-AQ*), cyclophosphamide (*Cytoxan, Neosar*), dacarbazine (*DTIC-Dome*), ifosfamide (*Ifex*), lomustine (*CeeNu, CCNU*), mechlorethamine (*Mustargen*), melphalan (*Alkeran*), oxaliplatin (*Eloxatin*), procarbazine (*Matulane*), streptozocin (*Zanosar*), temozolomide (*Temodar*), thiotepa (*Thioplex*). **Antibiotics:** bleomycin (*Blenoxane*), dactinomycin (*Cosmegen*), daunorubicin (*DaunoXome, Cerubidine*), doxorubicin liposomal (*Doxil*), doxorubicin non-liposomal (*Adriamycin, Rubex*), epirubicin (*Ellence*), idarubicin (*Idamycin*), mitomycin (*Mutamycin, Mitomycin-C*), mitoxantrone (*Novantrone*), plicamycin (*mithramycin, Mithracin*), valrubicin (*Valstar*). **Antimetabolites:** capecitabine (*Xeloda*), cladribine (*Leustatin*), cytarabine (*Cytosar-U, Tarabine, Depo-Cyt, AraC*), floxuridine (*FUDR*), fludarabine (*Fludara*), fluorouracil (*Adrucil, 5-FU*), gemcitabine (*Gemzar*), hydroxyurea (*Hydrea*), mercaptopurine (6-MP) (*Purinethol*), methotrexate (*Rheumatrex, Trexall*), pentostatin (*Nipent*), thioguanine. **Cytoprotective Agents:** amifostine (*Ethyol*), dexrazoxane (*Zinecard*), mesna (*Mesnex*). **Hormones:** anastrozole (*Arimidex*), bicalutamide (*Casodex*), estramustine (*Emcyt*), exemestane (*Aromasin*), flutamide (*Eulexin,* 🍁*Euflex*), fulvestrant (*Faslodex*), goserelin (*Zoladex*), letrozole (*Femara*), leuprolide (*Eligard, Leupron, Viadur*), medroxyprogesterone acetate (*Depo-Provera*), megestrol (*Megace*), nilutamide (*Nilandron*), tamoxifen (*Nolvadex, Tamone*), testolactone (*Teslac*), toremifene (*Fareston*), triptorelin (*Trelstar Depot*).

Immunomodulators: aldesleukin (*Proleukin, interleukin-2*), alemtuzumab (*Campath*), BCG (*Bacillus of Calmette & Guerin, Pacis, TheraCys, TICE BCG*), denileukin diftitox (*Ontak*), ibritumomab (*Zevalin*), imatinib mesylate (*Gleevec*), interferon alfa-2a (*Roferon-A*), interferon alfa-2b (*Intron A*), interferon alfa-n3 (*Alferon N*), rituximab (*Rituxan*), trastuzumab (*Herceptin*). **Mitotic Inhibitors:** docetaxel (*Taxotere*), etoposide (*VP 16, Etopophos, Toposar, VePesid*), paclitaxel (*Taxol, Onxol*), teniposide (*Vumon, VM-26*), vinblastine (*Velban, VLB, ♣Velbe*), vincristine (*Oncovin, Vincasar, VCR*), vinorelbine (*Navelbine*). **Radiopharmaceuticals:** samarium 153 (*Quadramet*), strontium-89 (*Metastron*). **Miscellaneous:** arsenic trioxide (*Trisenox*), asparaginase (*Elspar, ♣Kidrolase*), bexarotene (*Targretin*), irinotecan (*Camptosar*), leucovorin (*Wellcovorin, folinic acid*), levamisole (*Ergamisol*), mitotane (*Lysodren*), pegaspargase (*Oncaspar*), porfimer (*Photofrin*), topotecan (*Hycamtin*), tretinoin (*Vesanoid*).

OPHTHALMOLOGY

Antibacterials - Aminoglycosides

gentamicin (***Garamycin***): 1-2 gtts q4h; ½ inch ribbon of oint bid-tid. [Generic/Trade: solution 0.3%, ointment 0.3%.] ▸K ♀C ▸? $

tobramycin (***Tobrex***): 1-2 gtts q1-4h or ½ inch ribbon of ointment q3-4h or bid-tid. [Generic/Trade: solution 0.3%. Trade only: ointment 0.3%.] ▸K ♀B ▸- $

Antibacterials - Fluoroquinolones

ciprofloxacin (***Ciloxan***): 1-2 gtt q1-6h or ½ inch ribbon ointment bid-tid. [Trade only: solution 0.3%, ointment 0.3%.] ▸LK ♀C ▸? $$

levofloxacin (***Quixin***): 1-2 gtts q2h while awake up to 8 times/day on days 1 & 2, then 1-2 gtts q4h up to 4 times/day on days 3-7. [Trade only: solution 0.5%.] ▸KL ♀C ▸? $$

norfloxacin (***Chibroxin, Noroxin***): 1-2 gtts q2-6h. [Trade only: solution 0.3%.] ▸LK ♀C ▸? $

ofloxacin (***Ocuflox***): 1-2 gtts q1-6h x 7-10 days. [Trade only: solution 0.3%.] ▸LK ♀C ▸? $$

Antibacterials - Other

bacitracin (***AK Tracin***): Apply ½ inch ribbon of ointment q3-4h or bid-qid. [Generic/Trade: ointment 500 units/g.] ▸Minimal absorption ♀C ▸? $

erythromycin (***Ilotycin, AK-Mycin***): ½ inch ribbon of ointment q3-4h or bid-qid. [Generic/Trade: ointment 0.5%.] ▸L ♀B ▸+ $

Neosporin Ointment (neomycin + bacitracin + polymyxin B): ½ inch ribbon of ointment q3-4h x 7-10 days. [Generic/Trade: ointment.] ▸K ♀C ▸? $

Neosporin Solution (neomycin + polymyxin + gramicidin): 1-2 gtts q1-6h x 7-10 days. [Trade/generic: solution] ▸K ♀C ▸? $$

Polysporin (polymyxin B + bacitracin): ½ inch ribbon of ointment q3-4h x 7-10 days. [Generic/Trade: ointment.] ▸K ♀C ▸? $

Polytrim (polymyxin B + trimethoprim): 1 gtt q3-6h x 7-10d, max 6 gtts/day. [Trade only: solution.] ▸K ♀C ▸? $

sulfacetamide (***Sulamyd, Bleph-10, Sulf-10, Isopto Cetamide***): 1-2 gtts q2-6h x 7-10d or ½ inch ribbon of ointment q3-8h x 7-10d. [Generic/Trade: solution 1%, 10%, 15%, 30%. ointment 10%.] ▸K ♀C ▸- $

Antihistamines, Ocular

azelastine (***Optivar***): 1 gtt in each eye bid. [Trade only: soln 0.05%.] ▶L ♀C ▶? $$

emedastine (***Emadine***): 1 gtt in affected eye up to qid. [Trade only: solution 0.05%.] ▶L ♀B ▶? $$

levocabastine (***Livostin***): 1 gtt in each eye qid. [Trade only: suspension 0.05%.] ▶? ♀C ▶? $$$

Antiviral Agents

trifluridine (***Viroptic***): Herpes: 1 gtt q2-4h x 7-14d, max 9 gtts/day. [Trade only: solution 1%.] ▶Minimal absorption ♀C ▶- $$$

vidarabine (***Vira-A***): ½ inch ribbon of ointment 5 times daily (q3h) x 5-7 days. After re-epithelialization, ½ inch ribbon bid x 5-7 days. [Trade only: ointment 3%.] ▶Cornea ♀C ▶? $$$

Corticosteroid & Antibacterial Combinations

NOTE: Recommend that only ophthalmologists or optometrists prescribe due to infection and glaucoma risk. Monitor intraocular pressure.

Blephamide (prednisolone + sodium sulfacetamide, Vasocidin, FML-S): 1-2 gtts q1-8h or ½ inch ribbon of ointment qd-qid. [Generic/Trade: suspension, ointment.] ▶KL ♀C ▶? $

Cortisporin (neomycin + polymyxin + hydrocortisone): 1-2 gtts or ½ inch ribbon of ointment q3-4h or more frequently prn. [Generic/Trade: suspension, ointment.] ▶LK ♀C ▶? $

Maxitrol (dexamethasone + neomycin + polymyxin; Dexacidin): 1-2 gtts q1-8h or ½ -1 inch ribbon of ointment qd-qid. [Generic/Trade: suspension, ointment.] ▶KL ♀C ▶? $

Pred G (prednisolone acetate + gentamicin): 1-2 gtts q1-8h qd-qid or or ½ inch ribbon of ointment bid-qid. [Trade: suspension, ointment.] ▶KL ♀C ▶? $$

TobraDex (tobramycin + dexamethasone): 1-2 gtts q2-6h or ½ inch ribbon of ointment bid-qid. [Trade only: ointment. Trade/generic: suspension.] ▶L ♀C ▶? $$

Corticosteroids

NOTE: Recommend that only ophthalmologists or optometrists prescribe due to infection and glaucoma risk. Monitor intraocular pressure.

fluorometholone (***FML, FML Forte, Flarex***): 1-2 gtts q1-12h or ½ inch ribbon of ointment q4-24h. [Generic/Trade: suspension 0.1%. Trade only: suspension 0.25%. solution 0.1%, ointment 0.1%.] ▶L ♀C ▶? $$

loteprednol (***Alrex, Lotemax***): 1-2 gtts qid. [Trade only: suspension 0.2% (Alrex), 0.5% (Lotemax).] ▶L ♀C ▶? $$

prednisolone (***AK-Pred, Pred Forte, Pred Mild, Inflamase Forte***): 1 gtt q1-12h. [Generic/Trade: suspension 0.12,0.125,1%, solution 0.125,1%.] ▶L ♀C ▶? $$

rimexolone (***Vexol***): 1-2 gtts q1-6h. [Trade only: suspension 1%.] ▶L ♀C ▶? $$

Decongestants, Ocular

naphazoline (***Albalon, AK-Con, Vasocon, Naphcon, Allerest, Clear Eyes***): 1 gtt q3-4h prn up to qid. [OTC Generic/Trade: solution 0.012, 0.02, 0.03. Rx generic/trade: 0.1%.] ▶? ♀C ▶? $

Naphcon-A (naphazoline + pheniramine): 1-2 gtts bid-qid prn. [OTC Generic/Trade: solution (0.025% naphazoline + 0.3% pheniramine).] ▶L ♀C ▶? $

Glaucoma Agents - Beta Blockers (Use caution in cardiac conditions and asthma.)

betaxolol (***Betoptic, Betoptic S***): 1-2 gtts bid. [Trade only: suspension 0.25%. Generic/Trade: solution 0.5%.] ▶LK ♀C ▶? $$

carteolol (***Ocupress***): 1 gtt bid. [Generic/Trade: solution 1%.] ▶KL ♀C ▶? $

levobetaxolol (***Betaxon***): 1 gtt bid. [Trade only: solution 0.5%.] ▶KL ♀C ▶? ?

levobunolol (***Betagan***): 1- 2 gtts qd-bid. [Generic/Trade: soln 0.25,0.5%] ▶? ♀C ▶-$

timolol (***Timoptic, Timoptic XE***): 1 gtt bid. Timoptic XE: 1 gtt qd. [Generic/Trade: solution 0.25%, 0.5%, gel forming soln 0.25, 0.5% (Timoptic XE).] ▶LK ♀C ▶+ $

Glaucoma Agents - Carbonic Anhydrase Inhibitors

NOTE: Sulfonamide derivatives; verify absence of sulfa allergy before prescribing.

acetazolamide (***Diamox***): Glaucoma: 250 mg PO qd-qid (immediate release) or 500 mg PO qd-bid (extended release). [Generic/Trade: Tabs 125, 250 mg. Trade only: extended release Caps 500 mg.] ▶LK ♀C ▶+ $$

brinzolamide (***Azopt***): 1 gtt tid. [Trade only: suspension 1%.] ▶LK ♀C ▶? $$

dorzolamide (***Trusopt***): 1 gtt tid. [Trade only: solution 2%.] ▶KL ♀C ▶- $$

methazolamide (***Neptazane***): 25-50 mg PO qd-tid. [Generic/Trade: Tabs 25, 50 mg.] ▶LK ♀C ▶? $

Glaucoma Agents - Prostaglandin Analogs

bimatoprost (***Lumigan***): 1 gtt qhs. [Trade only: solution 0.03%.] ▶LK ♀C ▶? $$$

latanoprost (***Xalatan***): 1 gtt qhs. [Trade only: solution 0.005%.] ▶LK ♀C ▶? $$$

travoprost (***Travatan***): 1 gtt qhs. [Trade only: solution 0.004%.] ▶L ♀C ▶? $$

unoprostone (***Rescula***): 1 gtt bid. [Trade only: soln 0.15%.] ▶Plasma, K ♀C ▶? $$

Glaucoma Agents - Sympathomimetics

apraclonidine (***Iopidine***): 1-2 gtts tid. [Trade only: solution 0.5,1%.] ▶KL ♀C ▶? $$$

brimonidine (***Alphagan, Alphagan P***): 1 gtt tid. [Trade only: solution 0.15% (Alphagan P) 0.2% (Alphagan).] ▶L ♀B ▶? $$

dipivefrin (***Propine***): 1 gtt q12h. [Generic/Trade: soln 0.1%.] ▶Eye, plasma ♀B ▶? $

Glaucoma Agents - Other

Cosopt (dorzolamide + timolol): 1 gtt bid. [Trade only: solution (dorzolamide 2% + timolol 0.5%).] ▶LK ♀C ▶- $$

pilocarpine (***Pilocar, Pilopine qhs, Isopto Carpine, ✤Diocarpine***): 1-2 gtts tid-qid or ½ inch ribbon of gel qhs. [Generic/Trade: solution 0.5, 1, 2, 3, 4, 6, 8%. Trade only: 0.25,5,10%, gel 4%.] ▶Plasma ♀C ▶? $

MAST Cell Stabilizers, Ocular

cromolyn sodium (***Crolom, Opticrom***): 1-2 gtts in each eye 4-6 times per day. [Generic/Trade: solution 4%.] ▶LK ♀B ▶? $$$

ketotifen (***Zaditor***): 1 gtt in each eye q8-12h. [Trade only: soln 0.025%.] ▶Minimal absorption ♀C ▶? $$

lodoxamide tromethamine (***Alomide***): 1-2 gtts in each eye qid. [Trade only: solution 0.1%.] ▶K ♀B ▶? $$$

nedocromil (***Alocril, ✤Mireze***): 1-2 gtts in each eye bid. [Trade only: solution 2%.] ▶L ♀B ▶? $$

olopatadine (***Patanol***): 1-2 gtts in each eye bid. [Trade only: solution 0.1%.] ▶K ♀C ▶? $$$

pemirolast (***Alamast***): 1-2 gtts in each eye qid.[Trade only: soln 0.1%] ▶?♀C▶?$$$

Mydriatics & Cycloplegics

atropine (***Isopto Atropine***): 1-2 gtts before procedure or qd-qid, 1/8-1/4 inch ointment before procedure or qd-tid. Cycloplegia lasts 5-10d; mydriasis lasts 7-14d. [Generic/Trade: solution 1,2%, ointment 1%. Trade only: soln 0.5%.] ▶K ♀C ▶+ $

cyclopentolate (***AK-Pentolate, Cyclogyl, Pentolair***): 1-2 gtts x 1-2 doses before procedure. Cycloplegia lasts 6-24h; mydriasis lasts 1 day. [Generic/Trade: solution 1%. Trade only: 0.5,2%.] ▶? ♀C ▶? $

homatropine (***Isopto Homatropine***): 1-2 gtts before procedure or bid-tid. Cycloplegia & mydriasis lasts 1-3 days. [Trade only: solution 2%. Generic/Trade: solution 5%.] ▶? ♀C ▶? $

phenylephrine (***Neo-Synephrine, Mydfrin, Relief***): 1-2 gtts before procedure or tid-qid with atropine. No cycloplegia; mydriasis lasts 5 hours. [OTC Generic/Trade: solution 0.12, 2.5, 10%.] ▶Plasma ♀C ▶? $

tropicamide (***Mydriacyl***): 1-2 gtts before procedure. Mydriasis lasts 6 hours. [Generic/Trade: solution 0.5, 1%.] ▶? ♀? ▶? $

Nonsteroidal Anti-Inflammatories

diclofenac (***Voltaren***, ✤***Vofenal***): 1 gtt qid and/or before procedure. [Trade: solution 0.1%.] ▶L ♀B ▶? $$

ketorolac (***Acular***): 1 gtt qid. [Trade only: solution 0.5%. Preservative free 0.5% unit dose (0.4 ml).] ▶L ♀C ▶? $$$

Other Ophthalmologic Agents

artificial tears (***Tears Naturale, Hypotears, Refresh Tears, Lacrilube, GenTeal***): 1-2 gtts tid-qid prn. [OTC solution.] ▶Minimal absorption ♀A ▶+ $

dapiprazole (***Rev-Eyes***): 2 gtt in each eye, repeat in 5 mins. [Trade only: solution 0.5%.] ▶Minimal absorption ♀B ▶? $

petrolatum (***Lacrilube, Dry Eyes, Refresh PM***): Apply ¼ inch ointment to inside of lower lid prn. [OTC ointment.] ▶Minimal absorption ♀A ▶+ $

proparacaine (***Ophthaine, Ophthetic***, ✤***Alcaine***): Do not prescribe for unsupervised or prolonged use. Corneal toxicity and ocular infections may occur with repeated use. 1-2 gtts before procedure. [Generic/Trade: soln 0.5%.] ▶L ♀C ▶? $

tetracaine (***Pontocaine***): Do not prescribe for unsupervised or prolonged use. Corneal toxicity and ocular infections may occur with repeated use. 1-2 gtts or ½-1 inch ribbon of ointment before procedure. [Generic/Trade: solution 0.5%.] ▶Plasma ♀C ▶? $

verteporfin (***Visudyne***): 6 mg/m2 IV over 10 minutes; laser light therapy 15 minutes after start of infusion. ▶L/plasma ♀C ▶? $$$$$

PSYCHIATRY

Antidepressants - Heterocyclic Compounds

amitriptyline (***Elavil, Vanatrip***): Start 25-100 mg PO qhs, gradually increase to usual effective dose of 50-300 mg/d. Primarily serotonin. Demethylated to nortriptyline. [Generic/Trade: Tabs 10, 25, 50, 75, 100, 150 mg.] ▶L ♀D ▶- $

amoxapine (***Asendin***): Rarely used. Initiate 25-50 mg PO bid-tid, increase by 50-100 mg bid- tid after 1 week. Usual effective dose is 150- 400 mg/day. [Generic/Trade: Tabs 25, 50, 100, 150 mg.] ▶L ♀C ▶- $$$

clomipramine (***Anafranil***): Start 25 mg PO qhs, gradually increase to usual effective dose of 150-250 mg/day, max 250 mg/day. Primarily serotonin. Seizures. [Generic/Trade: Caps 25, 50, 75 mg.] ▶L ♀C ▶+ $$$

desipramine (***Norpramin***): Start 25 mg PO qd or in divided doses. Gradually increase to usual effective dose of 100-300 mg/d. Primarily norepinephrine. [Generic/Trade: Tabs 10, 25, 50, 75, 100, 150 mg.] ▶L ♀C ▶+ $

doxepin (***Sinequan, Zonalon***): Start 25 mg PO qhs. Usual effective dose 75-300 mg/day. Primarily norepinephrine. [Generic/Trade: Caps 10, 25, 50, 75, 100, 150 mg. oral concentrate 10 mg/ml.] ▶L ♀C ▶- $

imipramine (***Tofranil***): Start 25 mg PO qhs, gradually ↑ to usual effective 50-300 mg/d. Mixed serotonin & norepinephrine. Demethylated to desipramine. [Generic/Trade: Tabs 10,25,50 mg. Trade only: Caps 75,100,125,150 mg.] ▶L ♀D ▶- $

maprotiline (***Ludiomil***): Rarely used. Initiate 25 mg PO qd, gradually increase by 25 mg q2 weeks. Usual effective dose is 150 - 225 mg/day. [Generic/Trade: Tabs 25, 50, 75 mg.] ▶KL ♀B ▶? $$

nortriptyline (***Aventyl, Pamelor***): Start 25 mg PO qd- qid. Usual effective dose 50-150 mg/day. Primarily norepinephrine. [Generic/Trade: Caps 10, 25, 50, 75 mg. Trade only: oral solution 10 mg/ 5 ml.] ▶L ♀D ▶+ $

protriptyline (***Vivactil***, ***✤Triptil***): 15-40 mg/day PO divided tid-qid. [Generic/Trade: Tabs 5, 10 mg.] ▶L ♀C ▶+ $$

trimipramine (***Surmontil***): Initiate 25 mg PO qhs, increase gradually to 75-150 mg/day. [Trade: Caps 25, 50, 100 mg.] ▶L ♀C ▶? $$$

Antidepressants - Monoamine Oxidase Inhibitors (MAOIs)

NOTE: Must be on tyramine-free diet, stay on diet for 2 weeks after stopping. Risk of hypertensive crisis and serotonin syndrome with many medications, including OTC. Evaluate thoroughly for drug interactions. Allow at least 2 weeks wash-out between MAOIs and SSRIs (up to 6 weeks with fluoxetine), TCAs, and other antidepressants.

isocarboxazid (***Marplan***): Start 10 mg PO bid, increase by 10 mg q2-4 days. Usual effective dose is 20- 40 mg/day. [Trade: Tabs 10 mg.] ▶L ♀C ▶? $$$

phenelzine (***Nardil***): Start 15 mg PO tid. Usual effective dose is 60-90 mg/day in divided doses. [Trade: Tabs 15 mg.] ▶L ♀C ▶? $$

tranylcypromine (***Parnate***): Start 10 mg PO qam, increase by 10 mg/day at 1-3 week intervals to usual effective dose of 10-40 mg/day divided bid. [Trade: Tabs 10 mg.] ▶L ♀C ▶- $$$

Antidepressants - Selective Serotonin Reuptake Inhibitors (SSRIs)

citalopram (***Celexa***): Depression: Start 20 mg PO qd, max 60 mg/day. [Trade: Tabs 10, 20, 40 mg. oral solution 10 mg/5 ml.] ▶LK ♀C ▶- $$$

escitalopram (***Lexapro***): Depression: Start 10 mg PO qd, usual effective dose 10-20 mg/day. [Trade: tablets 10, 20 mg, both scored.] ▶LK ♀C ▶- $$$

fluoxetine (***Prozac, Prozac Weekly***): Depression & OCD: Start 20 mg PO q am, usual effective dose 20-40 mg/day, max 80 mg/day. Depression, maintenance: 20-40 mg/day OR 90 mg PO once weekly delayed release (start 7 days after last dose of 20 mg/day). Bulimia: 60 mg PO qd; may need to titrate up to 60 mg/day over several days. [Trade: tablets 10, 20 mg. Capsules 40 mg. Capsules, delayed release (Prozac Weekly) 90 mg. Generic: capsules 10, 20 mg, tablets 10 mg, 20 mg. Oral solution 20 mg/5 ml.] ▶L ♀C ▶- $$$

fluvoxamine (***Luvox***): OCD: Start 50 mg PO qhs, usual effective dose 100-300 mg/day divided bid, max 300 mg/day. OCD and ≥8 yo: Start 25 mg PO qhs, usual effective dose 50-200 mg/day divided bid, max 200 mg/day. Avoid with cisapride, diazepam, pimozide, and MAOIs; caution with benzodiazepines, TCAs, theophylline, and warfarin. [Generic/Trade: Tabs 25, 50, 100 mg. Trade discontinued indefinitely 5/02.] ▶L ♀C ▶- $$$$

paroxetine (***Paxil***): Start 20 mg PO qam, usual effective dose 20-50 mg/day, max 50 mg/day. Controlled release: start 25 mg/d, max 62.5 mg/d. OCD/ social phobia: Start 10-20 mg/day, usual effective dose 10-60 mg/day, max 60 mg/day. Panic disorder: Start 10 mg PO qam, increase by 10 mg/day at intervals ≥ 1 week to usual effective dose of 10-60 mg/day. Max 60 mg/day. Controlled-release: Start 12.5 mg/d, max 75 mg/d. Post-traumatic stress disorder: Start 20 mg PO qam, usual effective dose 20-40 mg/day, max 50 mg per day. [Trade: Tabs 10, 20, 30, 40 mg. tabs, controlled-release 12.5 mg and 25 mg. Oral suspension 10 mg/ 5 ml.] ▶LK ♀C ◗? $$$

sertraline (***Zoloft***): Depression/OCD: Start 50 mg PO qd, usual effective dose 50-200 mg/day, max 200 mg/day. Panic disorder/ Posttraumatic stress disorder: Start 25 mg PO qd, max 200 mg/day. Premenstrual dysphoric disorder: Start 50 mg PO qd (continuous) or 14 days prior to menses (intermittent), max 150 mg daily continuous or 100 mg daily intermittent. If used intemittently, start 50 mg PO qd x 3 days then increase to 100 mg. [Trade: Tabs 25, 50, 100 mg. oral concentrate 20 mg/ml.] ▶LK ♀C ◗+ $$$

Antidepressants - Other

bupropion (***Wellbutrin, Wellbutrin SR***): Depression: Start 100 mg PO bid, after 4-7 days can increase to 100 mg tid. Usual effective dose 300-450 mg/day. Max 150 mg/dose and 450 mg/day. Sustained release: Start 100-150 mg PO q am, after 4-7 days may increase to 150 mg bid, max 400 mg/d. Last dose no later than 5 pm. Contraindicated with seizures, bulimia, anorexia. Seizures in 0.4% at 300- 450 mg/d. [Generic/Trade: Tabs 75,100 mg. Trade only: sustained release Tabs 100, 150, 200 mg (Wellbutrin SR).] ▶LK ♀B ◗- $$$

mirtazapine (***Remeron, Remeron SolTab***): Start 15 mg PO qhs. Usual effective dose 15-45 mg/day. Agranulocytosis 0.1%. [Trade: Tabs 15, 30, 45 mg. Tabs, orally disintegrating (SolTab) 15, 30, 45 mg.] ▶LK ♀C ◗? $$$

nefazodone (***Serzone***): Start 100 mg PO bid, usual effective dose 150-300 mg PO bid, max 600 mg/day. Hepatotoxicity. Avoid with cisapride, MAOIs, or triazolam. [Trade: Tabs 50, 100, 150, 200, 250 mg.] ▶L ♀C ◗? $$$

trazodone (***Desyrel***): Start 50-150 mg/day PO in divided doses. Usual effective dose is 400-600 mg/day in divided doses. [Generic/Trade: Tabs 50, 100, 150. Trade only: Tabs 300 mg.] ▶L ♀C ◗- $$

venlafaxine (***Effexor, Effexor XR***): Depression/ anxiety: Start 37.5-75 mg PO qd (Effexor XR), max 225 mg/day; 75 mg/day (Effexor) PO divided bid-tid, max 375 mg/day. Usual effective dose 150-225 mg/day [Trade: Caps, extended release 37.5, 75, 150 mg. Tabs 25, 37.5, 50, 75, 100 mg.] ▶LK ♀C ◗? $$$$

Antimanic (Bipolar) Agents

carbamazepine (***Tegretol, Tegretol XR, Carbatrol, Epitol, Mazepine***): Mania: 200 mg PO qd- bid, increase by 200 mg/day q2-4 days. Mean effective dose = 1,000 mg/day. Aplastic anemia. [Trade: Tabs 200 mg (Tegretol, Epitol, Atretol) chew tabs 100 mg (Tegretol) Susp 100 mg/5 ml (Tegretol) extended release tabs 100, 200, 400 mg (Tegretol XR) extended release caps 200, 300 mg (Carbatrol). Generic: Tabs 200 mg. chew tabs 100 mg. susp 100 mg/5 ml.] ▶LK ♀D ◗+ $

gabapentin (***Neurontin***): Bipolar disorder (unapproved): Start 300 mg PO qhs, and increase over a few days to 300-600 mg PO tid, maximum 3600 mg/day. [Trade: Caps 100, 300, 400 mg. Tabs 600, 800 mg. solution 50 mg/ml.] ▶K ♀C ◗? $$$$

lamotrigine (***Lamictal, Lamictal CD***): Bipolar disorder (unapproved): Start 25-50 mg PO qd, titrate to 100-500 mg/day divided bid. Life-threatening rashes in 1:1000 adults and 1:50 children; discontinue if rash. Drug interaction with valproic acid (risk of rash increases); see product information for dosing guidelines. [Trade: Tabs 25,100,150,200 mg. Chewtabs 5,25 mg.] ▶LK ♀C ▶- $$$$

lithium (***Eskalith, Eskalith CR, Lithobid, Lithonate***, ***✤Lithane, Carbolith, Duralith***): Acute mania: Start 300-600 mg PO bid-tid, usual effective dose 900-1800 mg/d. 300 mg = 8 mEq or mmol. Steady state in 5d. Trough levels for acute mania 1.0-1.5 mEq/L, maintenance 0.6-1.2 mEq/L. Dose increase of 300 mg/day raises level by approx 0.2 mEq/L. Monitor renal, thyroid function. Diuretics and ACE inhibitors increase levels. Avoid dehydration, salt restriction and many NSAIDS (ASA & sulindac OK). [Generic/Trade: caps 150, 300, 600 mg, tabs 300 mg. Extended release tabs 300 mg. Trade only: 450 mg (Eskalith CR). Syrup 300 mg/5 ml.] ▶K ♀D ▶- $

topiramate (***Topamax***): Bipolar disorder (unapproved): Start 25-50 mg/day PO, titrate prn to max 400 mg/day. [Trade only: tabs 25, 100, 200 mg. sprinkle caps 15, 25 mg.] ▶K ♀C ▶? $$$$$

valproic acid (***Depakene, Depakote, Depakote ER, Depacon***, ***✤Epiject, Epival, Deproic***): Mania: 250 mg PO tid. Hepatotoxicity, drug interactions, reduce dose in elderly. [Generic/Trade: Caps (Depakene) 250 mg. syrup (Depakene) 250 mg/ 5 ml. Trade only: sprinkle Caps (Depakote) 125 mg. Tabs, delayed release (Depakote) 125, 250, 500 mg. Tabs, ext'd release (Depakote ER) 500 mg.] ▶L ♀D ▶+ $

Antipsychotics - Atypical - Serotonin Dopamine Receptor Antagonists

clozapine (***Clozaril***): Start 12.5 mg PO qd-bid. Usual effective dose 300-450 mg/ day divided bid. Max 900 mg/day. Agranulocytosis 1-2%; check WBC counts q week x 6 months, then q2 weeks. [Generic/Trade: Tabs 25, 100 mg.] ▶L ♀B ▶- $$$$$

olanzapine (***Zyprexa, Zyprexa Zydis***): Start 5-10 mg PO qd; usual effective dose 10-15 mg/day. Bipolar mania: Start 10-15 mg PO qd, usual effective dose 5-20 mg/day. Max 20 mg/day. [Trade: Tabs 2.5, 5, 7.5, 10, 15 mg. Tabs, orally disintegrating 5,10 mg (Zydis)] ▶L ♀C ▶- $$$$$

quetiapine (***Seroquel***): Psychotic disorders: Start 25 mg PO bid, increase by 25-50 mg bid-tid on day 2-3, to target dose of 300-400 mg/day divided bid-tid. Usual effective dose is150-750 mg/day. Max dose is 800 mg/day. Eye exam for cataracts recommended q 6 months. [Trade: Tabs 25, 100, 200 mg.] ▶LK ♀C ▶- $$$$$

risperidone (***Risperdal***): Start 1 mg PO bid (0.5 mg/dose in the elderly), slowly increase to usual effective dose of 4-8 mg/day divided qd-bid. Max 16 mg/day. Low EPS risk under 10 mg/day. [Trade: Tabs 0.25, 0.5, 1, 2, 3, 4 mg. oral solution 1 mg/ml.] ▶LK ♀C ▶- $$$$$

ziprasidone (***Geodon***): Start 20 mg PO bid with food, adjust at >2 day intervals to max 80 mg PO bid. Acute agitation: 10-20 mg IM, max 40 mg per day. [Trade: Caps 20,40,60,80 mg.] ▶L ♀C ▶- $$$$$

Antipsychotics - D2 Antagonists - High Potency (1-5 mg = 100 mg CPZ)

fluphenazine (***Prolixin, Permitil***, ***✤Modecate, Moditen***): 1.25- 10 mg/day IM divided q6-8h. Start 0.5- 10 mg/day PO divided q6-8h. Usual effective dose 1-20 mg/day. 2 mg = 100 CPZ. Depot (fluphenazine decanoate/ enanthate): 12.5-25 mg IM/SC q3 weeks = 10-20 mg/day PO fluphenazine. [Generic/Trade: Tabs 1, 2.5, 5, 10 mg. elixir 2.5 mg/5 ml. oral concentrate 5 mg/ml.] ▶LK ♀C ▶? $$

haloperidol (***Haldol***): 2-5 mg IM. Start 0.5- 5 mg PO bid-tid, usual effective dose 6-

20 mg/day. Therapeutic range 2-15 ng/ml. 2 mg = 100 mg CPZ. Depot haloperidol (haloperidol decanoate): 100-200 mg IM q4 weeks = 10 mg/day oral haloperidol. [Generic/Trade: Tabs 0.5,1,2,5,10,20 mg, oral concentrate 2 mg/ml] ▶LK ♀C ▶- $

perphenazine (***Trilafon***): Start 4-8 mg PO tid or 8-16 mg PO bid-qid (hospitalized patients), maximum 64 mg/day PO. Can give 5-10 mg IM q6h, maximum 30 mg/day IM. [Generic/Trade: Tabs 2, 4, 8, 16 mg. Oral concentrate 16 mg/5 ml.] ▶LK ♀C ▶? $$

pimozide (***Orap***): Tourette's: Start 1-2 mg/day PO in divided doses, increase q2 days to usual effective dose of 1-10 mg/day. [Trade only: Tabs 1, 2 mg.] ▶L ♀C ▶- $$$

thiothixene (***Navane***): Start 2 mg PO tid. Usual effective dose is 20-30 mg/day, maximum 60 mg/day PO. Can give 4 mg IM bid-qid. Usual effective dose is 16-20 mg/day IM, maximum 30 mg/day IM. [Generic/Trade: Caps 1, 2, 5, 10. oral concentrate 5 mg/ml. Trade only: Caps 20 mg.] ▶LK ♀C ▶? $$

trifluoperazine (***Stelazine***): Start 2-5 mg PO bid. Usual effective dose is 15- 20 mg/day. Can give 1-2 mg IM q4-6h prn, maximum 10 mg/day IM. [Generic/Trade: Tabs 1, 2, 5, 10 mg. Trade only: oral concentrate 10 mg/ml.] ▶LK ♀C ▶- $$

Antipsychotics - D2 Antagonists - Mid Potency (10 mg = 100 mg CPZ)

loxapine (***Loxitane***): 12.5-50 mg IM q4-12h. Start 10 mg PO bid, usual effective dose 60-100 mg/day. Max 250 mg/day. 15 mg = 100 mg CPZ. [Generic/Trade: Caps 5, 10, 25, 50 mg. Trade only: oral concentrate 25 mg/ml.] ▶LK ♀C ▶- $$$

molindone (***Moban***): Start 50- 75 mg/day PO divided tid- qid, usual effective dose 50-100 mg/day. Max 225 mg/day. 10 mg = 100 mg CPZ. [Trade: Tabs 5, 10, 25, 50, 100 mg. oral concentrate 20 mg/ml.] ▶LK ♀C ▶? $$$$$

Antipsychotics - D2 Antagonists - Low Potency (50-100 mg = 100 mg CPZ)

chlorpromazine (***Thorazine***): Start 10-50 mg PO/IM bid-tid, usual dose 300-800 mg/d. [Generic/Trade: Tabs 10, 25, 50, 100, 200 mg. oral concentrate 30 mg/ml, 100 mg/ml. Trade only: sustained release Caps 30, 75, 150 mg. syrup 10 mg/5 ml. suppositories 25, 100 mg.] ▶LK ♀C ▶- $

mesoridazine (***Serentil***): Schizophrenia: 50 mg PO tid, usual effective dose is 100-400 mg/day. Can prolong QT interval. [Trade: Tabs 10, 25, 50, 100 mg. oral concentrate 25 mg/ml.] ▶LK ♀C ▶- $$$$

thioridazine (***Mellaril***): Start 50-100 mg PO tid, usual dose 200-800 mg/day. 100 mg = 100 mg CPZ. Not first-line therapy. Causes QTc prolongation, torsade de pointes, and sudden death. Contraindicated with SSRIs, propranolol, pindolol. Monitor baseline ECG and potassium. Pigmentary retinopathy with doses> 800 mg/d. [Generic/Trade: Tabs 10, 15, 25, 50, 100, 150, 200 mg. oral concentrate 30, 100 mg/ml. Trade only: oral suspension 25, 100 mg/5 ml.] ▶LK ♀C ▶? $

Anxiolytics / Hypnotics - Benzodiazepines - Long Half-life (25-100 hours)

chlordiazepoxide (***Librium***): Anxiety: 5-25 mg PO or 25-50 mg IM/IV tid-qid. Acute alcohol withdrawal: 50-100 mg PO/IM/IV, repeat q3-4h prn up to 300 mg/day. Half-life 5-30 h. [Generic/Trade: Caps 5, 10, 25 mg.] ▶LK ♀D ▶- ©IV $

clonazepam (***Klonopin***, ***♣Rivotril***): Start 0.25-0.5 mg PO bid-tid, max 4 mg/day. Half-life 18- 50 h. [Generic/Trade: Tabs 0.5, 1, 2 mg.] ▶LK ♀D ▶? ©IV $$

clorazepate (***Tranxene***): Start 7.5-15 mg PO qhs or bid-tid, usual effective dose is 15-60 mg/day. Acute alcohol withdrawal: 60-90 mg/day on first day divided bid-tid, reduce dose to 7.5-15 mg/day over 5 days. [Generic/Trade: Tabs 3.75, 7.5, 15 mg. Trade only: sustained release Tabs 11.25, 22.5 mg.] ▶LK ♀D ▶- ©IV $$

diazepam (***Valium***): Anxiety: 2-10 mg PO bid-qid. Half-life 20-80h. [Generic/Trade: Tabs 2, 5, 10 mg. oral solution 5 mg/ 5 ml. Trade only: oral concentrate (Intensol) 5 mg/ml.] ▶LK ♀D ▶- ©IV $

flurazepam (***Dalmane***): 15-30 mg PO qhs. Half-life 70-90h. [Generic/Trade: Caps 15, 30 mg.] ▶LK ♀X ▶- ©IV $

Anxiolytics / Hypnotics - Benzodiazepines - Medium Half-Life (10-15 hours)

estazolam (***ProSom***): 1-2 mg PO qhs. [Generic/Trade: Tabs 1, 2 mg.] ▶LK ♀X ▶- ©IV $$

lorazepam (***Ativan***): 0.5-2 mg IV/IM/PO q6-8h, max 10 mg/d. Half-life 10-20h. [Generic/Trade: Tabs 0.5, 1, 2 mg. Trade only: oral concentrate 2 mg/ml.] ▶LK ♀D ▶- ©IV $$$

temazepam (***Restoril***): 7.5-30 mg PO qhs. Half-life 8-25h. [Generic/Trade: Caps 7.5, 15, 30 mg.] ▶LK ♀X ▶- ©IV $

Anxiolytics / Hypnotics - Benzodiazepines - Short Half-Life (<12 hours)

alprazolam (***Xanax***): 0.25-0.5 mg PO bid-tid. Half-life 12h. Multiple drug interactions. [Generic/Trade: Tabs 0.25, 0.5, 1, 2 mg. Trade only: oral concentrate 1 mg/ml.] ▶LK ♀D ▶- ©IV $

oxazepam (***Serax***): 10-30 mg PO tid-qid. Half-life 8h. [Generic/Trade: Caps 10, 15, 30 mg.] ▶LK ♀D ▶- ©IV $$

triazolam (***Halcion***): 0.125-0.5 mg PO qhs. 0.125 mg/day in elderly. Half-life 2-3h. [Generic/Trade: Tabs 0.125, 0.25 mg.] ▶LK ♀X ▶- ©IV $

Anxiolytics / Hypnotics - Other

buspirone (***BuSpar***): Anxiety: Start 15 mg "dividose" daily (7.5 mg PO bid), usual effective dose 30 mg/day. Max 60 mg/day. [Generic/Trade: tabs 5, 7.5,10, 15 mg. Trade only: dividose tab 15,30 mg (scored to be easily bisected or trisected).] ▶K ♀B ▶- $$$

chloral hydrate (***Somnote, Aquachloral Supprettes***): 25-50 mg/kg/day up to 1000 mg PO/PR. Many physicians use higher than recommended doses in children (eg, 75 mg/kg). [Generic/Trade: Caps 500 mg, syrup 500 mg/ 5 ml, suppositories 500 mg. Trade only: suppositories: 324, 648 mg.] ▶LK ♀C ▶+ ©IV $

diphenhydramine (***Benadryl, Banaril, Allermax, Diphen, Dytuss, Sominex, Tusstat, Truxadryl***): Insomnia: 25-50 mg PO qhs. Peds ≥12 yo: 50 mg PO qhs. [OTC/Generic/Trade: Tabs 25, 50 mg. OTC/Trade only: chew Tabs 12.5 mg. OTC/Rx/Generic/Trade: Caps 25, 50 mg. oral solution 12.5 mg/5 ml.] ▶LK ♀B(- in 1st trimester) ▶- $

pentobarbital (***Nembutal***): 20-150 mg PO/IV/IM/PR tid-qid. Peds: 2-6 mg/kg/day. [Trade: Caps 50, 100 mg. suppositories 60, 200 mg.] ▶LK ♀D ▶? ©II $

zaleplon (***Sonata***, ***✦Starnoc***): 5-10 mg PO qhs prn, max 20 mg. Do not use for benzodiazepine or alcohol withdrawal. [Trade: Caps 5, 10 mg.] ▶L ♀C ▶- ©IV $$$

zolpidem (***Ambien***): 5-10 mg PO qhs. Do not use for benzodiazepine or alcohol withdrawal. [Trade: Tabs 5, 10 mg.] ▶L ♀B ▶+ ©IV $$$

Combination Drugs

Etrafon, Triavil (perphenazine + amitriptyline): Rarely used. 1 tablet (2-25 or 4-25) PO tid-qid or 1 tablet (4-50) PO bid. [Generic/Trade: Tabs, perphenazine/amitriptyline: 2/10, 2/25, 4/10, 4/25, 4/50.] ▶LK ♀D ▶? $

Limbitrol (chlordiazepoxide + amitriptyline): Rarely used. 1 tablet PO tid-qid. [Generic/Trade: Tabs, chlordiazepoxide/amitript.: 5/12.5,10/25.] ▶LK ♀D ▶- ©IV $$

Drug Dependence Therapy

bupropion (**Zyban**): Start 150 mg PO qam x 3d, then increase to 150 mg PO bid x 7-12 wks. Max dose 150 mg PO bid. Last dose no later than 5 pm. Contraindicated with seizures, bulimia, anorexia. Seizures in 0.4% at 300-450 mg/day. [Trade: sustained release Tabs 150 mg.] ▶LK ♀B ▶- $$$

clonidine (**Catapres, Catapres TTS**): Opioid/ nicotine withdrawal, alcohol withdrawal adjunct (not FDA approved): 0.1- 0.3 mg PO tid- qid. Transdermal Therapeutic System (TTS) is designed for seven day use so that a TTS-1 delivers 0.1 mg/day x 7 days. May supplement first dose of TTS with oral x 2-3 days while therapeutic level is achieved. [Generic/Trade: Tabs 0.1, 0.2, 0.3 mg. Trade only: patch TTS-1, TTS- 2, TTS- 3.] ▶LK ♀C ▶? $

disulfiram (**Antabuse**): Sobriety: 125-500 mg PO qd. Patient must abstain from any alcohol for ≥12 h before using. Metronidazole & alcohol in any form (cough syrups, tonics, etc.) contraindicated. [Generic/Trade: Tabs 250,500 mg.] ▶L ♀C ▶? $

methadone (**Dolophine, Methadose**): Narcotic dependence: 15-60 mg PO q6-8h. Treatment >3 wks is maintenance and only permitted in approved treatment programs. [Generic/Trade: Tabs 5, 10, 40 mg. oral solution 5 & 10 mg/5 ml. oral concentrate 10 mg/ml.] ▶L ♀B ▶? ©II $$

naltrexone (**ReVia, Depade**): Alcohol/narcotic dependence: 25-50 mg PO qd. Avoid if recent ingestion of opioids (past 7-10 days). Hepatotoxicity with higher than approved doses. [Generic/Trade: Tabs 50 mg.] ▶LK ♀C ▶? $$$$

nicotine gum (**Nicorette, Nicorette DS**): Smoking cessation: Gradually taper 1 piece q1-2h x 6 weeks, 1 piece q2-4h x 3 weeks, then 1 piece q4-8h x 3 weeks, max 30 pieces/day of 2 mg or 24 pieces/day of 4 mg. Use Nicorette DS 4 mg/piece in high cigarette use (> 24 cigarettes/day). [OTC/Generic/Trade: gum 2, 4 mg.] ▶LK ♀X ▶- $$$$$

nicotine inhalation system (**Nicotrol Inhaler**): 6-16 cartridges/day x 12 weeks [Trade: Oral inhaler 10 mg/cartridge (4 mg nicotine delivered), 42 cartridges/box.] ▶LK ♀D ▶- $$$$$

nicotine nasal spray (**Nicotrol NS**): Smoking cessation:1-2 doses each hour, with each dose = 2 sprays, one in each nostril (1 spray = 0.5 mg nicotine). Minimum recommended: 8 doses/day, max 40 doses/day. [Trade: nasal solution 10 mg/ml (0.5 mg/inhalation); 10 ml bottles.] ▶LK ♀D ▶- $$$$$

nicotine patches (**Habitrol, Nicoderm, Nicotrol**): Smoking cessation: Start one patch (14-22 mg) qd, taper after 6 wks. Ensure patient has stopped smoking. [OTC/Rx/Generic/Trade: patches 11, 22 mg/ 24 hours. 7, 14, 21 mg/ 24 h (Habitrol & Nicoderm). OTC/Trade: 15 mg/ 16 h (Nicotrol).] ▶LK ♀D ▶- $$$

Sympathomimetics / Stimulants / Anorexiants

Adderall (dextroamphetamine + racemic amphetamine): ADHD: Start 2.5 mg (3-5 yo) or 5 mg (≥6 yo) PO qd-bid, increase by 2.5-5 mg every week, max 40 mg/d. May give 10 mg PO qd (Adderall XR); max 30 mg/d. Narcolepsy: Start 5-10 mg PO q am, increase by 5-10 mg q week, max 60 mg/d. Avoid evening doses. Monitor growth and use drug holidays when appropriate. [Trade/Generic: Tabs 5, 10, 20, 30 mg. Trade: Capsules, extended release (Adderall XR) 10, 20, 30 mg.] ▶L ♀C ▶- ©II $$

caffeine (**NoDoz, Vivarin, Caffedrine, Stay Awake, Quick-Pep**): 100-200 mg PO q3-4h prn. [OTC/Generic/Trade: Tabs 200 mg. OTC/Trade: extended release Tabs 200 mg.] ▶L ♀B ▶? $

dexmethylphenidate (**Focalin**): ADHD: Patients not taking stimulants start 2.5 mg

PO bid, max 20 mg/24 hr. Patients taking racemic methylphenidate use conversion of 2.5 mg for each 5 mg of methylphenidate, max 20 mg/d. [Trade: tabs 2.5 mg, 5 mg, 10 mg.] ▶LK ♀C ▶? ©II $$

dextroamphetamine (***Dexedrine, Dextrostat***): Narcolepsy/ADHD: 2.5-10 mg PO qam or bid-tid or 10-15 mg PO qd (sustained release), max 60 mg/d. Avoid evening doses. Monitor growth & use drug holidays when appropriate. [Trade: Tabs 5, 10 mg. Trade/Generic: Sust'd release caps 5, 10, 15 mg.] ▶L ♀C ▶- ©II $$

methylphenidate (***Ritalin, Ritalin LA, Ritalin SR, Methylin, Methylin ER, Metadate ER, Metadate CD, Concerta***): ADHD/Narcolepsy: 5-10 mg PO bid-tid or 20 mg PO qam (sustained and extended release), max 60 mg/d. Or 18-36 mg PO qam (Concerta), max 54 mg/day. Avoid evening doses. Monitor growth and use drug holidays when appropriate. [Trade: tabs 5, 10, 20 mg (Ritalin, Methylin, Metadate). Extended release tabs 10, 20 mg (Methylin ER, Metadate ER). Extended release tabs 18, 27, 36, 54 mg (Concerta). Extended release caps 20 mg (Metadate CD). Sustained-release tabs 20 mg (Ritalin SR). Extended release caps 20, 30, 40 mg (Ritalin LA). Generic: tabs 5, 10, 20 mg, extended release tabs 20 mg, sustained-release tabs 20 mg.] ▶LK ♀C ▶? ©II $

modafinil (***Provigil, Alertec***): 200 mg PO qam. [Trade: Tabs 100, 200 mg.] ▶L ♀C ▶? ©IV $$$$

phentermine (***Adipex-P, Ionamin, Phentride, Phentercot, Teramine, Pro-Fast, OBY-Trim***): 8 mg PO tid or 15-37.5 mg/day q am or 10-14 h before retiring. For short-term use. [Generic/Trade: Caps 15, 18.75, 30, 37.5 mg. Tabs 8, 37.5 mg. Trade only: extended release Caps 15, 30 mg (Ionamin).] ▶KL ♀C ▶- ©IV $

sibutramine (***Meridia***): Start 10 mg PO q am, max 15 mg/d. Monitor pulse and BP. [Trade: Caps 5, 10, 15 mg.] ▶KL ♀C ▶- ©IV $$$

BODY MASS INDEX*		Heights are in feet and inches; weights are in pounds					
BMI	*Classification*	*4'10"*	*5'0"*	*5'4"*	*5'8"*	*6'0"*	*6'4"*
<18	Underweight	<91	<97	<110	<125	<140	<156
18-24	Healthy Weight	91-119	97-127	110-144	125-163	140-183	156-204
25-29	Overweight	120-143	128-152	145-173	164-196	184-220	205-245
30-40	Obese	144-191	153-204	174-233	197-262	221-293	246-328
>40	Very Obese	>191	>204	>233	>262	>293	>328

*BMI = kg/m^2 = (weight in pounds)(703)/(height in inches)^2. Anorectants appropriate if BMI ≥30 (with comoribidities ≥27); surgery an option if BMI >40 (with comorbidities 35-40). www.nhlbi.nih.gov

Other Agents

benztropine (***Cogentin, Bensylate***): EPS: 1-4 mg PO/IM/IV qd-bid. [Generic/Trade: Tabs 0.5, 1, 2 mg.] ▶LK ♀C ▶? $

clonidine (***Catapres***): ADHD (unapproved peds): 5 mcg/kg/day PO x 8 weeks. [Generic/Trade: Tabs 0.1, 0.2, 0.3 mg. Trade only: patch TTS-1, TTS-2, TTS-3.] ▶LK ♀C ▶? $

diphenhydramine (***Benadryl, Banaril, Allermax Diphen, Dytuss, Sominex, Tusstat, Truxadryl, ✤Allerdryl, Allernix***): EPS: 25-50 mg PO tid-qid or 10-50 mg IV/IM tid-qid. [OTC/Generic/Trade: Tabs 25, 50 mg. OTC/Trade only: chew Tabs 12.5 mg. OTC/Rx/Generic/Trade: Caps 25, 50 mg. oral solution 12.5 mg/5 ml.] ▶LK ♀B(- in 1st trimester) ▶- $

fluoxetine (***Sarafem***): Premenstrual Dysphoric Disorder (PMDD): 20 mg PO qd continuously, or 20 mg PO qd for 14 days prior to menses, max 80 mg daily. [Trade: Caps 10, 20 mg.] ▶L ♀C ▶- $$$

guanfacine (***Tenex***): ADHD (unapproved peds): Start 0.5 mg PO qd, titrate by 0.5 mg q3-4 days as tolerated to 0.5 mg PO tid. [Generic/Trade: Tabs 1, 2 mg.] ▶K ♀B ▶? $$

PULMONARY

Beta Agonists

albuterol (***Ventolin, Ventolin HFA, Proventil, Proventil HFA, Volmax, Ventodisk, ♣Alromir, Asmavent, Salbutamol***): MDI 2 puffs q4-6h prn. 0.5 ml of 0.5% soln (2.5 mg) nebulized tid-qid. One 3 ml unit dose (0.083%) nebulized tid-qid. Caps for inhalation 200-400 mcg q4-6h. 2-4 mg PO tid-qid or extended release 4-8 mg PO q12h up to 16 mg PO q12h. Children 2-5 yo: 0.1-0.2 mg/kg/dose PO tid up to 4 mg tid; 6-12 yo: 2-4 mg. [Generic/Trade: MDI 90 mcg/actuation, 200/canister. "HFA" inhalers use hydrofluoroalkane propellant instead of CFCs but are otherwise equivalent. Soln for inhalation 0.5% (5 mg/ml) in 20 ml with dropper. Nebules for inhalation 3 ml unit dose 0.083%. Trade only:1.25 mg & 0.63 mg/3 ml unit dose.Tabs 2 & 4 mg. Syrup 2 mg/5 ml. Trade: extended release tabs 4 & 8 mg. Caps for inhalation 200 mcg microfine in 24s & 96s w/ Rotahaler.] ▶L ♀C ▶? $

bitolterol (***Tornalate***): Soln for inhalation 0.5-1 ml tid-qid via intermittent flow or 1.25 ml tid-qid via continuous flow. [Trade: Soln for inhalation 0.2% (2 mg/ml) with dropper.] ▶L ♀C ▶? $$

formoterol (***Foradil Aerolizer***): 1 puff bid. Not for acute bronchospasm. [Trade: DPI 12 mcg, 60 blisters/pack.] ▶L ♀C ▶? $$$

levalbuterol (***Xopenex***): 0.63-1.25 mg nebulized q6-8h. 6-11 yo: 0.31 mg nebulized tid. [Trade: soln for inhalation 0.63 & 1.25 mg in 3 ml unit-dose vials.] ▶L ♀C ▶? $$$$

metaproterenol (***Alupent, Metaprel, Pro-Meta***): MDI 2-3 puffs q3-4h: 0.2-0.3 ml 5% soln nebulized q4h. 20 mg PO tid-qid > 9 yo, 10 mg PO tid-qid if 6-9 yo, 1.3-2.6 mg/kg/day divided tid-qid if 2-5 yo. [Trade: MDI 0.65 mg/actuation in 100 & 200/canister. Trade/Generic: Soln for inhalation 0.4, 0.6% in unit-dose vials; 5% in 10 & 30 ml with dropper. Syrup 10 mg/5 ml. Generic: Tabs 10 & 20 mg.] ▶L ♀C ▶? $$

pirbuterol (***Maxair Autohaler***): 1-2 puffs q4-6h. [Trade: MDI 0.2 mg/actuation, 400/canister.] ▶L ♀C ▶? $$

salmeterol (***Serevent, Serevent Diskus***): 2 puffs bid (Serevent). 1 puff bid (Serevent Diskus). Not for acute bronchospasm. [Trade: MDI: 25 mcg/actuation, 60 & 120/canister. DPI (Diskus): 50 mcg, 60 blisters.] ▶L ♀C ▶? $$$

terbutaline (***Brethine, Bricanyl***): 2.5-5 mg PO q6h while awake in >12 yo. 0.25 mg SC. [Trade: Tabs 2.5 & 5 mg (Brethine scored).] ▶L ♀B ▶- $$

Combinations

Advair Diskus (fluticasone + salmeterol): 1 puff bid. [Trade: DPI: 100/50, 250/50, 500/50 mcg fluticasone propionate/mcg salmeterol per actuation.] ▶L ♀C ▶? $$$-$$$$

Combivent (albuterol + ipratropium): 2 puffs qid, max 12 puffs/day. Contraindicated with soy & peanut allergy. [Trade: MDI: 90 mcg albuterol sulfate/18 mcg ipratropium bromide per actuation, 200/canister.] ▶L ♀C ▶? $$

DuoNeb (albuterol + ipratropium): One unit dose qid. [Trade: Unit dose: 3 mg albuterol sulfate/0.5 mg ipratropium bromide per 3 ml vial, premixed. 30 & 60 vials/carton.] ▶L ♀C ▶? $$$$

INHALED STEROIDS: ESTIMATED COMPARATIVE DAILY DOSES*

Drug	*Form*	*ADULT*			*CHILD (≤12 yo)*		
		Low	*Medium*	*High*	*Low*	*Medium*	*High*
beclomethasone MDI	40 mcg/puff	2-6	6-12	>12	2-4	4-8	>8
	80 mcg/puff	1-3	3-6	>6	1-2	2-4	>4
budesonide DPI	200 mcg/dose	1-3	3-6	>6	1-2	2-4	>4
	Soln for nebs	-	-	-	0.5 mg	1 mg	2 mg
flunisolide MDI	250 mcg/puff	2-4	4-8	>8	2-3	4-5	>5
fluticasone MDI	44 mcg/puff	2-6	6-15	>15	2-4	4-10	>10
	110 mcg/puff	1-2	3-6	>6	1	1-4	>4
	220 mcg/puff	1	2-3	>3	n/a	1-2	>2
fluticasone DPI	50 mcg/dose	2-6	6-12	>12	2-4	4-8	>8
	100 mcg/dose	1-3	3-6	>6	1-2	2-4	>4
	250 mcg/dose	1	2	>2	n/a	1	>1
triamcinolone MDI	100 mcg/puff	4-10	10-20	>20	4-8	8-12	>12

*MDI=metered dose inhaler. DPI=dry powder inhaler. All doses in puffs (MDI) or inhalations (DPI).
Reference: http://www.nhlbi.nih.gov/guidelines/asthma/execsumm.pdf

Inhaled Steroids (See Endocrine-Corticosteroids when oral steroids necessary)

beclomethasone dipropionate (***Beclovent, Vanceril, QVAR***, ✤***Beclodisk***): Beclovent, Vanceril: 2 puffs tid-qid or 4 puffs bid. QVAR: 1-4 puffs bid (40 mcg). 1-2 puffs bid (80 mcg). [Trade: Beclovent, Vanceril MDI: 42mcg/ actuation, 80 & 200/canister. QVAR MDI (non-CFC): 40 mcg & 80 mcg/actuation, 100 actuations/canister.] ▶L ♀C ◗? $$

budesonide (***Pulmicort Turbuhaler, Pulmicort Respules***): 1-2 puffs qd-bid. [Trade: DPI: 200 mcg powder/actuation, 200/canister. Respules: 0.25 mg/2 ml & 0.5 mg/2 ml unit dose.] ▶L ♀B ◗? $$$$

flunisolide (***AeroBid, AeroBid-M***, ✤***Rhinalar***): 2-4 puffs bid. [Trade: MDI: 250 mcg/actuation, 100/canister. AeroBid-M: menthol flavor.] ▶L ♀C ◗? $$$

fluticasone (***Flovent, Flovent Rotadisk***): MDI: 2-4 puffs bid. DPI: 1 puff bid, max 2 puffs bid. [Trade: MDI: 44, 110, 220 mcg/actuation in 60 & 120/canister. DPI (Rotadisk): 50, 100, & 250 mcg/actuation, in 4 blisters containing 15 Rotadisks (total of 60 doses) with inhalation device.] ▶L ♀C ◗? $$$

triamcinolone acetonide (***Azmacort***): 2 puffs tid-qid or 4 puffs bid; max 16 puffs/day. [Trade: MDI: 100 mcg/actuation, 240/canister. Built-in spacer.] ▶L ♀D ◗? $$$

Leukotriene Inhibitors

montelukast (***Singulair***): Adults: 10 mg PO qpm. Children 2-5 yo: 4 mg po q pm. 6-14 yo: 5 mg PO q pm. [Trade: Tabs 4, 5 mg (chew cherry flavored) & 10 mg. Oral granules 4 mg packet, 30/box.] ▶L ♀B ◗? $$$

PREDICTED PEAK EXPIRATORY FLOW (liters/min) *Am Rev Resp Dis* 1963; 88:644

Age (yrs)	**Women** *(height in inches)* 55"	60"	65"	70"	75"	**Men** *(height in inches)* 60"	65"	70"	75"	80"	**Child** *(height in inches)*	
20	390	423	460	496	529	554	602	649	693	740	44"	160
30	380	413	448	483	516	532	577	622	664	710	46"	187
40	370	402	436	470	502	509	552	596	636	680	48"	214
50	360	391	424	457	488	486	527	569	607	649	50"	240
60	350	380	412	445	475	463	502	542	578	618	52"	267
70	340	369	400	432	461	440	477	515	550	587	54"	293

zafirlukast (***Accolate***): 20 mg PO bid. Peds 5-11 yo, 10 mg PO bid. Take 1h ac or 2h pc. Potentiates warfarin & theophylline. [Trade: Tabs 10,20 mg.] ▶L ♀B ▶- $$$

zileuton (***Zyflo***): 600 mg PO qid. Hepatotoxicity, potentiates warfarin & theophylline. [Trade: Tabs 600 mg.] ▶L ♀C ▶? $$$$

WHAT COLOR IS WHAT INHALER? (Body then cap - Generics may differ)

Advair	purple	*Flovent*	orange/ peach	*Pulmicort*	white/brown
Aerobid	grey/purple	*Foradil*	grey/beige	*QVAR* 40mcg	beige/grey
Aerobid-M	grey/green	*Intal*	white/blue	*QVAR* 80mcg	mauve/grey
Alupent	clear/blue	*Maxair*	blue/white	*Serevent*	teal/light teal
Atrovent	clear/green	*Maxair Autohaler*	white/white	*Tilade*	white/white
Azmacort	white/white			*Tornalate*	blue/blue
Combivent	clear/orange	*Proventil*	yellow/ orange	*Ventolin*	light blue/navy

Other Pulmonary Medications

acetylcysteine (***Mucomyst, Mucosil-10, Mucosil-20, Parvolex***): Mucolytic: 3-5 ml of 20% or 6-10 ml of 10% soln nebulized tid-qid. [Generic/Trade: soln 10 & 20% in 4,10, & 30 ml vials.] ▶L ♀B ▶? $$$

aminophylline: Asthma: loading dose: 6 mg/kg IV over 20-30 min. Maintenance 0.5-0.7 mg/kg/h IV. [Generic: Tabs 100 & 200 mg. Oral liquid 105 mg/5 ml. Trade: Tabs controlled release (12hr) 225 mg, scored.] ▶L ♀C ▶? $

cromolyn sodium (***Intal, Gastrocrom, Nalcrom***): Asthma: 2-4 puffs qid or 20 mg nebs qid. Prevention of exercise-induced bronchospasm: 2 puffs 10-15 min prior to exercise. Mastocytosis: Oral concentrate 200 mg PO qid for adults, 100 mg qid in children 2-12 yo. [Trade: MDI 800 mcg/actuation, 112 & 200/canister. Oral concentrate 5 ml/100 mg in 8 amps/foil pouch. Generic/Trade: Soln for nebs: 20 mg/2 ml.] ▶LK ♀B ▶? $$$

dexamethasone (***Decadron***): BPD preterm infants: 0.5 mg/kg PO/IV divided q12h x 3 days, then taper. Croup: 0.15-0.6 mg/kg PO or IM x 1. Acute asthma: >2 yo: 0.6 mg/kg to max 16 mg PO qd x 2 days. [Generic/Trade: Tabs 0.25, 0.5, 0.75, 1, 1.5, 2, 4, & 6 mg, various scored. Elixir: 0.5 mg/5 ml. Oral soln: 0.5 mg/5 ml & 0.5 mg/0.5 ml.] ▶L ♀C ▶- $

dornase alfa (***Pulmozyme***): Cystic fibrosis: 2.5 mg nebulized qd-bid. [Trade: soln for inhalation: 1 mg/ml in 2.5 ml vials.] ▶L ♀B ▶? $$$$$

epinephrine (***EpiPen, EpiPen Jr.***): Acute asthma & hypersensitivity reactions in adults: 0.1 to 0.3 mg of 1:1,000 soln SC. Peds: 0.01 mg/kg (up to 0.3 mg) of 1:1,000 soln SC. Sustained release: 0.005 mg/kg (up to 0.15 mg) of 1:200 soln SC. [Soln for inj: 1:1,000 (1 mg/ml in 1 ml amps). Sust'd formulation (Sus-Phrine): 1:200 (5 mg/ml) in 0.3 ml amps or 5 ml multi-dose vials. Injectable allergy kit in single-dose auto-injectors: Epipen (0.3 mg), Epipen Jr (0.15 mg).] ▶Plasma ♀C ▶- $$

epinephrine racemic (***AsthmaNefrin, MicroNefrin, Nephron, S-2***): Severe croup: 0.05 ml/kg/dose diluted to 3 ml w/NS. Max dose 0.5 ml. [Trade: soln for inhalation: 2.25% racepinephrine in 15 & 30 ml.] ▶Plasma ♀C ▶- $

ipratropium (***Atrovent***): 2-3 puffs qid, or one 500 mcg vial neb tid-qid. Contraindicated with soy & peanut allergy. [Trade: MDI: 18mcg/actuation, 200/canister. Generic/Trade: Soln for nebulization: 0.02% (500 mcg/vial) in unit dose vials.] ▶Lung ♀B ▶? $$

nedocromil (***Tilade***): 2 puffs qid. Reduce as tolerated [Trade: MDI: 1.75 mg/actuation, 112/canister.] ▶L ♀B ▶? $$

theophylline (***Elixophyllin, Uniphyl, Theo-24, T-Phyl***): 5-13 mg/kg/day PO in divided doses. Max dose 900 mg/day. Peds dosing variable. [Trade: Elixophyllin Liquid 80 mg/15 ml. Qd sustained release tabs: Uniphyl 400, 600 mg. Caps:Theo-24: 100, 200, 300, 400 mg. Bid sustained release tabs: T-Phyl 200 mg. Generic: Theophylline ER tabs: 100, 200, 300 mg. Caps: 125, 200, 300 mg.] ▶L ♀C ▶+ $

TOXICOLOGY

acetylcysteine (***Mucomyst***): Acetaminophen toxicity: Load 140 mg/kg PO or NG, then 70 mg/kg q4h x 17 doses. May be mixed in water or soft drink diluted to a 5% solution. IV use possible (orphan drug); consult poison center. Renal impairment, prophylaxis prior to contrast agents: 600 mg PO bid on the day before and on the day of administration of contrast agents. [Generic/Trade: solution 10%, 20%.] ▶L ♀B ▶? $$$$

charcoal (**activated charcoal, *Actidose-Aqua, CharcoAid, EZ-Char*, *✤Charcodate***): 0.5-1 g/kg up to 100 g PO. May repeat q4h. When sorbitol is coadministered, use only with the first dose if repeated doses are to be given. [OTC/Generic/Trade: Tabs 250 mg, Caps 260 mg, Pellets 25 g, solution 15 g/72 ml, 25 g/ 120 ml, 50 g/240 ml.] ▶Not absorbed ♀+ ▶+ $

deferoxamine (***Desferal***): Chronic iron overload: 500-1000 mg IM qd and 2 g IV infusion (≤15 mg/kg/hr) with each unit of blood or 1-2 g SC qd (20-40 mg/kg/day) over 8-24 h via continuous infusion pump. Acute iron toxicity: IV infusion up to 15 mg/kg/hr (consult poison center). ▶K ♀C ▶? $$$$$

dimercaprol (***BAL in oil***): Specialized dosing for arsenic, mercury, gold, lead toxicity; consult poison center. ▶KL ♀C ▶? $$$$$

edetate disodium (***EDTA, Endrate, Meritate***): Specialized dosing for lead toxicity; consult poison center. ▶K ♀C ▶- $$$

ethanol: Specialized dosing for methanol, ethylene glycol toxicity if fomepizole is unavailable or delayed. ▶L ♀D ▶+ ?

flumazenil (***Romazicon, ✤Anexate***): benzodiazepine sedation reversal: 0.2 mg IV over 15 sec, then 0.2 mg q1 min prn up to 1 mg total dose. Overdose reversal: 0.2 mg IV over 30 sec, then 0.3-0.5 mg q30 sec prn up to 3 mg total dose. Contraindicated in mixed drug OD or chronic benzodiazepine use. ▶LK ♀C ▶? $$$

fomepizole (***Antizol***): Specialized dosing in ethylene glycol or methanol toxicity. ▶L ♀C ▶? $$$$$

ipecac syrup: Emesis: 30 ml PO for adults, 15 ml if 1-12 yo. [Generic/OTC: syrup.] ▶Gut ♀C ▶? $

methylene blue (***Urolene blue***): Methemoglobinemia: 1-2 mg/kg IV over 5 min. ▶K ♀C ▶? $$

penicillamine (***Cuprimine, Depen***): Specialized dosing for copper toxicity. [Trade: Caps 125, 250 mg; Tabs 250 mg.] ▶K ♀D ▶- $$$$

pralidoxime (***Protopam***): Organophosphate poisoning; consult poison center: 1-2 g IV infusion over 15-30 min or slow IV injection ≥5 min (max rate 200 mg/min). May repeat dose after 1 h if muscle weakness persists. Peds: 20-50 mg/kg/dose IV over 15-30 min. ▶K ♀C ▶? $$$

sorbitol: Cathartic: 30- 50 ml of 70% soln PO. [Generic: oral solution 70%.] ▶Not absorbed ♀+ ▶+ $

succimer (***Chemet***): Lead toxicity in children ≥1 yo: Start 10 mg/kg PO or 350 mg/m2 q8h x 5 days, then reduce the frequency to q12h x 2 weeks. [Trade: Caps 100 mg.] ▶K ♀C ▶? $$$$$

ANTIDOTES

Toxin	Antidote/Treatment	Toxin	Antidote/Treatment
acetaminophen	N-acetylcysteine	ethylene glycol	fomepizole
antidepressants	bicarbonate	heparin	protamine
arsenic, mercury	dimercaprol (BAL)	iron	deferoxamine
benzodiazepine	flumazenil	lead	EDTA, succimer
beta blockers	glucagon	methanol	fomepizole
calcium channel blockers	calcium chloride, glucagon	methemoglobin	methylene blue
		narcotics	naloxone
cyanide	Lilly cyanide kit	organophosphates	atropine+pralidoxime
digoxin	dig immune Fab	warfarin	vitamin K, FFP

UROLOGY

Benign Prostatic Hyperplasia

doxazosin (***Cardura***): Start 1 mg PO qhs, max 8 mg/day. [Generic/Trade: Tabs 1, 2, 4, 8 mg.] ▶L ♀C ▶? $$$

finasteride (***Proscar***): 5 mg PO qd [Trade: Tabs 5 mg.] ▶L ♀X ▶- $$$

tamsulosin (***Flomax***): 0.4 mg PO qd, given 30 min after a meal. Maximum 0.8 mg/day. [Trade: Caps 0.4 mg.] ▶LK ♀B ▶- $$$

terazosin (***Hytrin***): Start 1 mg PO qhs, usual effective dose 10 mg/day, max 20 mg/day. [Generic/Trade: Caps 1, 2, 5, 10 mg.] ▶LK ♀C ▶? $

Bladder Agents

bethanechol (***Urecholine***, ***✤Duvoid, Myotonachol***): Urinary retention: 10-50 mg PO tid-qid. [Generic/Trade: Tabs 5, 10, 25, 50 mg.] ▶L ♀C ▶? $

desmopressin (***DDAVP***, ***✤Octostim***): Enuresis: 10-40 mcg intranasally qhs or 0.2-0.6 mg PO qhs. Not for children <6 yo. [Generic/Trade: Tabs 0.1, 0.2 mg; Nasal solution 0.1 mg/ml (10 mcg/ spray).] ▶LK ♀B ▶? $$$

flavoxate (***Urispas***): 100-200 mg PO tid-qid. [Trade: Tabs 100 mg.] ▶K ♀B ▶? $$$$

hyoscyamine (***Anaspaz, A-spaz, Cystospaz, ED Spaz, Hyosol, Hyospaz, Levbid, Levsin, Levsinex, Medispaz, NuLev, Spacol, Spasdel, Symax***): 0.125-0.25 mg PO/SL q4h or prn or 0.375-0.75 mg PO q12h (ext release); max 1.5 mg/day. [Generic/Trade: Tabs 0.125; sublingual Tabs 0.125 mg; extended release Tabs 0.375 mg; extended release Caps 0.375 mg; elixir 0.125 mg/ 5 ml; drops 0.125 mg/1 ml; Trade only: Tabs 0.15 mg (Hyospaz, Cystospaz). Tabs, orally disintegrating 0.125 (NuLev).] ▶LK ♀C ▶- $$

imipramine (***Tofranil, Tofranil-PM***): Enuresis: 25-75 mg PO qhs. [Generic/Trade: Tabs 10,25,50 mg. Trade only: Caps (Tofranil-PM) 75,100,125,150 mg] ▶L♀B▶?$

methylene blue (***Methblue 65, Urolene blue***): Dysuria: 65-130 mg PO tid after meals with liberal water. May turn urine/contact lenses blue. [Trade only: Tabs 65 mg.] ▶Gut/K ♀C ▶? $

oxybutynin (***Ditropan, Ditropan XL***, ***✤Oxybutyn***): Bladder instability: 5 mg PO bid-tid (Ditropan) or 5-30 mg PO qd Ditropan XL). [Generic/Trade: Tabs 5 mg; syrup 5 mg/5 ml. Trade only: ext'd release tabs (Ditropan XL) 5,10,15 mg] ▶LK ♀B ▶? $

pentosan polysulfate (***Elmiron***): Interstitial cystitis: 100 mg PO tid. [Trade: Caps 100 mg.] ▶LK ♀B ▶? $$$$

phenazopyridine (***Pyridium, Azo-Standard, Urogesic, Prodium, Pyridiate, Urodol, Baridium, UTI Relief***, ***✤Pyronium, Phenazo Tab***): Dysuria: 200 mg PO tid x 2 days. May turn urine/contact lenses orange. [OTC/Generic/Trade: Tabs 95, 97.2 mg. Generic/Trade: Tabs 100, 200 mg.] ▶K ♀B ▶? $

Prosed DS (methenamine + phenyl salicylate + methylene blue + benzoic acid + atropine sulfate + hyoscyamine sulfate): 1 tab qid with liberal fluids. May turn urine/contact lenses blue. [Trade only: Tabs (methenamine 81.6 mg + phenyl salicylate 36.2 mg + methylene blue 10.8 mg + benzoic acid 9.0 mg + atropine sulfate 0.06 mg + hyoscyamine sulfate 0.06 mg).] ▶KL ♀C ▶? $$$

tolterodine (***Detrol, Detrol LA***): Overactive bladder: 1-2 mg PO bid (Detrol) or 2-4 mg PO qd (Detrol LA). [Trade: Tabs 1, 2 mg. Caps, extended release 2, 4 mg.] ▶L ♀C ▶- $$$

Urised (methenamine + phenyl salicylate + atropine + hyoscyamine + benzoic acid + methylene blue, Usept): Dysuria: 2 tabs PO qid. May turn urine/contact lenses blue, don't use with sulfa. [Trade: Tab (methenamine 40.8 mg + phenyl salicylate 18.1 mg + atropine 0.03 mg + hyoscyamine 0.03 mg + 4.5 mg benzoic acid + 5.4 mg methylene blue).] ▶K ♀C ▶? $$$$

Erectile Dysfunction

alprostadil (***Muse, Caverject, Edex***): 1 intraurethral pellet (Muse) or intracavernosal injection (Caverject, Edex) at lowest dose that will produce erection. Onset of effect is 5-20 minutes. [Trade: Injection (Edex) 10,20,40 mcg; (Caverject) 6.15,11.9,23.3 mcg. Pellet (Muse) 125, 250, 500, 1000 mcg.] ▶L ♀- ▶- $$$$

sildenafil (***Viagra***): Start 50 mg PO 0.5-4 h prior to intercourse. Max 1 dose/day. Usual effective range 25-100 mg. Start at 25 mg if >65 yo, or liver/renal impairment. Contraindicated with nitrates - fatalities reported. Not FDA approved for women. [Trade: Tabs 25, 50, 100 mg. Unscored tab but can be cut in half.] ▶LK ♀B ▶- $$$

Nephrolithiasis

acetohydroxamic acid (***Lithostat***): Chronic UTI adjunctive therapy: 250 mg PO tid-qid. [Trade: Tabs 250 mg.] ▶K ♀X ▶? $$$

allopurinol (***Zyloprim***): Recurrent calcium oxalate stones: 200-300 mg PO qd-bid. [Generic/Trade: Tabs 100, 300 mg.] ▶K ♀C ▶+ $

hydrochlorothiazide (***HCTZ, Esidrix, HydroDIURIL, Oretic, Microzide, Ezide, Hydrocot, Aquazide H***): Nephrolithiasis (unapproved use): 50-100 mg PO qd. [Generic/Trade: Tabs 25, 50, 100 mg; Solution 50 mg/ 5 mL; Caps 12.5 mg.] ▶L ♀D ▶+ $

potassium citrate (***Polycitra-K, Urocit-K***): Urinary alkalinization: 1 packet in water/juice PO tid-qid. [Trade: Polycitra-K packet (potassium 3300 mg + citric acid 1002 mg). Polycitra-K oral solution (5 ml = potassium 1100 mg + citric acid 334 mg). Urocit-K wax Tabs 5, 10 mEq.] ▶K ♀C ▶? $$$

Prostate Cancer

bicalutamide (***Casodex***): 50 mg PO qd. [Trade: Tabs 50 mg.] ▶L ♀X ▶- $$$$$

flutamide (***Eulexin, ♣Euflex***): 250 mg PO q8h. [Generic/Trade: Caps 125 mg.] ▶KL ♀D ▶- $$$$$

goserelin (***Zoladex***): 3.6 mg implant SC q28 days, or 10.8 mg implant SC q12 weeks. [Trade: Implants 3.6, 10.8 mg.] ▶L ♀X ▶- $$$$$

leuprolide (***Eligard, Lupron, Lupron Depot, Oaklide, Viadur***): 1 mg SC qd, 7.5 mg IM q month (Lupron Depot), 22.5 mg IM q3 months (Lupron Depot), or 30 mg IM q4 months (Lupron Depot), or 65 mg SC implant q12 month (Viadur). ▶L ♀X ▶- $$$$$

nilutamide (***Nilandron, ♣Anandron***): 300 mg PO qd for 30 days, then 150 mg qd. [Trade: Tabs 50 mg.] ▶K ♀C ▶? $$$$$

t = top of page
m = middle of page
b = bottom of page
D = for brevity in deluxe edition only

B

t = top of page
m = middle of page
b = bottom of page
D = for brevity in deluxe edition only

Index – 109

t = top of page
m = middle of page
b = bottom of page
D = for brevity in deluxe edition only

t = top of page
m = middle of page
b = bottom of page
D = for brevity in deluxe edition only

t = top of page
m = middle of page
b = bottom of page
D = for brevity in deluxe edition only

E

t = top of page
m = middle of page
b = bottom of page
D = for brevity in deluxe edition only

F

t = top of page
m = middle of page
b = bottom of page
D = for brevity in deluxe edition only

t = top of page
m = middle of page
b = bottom of page
D = for brevity in deluxe edition only

t = top of page
m = middle of page
b = bottom of page
D = for brevity in deluxe edition only

t = top of page
m = middle of page
b = bottom of page
D = for brevity in deluxe edition only

N

t = top of page
m = middle of page
b = bottom of page
D = for brevity in deluxe edition only

O

t = top of page
m = middle of page
b = bottom of page
D = for brevity in deluxe edition only

t = top of page
m = middle of page
b = bottom of page
D = for brevity in deluxe edition only

t = top of page
m = middle of page
b = bottom of page
D = for brevity in deluxe edition only

t = top of page
m = middle of page
b = bottom of page
D = for brevity in deluxe edition only

T

t = top of page
m = middle of page
b = bottom of page
D = for brevity in deluxe edition only

U

V

t = top of page
m = middle of page
b = bottom of page
D = for brevity in deluxe edition only

W

X

Y

Z

Page left blank for notes

Page left blank for notes

Page left blank for notes

Page left blank for notes

ADULT EMERGENCY DRUGS (selected)

ALLERGY	cimetidine (*Tagamet*): 300 mg IV/IM. diphenhydramine (*Benadryl*): 50 mg IV/IM. epinephrine: 0.1-0.5 mg SC (1:1000 solution), may repeat after 20 minutes. methylprednisolone (*Solu-Medrol*): 125 mg IV/IM.
DYSRHYTHMIAS / CARDIAC ARREST	adenosine (*Adenocard*): SVT (not A-fib/flutter): 6 mg rapid IV & flush, preferably through a central line. If no response after 1-2 minutes then 12 mg. A third dose of 12-18 mg may be given prn. amiodarone (*Cordarone, Pacerone*): Life-threatening ventricular arrhythmia: Load 150 mg IV over 10 min, then 1 mg/min x 6h, then 0.5 mg/min x 18h. atropine: 0.5-1.0 mg IV/ET. diltiazem (*Cardizem*): Rapid atrial fibrillation: bolus 0.25 mg/kg or 20 mg IV over 2 min. Infusion 5-15 mg/h. epinephrine: 1 mg IV/ET for cardiac arrest. [1:10,000 solution] lidocaine (*Xylocaine*): Load 1 mg/kg IV, then 0.5 mg/kg q8-10min as needed to max 3 mg/kg. Maintenance 2g in 250ml D5W (8 mg/ml) at 1-4 mg/min drip (7-30 ml/h). procainamide (*Pronestyl*): 100 mg IV q10min or run infusion below at 20 mg/min (150 ml/h) until: 1) QRS or PR widens >50%, 2) Dysrhythmia suppressed, 3) Hypotension, or 4) Total of 17 mg/kg or 1000 mg. Infusion 2g in 250ml D5W (8 mg/ml) at 2-6 mg/min (15-45 ml/h). vasopressin (*Pitressin,* ADH): Ventricular fibrillation: 40 units IV once.
PRESSORS	dobutamine (*Dobutrex*): 250 mg in 250ml D5W (1 mg/ml) at 2.5-15 mcg/kg/min. 70 kg: 21 ml/h = 5 mcg/kg/min. dopamine (*Intropin*): 400 mg in 250ml D5W (1600 mcg/ml) at 2-20 mcg/kg/min. 70 kg: 13 ml/h = 5 mcg/kg/min. Doses in mcg/kg/min: 2-5 = dopaminergic, 5-10 = beta, >10 = alpha. norepinephrine (*Levophed*): 4 mg in 500 ml D5W (8 mcg/ml) at 2-4 mcg/min. 20 ml/h = 3 mcg/min. phenylephrine (*Neo-Synephrine*): 50 mcg boluses IV. Infusion for hypotension: 20 mg in 250ml D5W (80 mcg/ml) at 40-180 mcg/min (35-160ml/h).
INTUBATION	etomidate (*Amidate*): 0.3 mg/kg IV. methohexital (*Brevital*): 1-1.5 mg/kg IV. rocuronium (*Zemuron*): 0.6-1.2 mg/kg IV. succinylcholine (*Anectine*): 1 mg/kg IV. Peds (<5 yo): 2 mg/kg IV preceded by atropine 0.02 mg/kg. thiopental (*Pentothal*): 3-5 mg/kg IV.
SEIZURES	diazepam (*Valium*): 5-10 mg IV, or 0.2-0.5 mg/kg rectal gel up to 20 mg PR. fosphenytoin (*Cerebyx*): Load 15-20 "phenytoin equivalents" per kg either IM, or IV no faster than 100-150 mg/min. lorazepam (*Ativan*): 0.05-0.15 mg/kg up to 3-4 mg IV/IM. magnesium sulfate: Eclampsia: 1-4 g IV over 2-4 min. phenobarbital: 200- 600 mg IV at rate ≤60 mg/min up to 20 mg/kg. phenytoin (*Dilantin*): Load 15-20 mg/kg up to 1000 mg IV no faster than 50 mg/min.

CARDIAC DYSRHYTHMIA PROTOCOLS (*Circulation* 2000; 102, suppl I)

Basic Life Support
All cases: Two initial breaths, then compressions 100 per minute
One or two rescuer: 15:2 ratio of compressions to ventilations

V-Fib, Pulseless V-Tach
CPR until defibrillator ready
Defibrillate 200 J
Defibrillate 200-300 J
Defibrillate 360 J
Intubate, IV, then *options:*
- Epinephrine 1 mg IV q3-5 minutes
- Vasopressin 40 units IV once only; switch to epi if no response
- Defibrillate 360 J after each drug dose

Options:
- Amiodarone 300 mg IV; repeat doses 150 mg
- Lidocaine 1.0-1.5 mg/kg IV q3-5 minutes to max 3 mg/kg
- Magnesium 1-2 g IV
- Procainamide 30 mg/min IV to max 17 mg/kg
- Bicarbonate 1 mEq/kg IV

Defibrillate 360 J after each drug dose

Pulseless Electrical Activity (PEA)
CPR, intubate, IV.
- Consider 5 H's: hypovolemia, hypoxia, H+ acidosis, hyper / hypokalemia, hypothermia
- Consider 5 T's: "tablets"-drug OD, tamponade-cardiac, tension pneumothorax, thrombosis-coronary, thrombosis-pulmonary embolism

Epinephrine 1 mg IV q3-5 minutes
If bradycardia, atropine 1 mg IV q3-5 min to max 0.04 mg/kg

Asystole
CPR, intubate, IV, assess code status
Confirm asystole in >1 load
Search for and treat reversible causes
Consider early transcutaneous pacing
Epinephrine 1 mg IV q3-5 minutes
Atropine 1 mg IV q3-5 min to max 0.04 mg/kg

Bradycardia (<60 bpm), symptomatic
Airway, oxygen, IV
Atropine 0.5-1 mg IV q3-5 min to max 0.04 mg/kg
Transcutaneous pacemaker
Options:
- Dopamine 5-20 mcg/kg/min
- Epinephrine 2-10 mcg/min

Unstable Tachycardia (>150 bpm)
Airway, oxygen, IV
Consider brief trial of medications
Premedicate whenever possible
Synchronized cardioversion 100 J
Synchronized cardioversion 200 J
Synchronized cardioversion 300 J
Synchronized cardioversion 360 J

Stable Monomorphic V-Tach
Airway, oxygen, IV
If no CHF, then choose just one top agent (procainamide, sotalol) or other agent (amiodarone, lidocaine)
If CHF (EF<40%), then DC cardioversion after pretreatment with either:
- Amiodarone 150 mg IV over 10 min; repeat q10-15 min prn
- Lidocaine 0.5-0.75 mg/kg IV; repeat q5-10 min prn to max 3 mg/kg

Stable Wide-Complex Tachycardia
Airway, oxygen, IV
If no CHF, then *options*:
- DC cardioversion
- Procainamide 20-30 mg/min IV to max 17 mg/kg
- Amiodarone

If CHF (EF<40%), then *options*:
- DC cardioversion
- Amiodarone

Stable Narrow-Complex SVT
Airway, oxygen, IV
Vagal stimulation
Adenosine
Further treatment based on specific rhythm (junctional tachycardia, PSVT, multifocal atrial tachycardia) and presence or absence of CHF.

Ordering Books From Tarascon Publishing

FAX	***PHONE***	***INTERNET***	***MAIL***
Fax credit card orders 24 hrs/day toll free to **877.929.9926**	For phone orders or customer service, call **800.929.9926**	Order through our OnLine store with your credit card at **www.tarascon.com**	Mail order & check to: **Tarascon Publishing PO Box 1159 Loma Linda, CA 92354**

Name		
Address		
City	State	Zip

Please send me:	*Number*	*Price ‡*
Tarascon Pocket Pharmacopoeia, Classic Shirt-Pocket Edition		$
Tarascon Pocket Pharmacopoeia, Deluxe Labcoat Pocket Edition		$
Tarascon Pediatric Emergency Pocketbook		$
Tarascon Adult Emergency Pocketbook		$
Tarascon Internal Medicine & Critical Care Pocketbook		$
Tarascon Pocket Orthopaedica		$
How to be a Truly Excellent Junior Medical Student		$
Sheet Magnifier – Fits in any book to make reading easier!		$

‡ Price per Copy by Number of Copies Ordered

Total # of each ordered	1–9	10–49	50-99	≥100
Pocket Pharmacop Classic	$ 8.95	$ 7.95	$ 6.95	$ 5.95
Pocket Pharmacop Deluxe	$17.95	$15.25	$13.45	$12.55
Peds Emerg Pocketbook	$11.95	$ 9.90	$ 8.95	$ 8.35
Adult Emerg Pocketbook	$11.95	$ 9.90	$ 8.95	$ 8.35
Internal Med Pocketbook	$11.95	$ 9.90	$ 8.95	$ 8.35
Pocket Orthopaedica	$11.95	$ 9.90	$ 8.95	$ 8.35
How…Truly Excellent JMS	$ 9.95	$ 8.25	$ 7.45	$ 6.95
Sheet Magnifier	$ 1.00	$ 0.89	$ 0.78	$ 0.66

Shipping & Handling

If subtotal is →	<$10	$10-29	$30-75	$76-300
Standard shipping	$ 1.00	$ 2.50	$ 6.00	$ 8.00
UPS 2-day air*	$12.00	$14.00	$16.00	$18.00

**No post office boxes*

Subtotal	$
California only add 7.75% sales tax	$
Shipping and handling (table)	$
TOTAL	$

❒ **Charge credit card**: ❒ VISA ❒ Mastercard ❒ AmEx ❒ Discover

Card number		Exp Date
Signature	E-mail	Phone